VALUES

FOR A NEW MILLENNIUM

Activating the Natural Law to:
- *Reduce Violence*
- *Revitalize Our Schools*
- *Promote Cross-Cultural Harmony*

ROBERT L. HUMPHREY, J.D.

THE LIFE VALUES PRESS
2005

VALUES
FOR A NEW MILLENNIUM
COPYRIGHT © 1992 BY ROBERT L. HUMPHREY, J.D.
COPYRIGHT © 2004 BY PEGGY HUMPHREY

ISBN# 0-915761-04-1

PUBLISHED BY:
THE LIFE VALUES PRESS
WWW.LIFEFVALUES.COM

IN ASSOCIATION WITH:
LIVING VALUES INSTITUTE
P.O. BOX 652
SPRING LAKE, NJ 07762

FIRST PRINTING 1992
SECOND PRINTING 2005

PRINTED IN CANADA

Dedicated to my former students, especially to Jack Hoban and Mark Hodel, who organized, cajoled, and financed this project.

WARRIOR CREED

Wherever I walk, everyone is safer.
Wherever I am, anyone in need has a friend.
Whenever I return home, everyone is happy I am there.

It's a better life!

Robert L. Humphrey (1923 – 1927)

FOREWORD

Alfred Adler observed that the consideration of human nature is the most important endeavor of the human mind. This work may solve that great riddle of human nature and demonstrate the problem-solving importance of The Natural Law.

I am an American business executive – product of the U.S. graduate schools. I am also a former U.S. Marine Corps Captain and long-time martial arts student. For as long as I can remember, even before I could put it into words, I had searched for the "spiritual" balance that would round out my intellectual and physical training. When I say "spiritual," I don't mean it in a religious way. I feel that I had a fine religious upbringing, including regular church attendance and parochial schooling. I mean that "horizontal" people-to-people spirituality.

It was in the early 1980's that I first encountered Dr. Humphrey as he addressed my graduate school class. Frankly, I was a hostile audience. I wondered how "Cross-Cultural Relations" could be justified as a required course for M.B.A. candidates. Suddenly though, as he talked, I felt that prickly sensation on the back of my neck. It was powerful and really quite physical. The things that he was saying, in such a matter-of-fact, common sense tone, began to touch me in a way that has literally changed me forever. I was stunned to hear him explaining, clearly, the meaning of life. The lessons he taught, the stories he told, are in this book.

Humphrey, himself, was a scholar/athlete, a graduate of Harvard Law School, and a collegiate and semi-professional boxer. He led a Marine rifle platoon on Iwo Jima, and was wounded there. After years overseas in many diverse countries solving major, en-masse cross-cultural problems for America, he became an itinerant professor for Pepperdine and National Universities. Most of his students were among the most knowledgeable, experienced, and skeptical of those who have ever graced our great universities – disillusioned military officers in post-Vietnam America. They were looking for deeper answers to the desperate global problems. What follows are a few of the reactions to the course from these men. Not being able to solicit permission for their use, I'll submit them without names. But they can be credited with absolute sincerity; they were returned directly, gratuitously to the universities after grades were in.

"Changed many of my attitudes toward making changes in my job and home."

– USMC (El Toro)

"The most relevant course yet, the best I've had in eighteen years."

– Air Force (Homestead)

"Super!! A true change agent course. Best leadership course (personal and professional) I have ever attended."

– Navy (Norfolk)

"One of the most significant events of my life."

– USMC (Parris Island)

Later, commendations on his work with high risk students (in southern California with Mexican/American street gangs and in Canada with Native Indian hard-core dropouts) were equally positive:

"The Humphreys have discovered the secret to learning."

– National City Chamber of Commerce

"The educational breakthrough of the decade."

– Athabasca University Native Program Education

Bob Humphrey passed away in July of 1997. But his life story and the lessons he taught live on in this book.

On behalf of the many Humphrey students, I encourage you to read (and study) this work. It can upgrade your life; it can make life better for all of us. As you shall see, directly or indirectly, *it probably has already.*

Jack Hoban

TABLE OF CONTENTS

BOOK TWO
THE ATTACHMENTS

PART I

Attachment B

Illustrations

ACKNOWLEDGMENTS

These documents summarize, literally, thousands of notes from half a century of formal studies, clippings, and observations in a score of countries and in two wars. After listing pages of key names that should be mentioned, on each review I have recalled almost an equal number of omissions. Finally, I gave up due to the sheer volume. Now, humbly, mainly as the reporter for this project, I say merely, thank you, to countless participating friends worldwide, and even to a few obstructionists. They helped too.

PREFACE

Familiar forms of grass-roots violence, ranging from child-abuse to street-gang warfare, seem to be increasing. Ethnic and class conflicts, in the East as well as in the West, revive foreboding recollections of the Nazis and group exterminations. Nations all around the world are retraining their police and military personnel to cope with (or practice) international terrorism and low-intensity warfare. Our little planet, on the edge of the cosmos, is not yet a fully civilized or friendly place to live.

The purpose of this work is to describe a new, scientific approach for solving human relations, or social problems, especially for reducing global violence. This methodology was research-developed and is research-guided. That is, the problem-solving method was, and the educational materials are, developed empirically from social-scientific research and experimentation, especially through programs designed to change attitudes among groups in conflict. These changed attitudes do not simply stop violence, as you will see, they *eliminate the causes* of violence by creating situations that conform to human nature.

Conforming to human nature means following the dictates of the universal human values that emanate from human nature, empirically perceived. When human nature's innate or instinct-like guidelines or values are violated, conflicts inevitably result. We have found that those conflicts can be eliminated or reduced on a mass scale by activating greater respect for the universal values. This is not an especially difficult process because one is not changing anyone's values; rather, the process simply reinforces the constructive (life-supporting) values quite generally endorsed in all of the world's cultures where we have conducted attitude studies. We have not found an exception—not in Africa, not in Asia, not in Europe, not in North America, and not in Latin America. *Universal values exist and persist despite all the violations.* There is a Natural Law in human affairs with automatic sanctions of unhappiness for its violations.

The basic conflict-resolving methodology was field-developed during a period of thirty years working in eight diverse cultures of the world. Its guiding principles were double-checked through research in twelve additional cultures. (Actually, the program was developed initially to *put out fires* in cross-cultural relations between overseas Americans and their foreign host-nationals in key hot spots of the world.)

At a deeper level, this method provides a human-nature-guided formula for meaningful educational reform. Considerably better, more synthesized (mind/body/art/values) education for all children is the only way to eliminate the general social injustices that stimulate much of the domestic violence and international warfare. We have applied the approach successfully in schools for students at risk and for hard-core dropouts for the past eight years. Besides educating *all* the children, better, it gives us a violence-reducing method for young persons that is much needed and whose time has come.

Most recently, as we go to print, I have encountered the book, *Inventing America, Jefferson's Declaration of Independence* (Doubleday, 1978), by Garry Wills.

Through exhaustive scholarship, Wills identifies Thomas Jefferson's ideology, enunciated in our Declaration of Independence, as a hardy, egalitarian flower of benevolence from the intellectual garden of the Scottish Enlightenment, rather than as a tricky tumbleweed from John Locke's relativistic backyard. This last-minute (for me) interpretation of Jefferson's philosophy corroborates the heartfelt description of human nature that I was given by the world's common folk in the streets and villages of the globe. Despite the convincing impact of those down-to-earth attitudes that I personally collected, the nuances were different enough from my academic learning that I could not avoid a tiny question. Now, however, the Willis Correction, (see his Part II, A Moral Paper) showing Jefferson's agreement with the thinkers of the Scottish Enlightenment, obliterates my tinge of doubt.

BOOK ONE

PART I

THE SEARCH FOR VALUES

CHAPTER 1

INTRODUCTION

THE WRITER'S ROLE

My unique job for seventeen years during the Cold War was to eliminate the Ugly Americanism demonstrated by our citizens in our *Little Americas* abroad, and then, reduce the anti-American attitudes among the surrounding overseas host-nationals. The work was conducted among six allied Eurasian peoples who helped us stop the spread of communism.

I moved into the conflict-resolution work as a lifetime specialty quite by chance. It happened as the result of a surprising success on a troubleshooting effort in a crucial multicultural crisis-situation in NATO, after all conflict resolution approaches known to the social sciences had already been tried and had failed. Eventual success for us depended on nothing less than developing a better understanding of human nature including identification of the chief, violence-controlling, universal human values and the means to reinforce those values effectively.

This new crash methodology was necessarily employed somewhat confidentially. And of course it was controversial. But that first effort and all others for two decades were successful enough that after each project we received another well-funded contract for the next program.

THIS NEW APPROACH TO PEACE: MASS DIPLOMACY OR IDEOLOGICAL WAR?

My official Data Sheet, prepared by corporate management, declares that I was America's leading ideologist during the Cold

War. That review of my work abroad pleases but amuses me. In my thirty years of world travel plus extensive study of world history, frankly, I encountered no other case of the equality/freedom ideology being used to motivate masses of persons in multicultural situations toward peaceful conflict resolution. If I was America's leading overseas ideologist during the Cold War, it was because I was the only one working directly, scientifically, in this field.

The world was, and still is, quite primitive, tribal, and dangerous. Keep that fact in mind. It necessitates courses such as this one in place of the historical reports that pass for international relations courses in most universities and high schools.

In 1955, when I first journeyed overseas for this work, Ugly Americanism had already become a definite, if unnamed, problem. To combat the phenomenon I first resorted to an embryonic values-activating approach in two countries in the volatile Mediterranean, Middle East arena—one Christian, one Muslim. As soon as I observed the inspiring effectiveness of the new ideological methodology, I was eager to try it on a larger scale. But since we were "teaching values," mainly *respect for human equality*, as the foundation for political freedom, the effort was soon identified as ideological warfare, in the sensitive context of the Cold War. This made leaders nervous. Only freedom, even to the point of license, was safe to teach as an American ideology.

Consequently, I was compelled to work at a very low profile—secretly in fact, as the ideologist in one major Vietnam program for the Marines. Nonetheless, the new approach received enough top-level commendations to document its acknowledged effectiveness. It solved problems for the leaders that had been resisting it.

U.S. EDUCATIONAL REFORM

We finally left the overseas scene when my children approached college age. One son, Bradford, then adapted the new guiding theory to the crisis in education. Through eight years of school programs with teenagers at risk and hard-core dropouts, we found that the crisis definitely can be solved. It can be solved relatively easily if leaders, in general, are interested. But the U.S. educational system is an elitist system with the children of leaders attending private schools. Few in the U.S. leadership classes are willing to change that. Secretly, even if subconsciously, it is comforting for them to know that their children are gaining an edge. Of course it is a foolish short-run comfort they are enjoying. They are leading our nation, including their own children, into decline by their failure to take drastic action. The worst possibility in this regard is that leadership is innocent in the sense of being blind about this problem. For example, the president of one of America's world-famous universities recently defended the university system against its critics. He devoted more words to the defense of the preferential education system (high-tuition colleges for the wealthy) than to any other topic.

GOALS AND TERMINOLOGY

In view of America's two closely related national needs, key goals of this work include (1) building America's health and constructive influence abroad, including material exports, and (2) solving the domestic crisis in our elitist (token public) educational system with its resulting academic failures, ethnic conflicts, drug culture, and obvious contribution to national decline. Consequently, it is time to set down on paper the details of this new values approach to social-scientific problem-solving and national re-strengthening through school reform.

Regarding terminology, we have called the new theory of human nature that guides the program either the *Balanced Life Value Theory or the Dual Life Value Theory*. It is known by both terms among my students. The term *values-based* is actually used as shorthand for *human-nature guided*. We also call the new values-based approach to education, descriptively, the *mind/body/art/values* curriculum.

To save endless space, we are not going to delve into the meanings, subtle distinctions, and changing uses of the terms *spiritual, ethical, moral, attitudes, values,* and *opinions* other than to mention that we'll go along with two customary connotations of the term "values:" We'll use it in a general sense to mean anything that humans desire, and then, frequently, in its special connotation to mean the earthly (person-to-person) spiritual values. For the particular meaning of any of these terms, at any particular place, we'll rely on the context.

ORGANIZATION

WARNING: A PROGRAM, NOT MERELY A BOOK

My students, especially Jack Hoban, and my own children have persuaded me to set these lessons down in print. Those young friends have all said in one tactful way or another, "Professor, Dad, MAN! You are getting old. You must write this all down before it is too late."

After years of resistance, finally, I said, okay; but I knew, as is said in the law, IT WON'T WRITE. The simplest description of the work is still too complicated; *it is not the work for a mere book.* A set of books might do it if accompanied by a good teacher/coach who knew the books well enough to integrate their messages in the classroom. Otherwise, the materials cannot be divided into several books without losing their combined message. In fact, the main enemy of effectiveness in this field, as in others, is the modern overspecialization or compartmentalization of education. This seems to be a necessary evil of modern education, overflowing as it is, with the flood of information. Yet, most of us recognize it as an evil that handicaps general understanding. In some fields it will not work at all. This new field of massive conflict resolution and violence reduction, obviously, is one such field.

If I were forced to write these materials into acceptable book form, I would use at least three books: one, an autobiography; another, a research document; the third, a self-development manual, and perhaps, fourth, a thought-piece on pure theory. That approach however is not the way the problem-solving method presented here was developed and used in the field. It is the latter, the successful approach to social problem-solving, complicated as it may be, that is most worth preserving. We need to dwell on this point even further for a moment.

The course of study presented here probably demands an oral training program with field assignments and the give-and-take of discussions backed with many reference materials. That is the way the program has always been taught or implemented successfully in the field. When presented in cold print alone, some readers will conclude in places: this is an illogical digression, or this is the reverse order of the way the theoretical propositions and facts should be studied, or this is an *unnecessary* redundancy, or this is just plain wrong, disagreeing as it does with all I have ever learned.

Meanwhile, ten years of teaching in the graduate classroom have proven that when these materials are edited to read well, they do not teach well. Consequently, for these teaching materials I have remained close to the kaleidoscope of realistic field confusion that is documented in my records of developing and implementing the program in the field. I have made only those concessions that were necessary to prevent the complete withdrawal of all editorial assistance. The one *major* artificial concession made here that I sometimes also use in the classroom, but that you will never find in the field, is the addition of some transition notes between the intellectual jumping around that is the only realistic preparation for actual field problems.

Nonetheless, my young associates are right: I cannot continue to teach in person. Still, equally true: This document is *not written as I would write a book; it cannot be. And it cannot be read rapidly as is possible with most books.*

Despite the difficulties, the goal, the treasured end, is here. This primitive, original pathway through the jungle maze, guided by human nature, did lead on every leg of the journey to massive attitude improvement and violence reduction on a major scale.

So I implore you, don't try to read these instructions like a mere book. Go slowly; learn the method; build the necessary tolerance for confusion. Study the possible relationship between ideas when they seem to change direction completely. Study these lines of words for what they really are: the written directions to go and get pieces from everywhere to put together some important puzzles. Be patient every endless time that I pull back and review lead-in lessons for repetitive introductions to different follow-on points. They are needed by most.

Understand that in this very digression itself, we are discussing one of the most basic problems of failed education. Modern school-oriented education has become the prisoner of the book, or of the written message. AND BOOKS OR MESSAGES THAT READ WELL, DON'T TEACH WELL. WHEREAS MATERIALS THAT TEACH WELL, DON'T READ FAST. RATHER, THEY FORCE YOU TO THINK. That takes time, not a favorite practice anymore for busy Americans. Perhaps programmed learning on the fascinating computers will help solve this problem. If you agree, please consider these materials to be a very complicated programmed-learning text.

In those places where you tend to get impatient with my constant reviews, don't read faster there; please slow down and read more thoughtfully. Know that you are in one of the places where I have learned to lower my voice, speak more slowly, and guide students carefully. It is one of the many tricky places in the maze, in the darkened pathway, where many, in retrospect, got confused. Or else they moved too carelessly and got lost in the bush. In those places, besides the tool of redundancy, used in these oral-like lessons, but usually not allowed by editors, I'll also insert comments that are quite personal and that would be considered unprofessional in the strict book-world of academia. I have learned from years of teaching, that students, in order to learn from you in the field of values, need those candid, personal confidentialities. Why would this be true when in most fields it is indeed extraneous?

The answer, I have found, is this: When you are "teaching" values, especially when the message is uplifting to a plateau above the modern philosophical deserts of doubt and cynicism, the students are interested to the point of excitement. But they inevitably wonder about your candor. After class, almost in whispers, they probe for that missing confidentiality and suspected secret motive: *What is your religious background,* they ask, or, *what is your alignment on the political spectrum?* Later, when they trust you, they admit having suspected some offbeat ideology that was lurking in a secret motive to suck them in. Conversely, if you level with them early about your background, revealing the understandable economic and generational sources of your original hypotheses and possible biases, it solves this ubiquitous problem of modern skepticism. That is, it does if it makes sense and is clearly well motivated. (Negative philosophies are easier to sell in the modern philosophical smog of skepticism; but they are accepted and promulgated aggressively by a different little leadership group.)

I have maintained, against editorial pressures, some of my oral grammar and vocabulary techniques that I learned to use in the field for effectiveness:

1. Occasionally some slang, especially if quoting others;

2. Embedded thoughts (with parentheses) or with hyphens when I want the listener to try to think of two ideas together;

3. Long sentences or other slightly complicated constructions that force the listener to figure out—a little—what is being said, and thereby remember it better;

4. Occasionally some faulty grammar—especially with pronouns, conjunctions, and prepositions—when proper grammar sounds stuffy in spoken English;

5. Slightly illogical sequences of thought that experience has shown "teach better" than logical ones;

6. A few coined—especially hyphenated—words when proper words failed me; and

7. Finally, again (and again) constant review or repetition, one top key to effective teaching if well spaced as convenient reviews or appropriate reminders.

Now, despite the fact that this is not just a book, I have organized it somewhat chronologically into intellectual parts, book-like. That was, indeed, necessary in order to place the materials in the hands of other change agents. There is no other means available to me, just now, that is appropriate.

Part I will take you on the fascinating field-search for, and the baffling struggle to activate, the universal human values that transcend cultures and ultimately control human behavior (peace and violence). We found that violation of, or deference to, these values, respectively, do in fact, cause, or resolve, conflicts. Do you appreciate the significance of this assertion? It means that universal, objective values, or standards of right and wrong, *do exist.* This is contrary to the position usually taught in school, often by default, that all is relative (that there are no universal values)—the position of ethical relativism.

Part II presents the most challenging case-studies of the cross-cultural problems that we encountered in eight countries during almost two decades in the field. Cross-group animosities (often with ancient roots in bloodletting) constitute feud-like inclinations toward cross-ethnic violence or little wars everywhere.

Human cultural and physical differences that cause negative attitudes are still little understood in our somewhat tribal world. Hence, once these differences are understood, cross-cultural violence can be stopped substantially through activation of the universal values via the method described here.

Cultural differences that seemed crazy, evil, or downright subhuman to outsiders will be presented to you as cross-cultural mysteries—just as they appeared to us when first encountered in the field. We will teach you, as *cross-cultural detectives,* how to solve these mysteries. This fascinating detective-like skill must be learned and used by many conflict-resolution professionals around the globe if we want to stop the human slaughter and cultural genocide that makes Earth, not Mars, the red planet of war.

Without a global commitment to activating the objective human values (or universal ethics) another holocaust is not unlikely. If you think it cannot happen again in Germany, Japan, Russia, or the U.S.A., spend a little time listening to group-conversations on the college campuses in any of those lands. To a degree, in several places, such evils are happening now. In human relations, we all know that human beings are still very primitive. We are still very tribal. And that is very dangerous to peace and tranquility, both domestic and international.

Attachment A expands on the history of the program's implementation in specific countries and institutions. Also, while highlighting one feature of the generally unknown history of what actually happened in Vietnam, it sets forth a values-guided global strategy for low-intensity warfare, and closely related, describes modernized training needs for America's future military personnel. What this adds up to is a peaceful strategy for protecting democracy in the coming century virtually without the use of force. This depends on us, on America, including our military, to establish our image as *Life Defenders* versus the negative tags of Ugly Americans, Gunboat Diplomats, or Killer Commandos.

I have collected and presented there, in *Attachment A*, in one coordinated section, several of the most significant entries on military strategy which are scattered appropriately through other sections of the book, but I have added significant details to fill out the picture. Readers with a determined interest in world peace through strength rather than (historically futile and usually self-deceptively tragic) disarmament, will find it especially interesting. Simultaneously, I have included details for trying to deal with the almost insurmountable barriers to institutional change.

Attachment B describes briefly how the new knowledge of human nature and human values can be (and has been) applied successfully inside our failing schools. Through the values-based, or unified mind/body/art/values, curriculum it is possible to educate *all* of our children well and happily. Again, here, we have supplied additional facts to provide warnings and insights for trying to cope with intransigent institutional-change obstructions.

Attachment C leads off with a summary of a document that was indispensable for reducing Ugly Americanism overseas during the height of the Cold War. It explains the real reason why underdeveloped countries are underdeveloped, versus the self-aggrandizing, "others"-insulting, ethnocentric reasons *usually* imagined by culture-shocked or culture-bound citizens from the industrialized economies. Until the forgotten field of geography regains its status as the queen of the social sciences, this Attachment, I fear, will be much needed. *Attachment C* also contains many loose ends of information that some readers will want; others won't.

PARALLEL ACCOUNTS:
INTELLECTUAL AND INSTITUTIONAL

Finally, I want to re-emphasize the complicated nature of these materials, and the need for redundancy in more specific terms than above. Why? Because I have found that the general approach employed above is effective with some students. This more specific approach with examples is needed by others.

Trying to dig out the details of human nature's guidelines for solving actual field-problems, while simultaneously trying to implement such a program, resembled the chaos of a first practice fire drill when everyone thought there was a real fire.

I'll emphasize the difficulty by drawing a second parallel: Assume you had to construct a building rapidly without a blueprint. With the structure deemed complete and the upstairs full of people, you see it teeter and realize that you have left a cornerstone out of the foundation. As you'll see, that happens. The exact parallel happened to me in Vietnam.

The sizable task now is to report the total methodology, corrected but realistic, so that others can duplicate its successes without our mistakes. Flexibility is a key to success in implementation. The best method, I find, for teaching college students to work on urban social problems is to announce the goals of the entire course and the goals of each lesson, but then, advise the students to go willingly wherever the class questions and discussion take us. School them constantly to deal with ambiguity and confusion, to remain flexible.

To re-emphasize this decisive need for flexibility, assume you have written a grant proposal to solve a city's race-relations problem or to reduce the equally tragic Arab/Israeli conflict. Then, visualize yourself winning the grant for your outstanding plan. Finally, face the fact that you have to give up the plan and, therefore, the grant, or else forsake all hope of solving the problem. Why? Because this work is similar to a football game. You start with a game plan, knowing that because of strong, inevitable opposition to solving any problem, you must keep much of the plan confidential and alter its details constantly, or fail.

In other words, the combined work of the cultural detective and the conflict-resolution specialist is truly holistic and jumbled in the field. In writing it up as completely as possible in this combined field report and teaching manual, I'll place as many balls in the air as is possible in some example cases, for your proper (harassed) orientation. (For better examples of the combat-like confusion, see *Attachments A and B*.) Meanwhile, throughout, I'll still follow the *two main developmental threads* that were followed or woven in the field:

1. The *search for the universal values* that make up the new guiding theory, or the values package; and

2. *The struggle,* against institutionalized opposition, *to implement* the guidelines derived from this new theory.

(Incidentally, many of my students complain that I should not refer to this new description of human nature as a theory; they insist that it is more of a truism that they have always known but just had not articulated.)

That second thread, the account of the program's broad implementation in several cultures, both in cold war and in combat (Vietnam), teaches a strategy for winning unavoidable conflicts with minimum use of force, and it provides a superior, grass-roots foundation for all facets of our foreign relations including economic. It can help us reduce our costly foreign trade deficit.

To reiterate, the full story of what happened in Vietnam has most definitely not yet been told. That war was lost for democracy because we Americans who fought there did not abide by our own American ideology. The struggle was not, as apologists for the loss often assert, merely a misunderstood conventional war.

Revealing that the Vietnamese conflict *and the burgeoning worldwide violence* were, and are, mainly ideological or values problems is also a primary purpose of this work.

HOLD TO THE THEORY

It is sometimes said in football, *when uncertain, kick.* In this work, when uncertain, go back to the fundamentals of the basic theory; repeat what you know of the theory; then try to go where the theory would suggest rather than where logic, otherwise, might take you. Especially, do not let the redundancy in that regard annoy you. I removed most of the redundancy once from a set of lesson plans for a couple of associate-teachers who had complained. But then tests revealed that without the redundancy, especially on matters of guiding theory, their students did not learn the material. We need constant review in order to bring the most important ideas to a level of strong, permanent, surface consciousness in all participants. Also, central ideas are repeated throughout the body of the work with slightly different but important nuances in each different context.

AUDIENCE

The book is written for persons who are energetic and courageous enough to give some effort and *take some hits* to help re-strengthen America and improve the fate of humankind.

Now, emphatically, be warned that to lead in this effort you must be tough-minded (thick skinned). If you try to *change things* constructively in the social sciences or try to reconcile conflicts, rather than take sides, you'll be attacked through character assassination and every other means of skullduggery not excluding physical assault. It is inevitable and inescapable. It will disgust you to the point of befuddlement and, at times, rage. That beautiful beatitude in the Bible should be changed to read:

Blessed are the peacemakers in heaven; because on Earth, they shall catch hell.

Nonetheless, I'll stress that the time is finally right, on our planet, for the expansive light of true civilization. Well-informed voices both prophesying and forcing that maturation, suddenly, are being heard everywhere.

THE NEW GRASS-ROOTS DEMANDS FOR JUSTICE

With the explosion of communication, through radio and television penetrating even into the world's jungles, the masses of common folk that I have interviewed in, and from, a score of countries insist that they are wising up. *They* express disgust with having been too long squeezed between the political oppression of dictatorship and the economic violence of rank capitalism. Religious or not, these voices agree with the views of the Pope: *There has been unacceptable oppression and exploitation in both Communist and capitalist countries.*

If these general allegations are true, why? Why does the oppression and misuse persist? Because there has been no *equal-vote democracy* in the Communist countries where power corrupts the ruling few, and also too little of it in the capitalistic economies where money (traded for undemocratic political power) also corrupts the ruling classes.

In response, the common folk of the earth, newly informed, are warning us more and more aggressively that the abuses of the actual or substantially disfranchised little people must stop. Similarly, as a result of this same amorphous common-folk *wising-up* to America's Vietnam and Russia's Afghanistan, the days of cannon-fodder armies, in which the masses *are not to reason why, but just to do or die,* are also probably over, at least in the industrialized societies.

THE LEADERSHIP TASK

Despite the recent, spreading enlightenment, the human species is still young on Earth. I am not trying to wax poetic when I suggest that we are still in the Late Dark Ages. With the extent of needless violence from unadulterated greed and childishness, this historic characterization will be seen clearly as accurate a thousand years from now if the human species survives, and matures culturally. Despite likely political chaos, an historic high point, suddenly, *does* offer an opportunity—*that opening that came in the Russian sky*— for a giant step toward world peace and happiness. But the Russians cannot be expected to understand democracy. The decisive task, now, is for us Americans to lead through an even higher perfection of democracy, into an era of global justice.

To enter this evolutionary period, the final *Age of Justice,* we average middle class Americans must lead. It must be leadership by example in the neighborhoods where we are in daily contact with "the people." How about the leadership of our elected representative and of our professional classes?

In answer, perhaps above all else for good leadership we must resist with satirical determination, the childish, greedy leadership of too many political and professional (congressional, medical, and legal) citizens to establish for themselves millionaire status while ignoring the unnecessary suffering of masses of their own people, never mind the rest of the globe. If most of us join in that scramble for materialistic wealth with ever-*decreasing* concern for others, it can only lead to more cynicism, more division, more bloody violence in our streets, and eventually, again, to attempted international recriminations, especially from the Third World. However, understand this, although I will not mention it again: Regarding the disgusting wealth-accumulation by leaders despite the suffering, or despite the poverty of many in the midst of plenty, there is a strong unspoken rationalization for this oppressive greed. The rationalization, or excuse, derives from the accepted inevitability of the Malthusian population problem, allegedly revealed in famine and homelessness.

Correcting that attitude and economic misuse of "the people" in America awaits full acquisition or recovery of democratic leadership by "the people." Because of campaign costs, top leadership in America has become a monopoly of millionaires. And millionaires almost inevitably withdraw from societies' cultures, the systems of values, that serve <u>all</u> the people. Millionaires tend to give their allegiance only to economies. And under the political control of cultural outsiders (millionaires), economies become monsters that eat "the people."

CHAPTER 2

THE PRIMARY IDEOLOGICAL CAUSE OF CONFLICT

Anyone who traveled extensively immediately after WWII could not help but be impressed with the *American presence*. One encountered numerous Americans in almost every country. One saw the signs of our bountiful economy everywhere. Our Hollywood movies were showing in every foreign city. Our sturdy old automobiles filled the world's highways. Most telling of all, in a strange way, was the fact that even our used tin cans and candy wrappers littered the streets and campgrounds of the entire world. It was indeed the American era. We Americans were the missionaries of economic aid, just as we had been the liberating champions of war.

Within a decade, the image was fading. Wherever you traveled you began to hear reluctant whispering about the "Ugly American." Having fought, and been shot, and having lost five of my closest Marine lieutenant friends on Iwo Jima, plus sacrificing all of that time, I was made sensitive to these new charges. I resented the new anti-Americanism. Being a college teacher of International Relations, I decided to take a government grant for a brief spell, go back overseas, and work on this new foreboding problem of anti-Americanism in a world being divided by a cold war.

My hope, of course, was to analyze the problem and make a quick contribution to its solution. It seemed that I was ideally prepared. I held degrees in accounting, law, and international diplomacy from the prestigious universities of Wisconsin, Harvard, and The Fletcher School of Diplomacy. I had taught International Relations and Economics at the Massachusetts Institute of Technology. I already had considerable overseas experience in the Marines and the merchant marines. For acceptability with the omnipresent military, besides having been a rifle platoon leader in the Pacific Theater, I had ten years experience in the amateur and semi-pro boxing ring. So I had no credibility problems. My accompanying family, including Mrs. Humphrey and four children (later five), promised a full sociological perspective on the new foreign scene. I took the grant for two years and stayed seventeen.

EASY ANALYSIS BUT NO SOLUTIONS

Despite my own sensitivities to the new anti-American allegations, once back overseas in the 1950s, I soon perceived that a fair-minded American had to acknowledge the justification for the foreign peoples' criticism. Have you ever had to accept assistance from someone who seemed to assume a superior attitude toward you in his giving? Gratitude is felt; but not gratitude alone; there is also resentment, and often detestation. Having been a teenager in the CCCs during the Great Depression, I knew about those ambivalent feelings.

Working overseas in a Third World country in the State Department's semiofficial, largely ignored, people-to-people program, which was institutionalized through *Binational Centers and America Houses* my job, simply stated, was to promote good relations between the host-nationals and our communities of overseas Americans. There were, however, no official pressures. All overseas diplomatic leaders seemed to assume there was no answer. My boss advised me: "These people are poor; we are rich; their resentment is inevitable." (I knew that was false; wealthy people who seem nice, can be loved.) No one expected anything more than a polite effort with the local elite, mainly through cocktail parties.

Nonetheless, seeking a better answer, I tried everything. For two years I filled that Binational Center with every type of social and cultural function known to civilization. Nothing worked. Confidential conversations and more open whispering, not to mention harsher conflicts in the streets revealed clearly that the Ugly Americanism and anti-Americanism were still with us, and growing.

A HOPEFUL CLUE

While packing my bags for the return to *the world,* as our overseas GIs often call America, I decided to conduct some attitude studies among the host nationals to try to find out why everything failed. From the hundred questions that I developed for the exploratory study, the answers to one small area of the investigation were surprising for their content and consistency. (Note: Being from the World War II generation, I use the term GI as a term of great respect as it was generally used then.)

The questions were:

What do you (host nationals) want from us Americans?

What can we Americans do, or stop doing, to promote better relations?

Fascinated by the unexpected responses, I constructed a more official-looking instrument limited to those two questions and took it to the embassy for approval. (Opinion studies were not yet used much.) A ranking officer advised against, but did not forbid, the study. He speculated that the answers would be "too embarrassing *if they got out.*" He thought the host nationals would insist that we Americans should either go home, or else give them more money.

Ever so carefully I distributed the questionnaires in two countries, one Christian and one Moslem. The results corroborated the first exploratory study. Approximately 80% of the answers from both countries carried one theme. It was not *Go home,* or *Give us more money.* Can you guess what it was? Contemplate the probable answer for a moment.

HUMANKIND'S SINGLE MOST CONSCIOUS CAUSE OF CONFLICT

Over the next three decades I conducted similar studies in a dozen countries, on all five major continents, in societies representing most of the world's major religions. The overwhelming theme in every study was the same. The worldwide attitude, even though seldom voiced in the absence of an obviously sincere study, I now ascertain, expressed the conscious value that substantially controls all human relations, controls the existence of crime or tranquillity in domestic relations, and controls the probabilities of peace or war in international affairs.

The answer was:

Respect us as Equals.

Did you anticipate this response? No one seemed to at that time. Currently, some school teachers guess it correctly in my seminars. Frankly, at that time, I was amazed.

Most overseas Americans had been warning me that the local nationals hated us just as most overseas Americans held the foreigners in low esteem. Yet, obviously, this response, *respect us,* is basically pro-American (Isn't it?). The most frequent responses making up that general category were these:

- *Show us more respect*

- *View us as equals*

- *Treat us as equal human beings*

- *Respect our human equality*

- *Respect our women*

- *Respect our culture*

- *Don't look down on us*

- *Don't consider us (stuff) in the grass*

- *Don't act like our bosses when you are not*

- *Don't call us names*

- *Respect our lives*

- *Don't consider our lives of less importance than your own*

[When you see these under-the-surface feelings in grass-roots foreign relations, can you understand why reducing the value of the U.S. dollar did not, as hoped, automatically recover our lost sales of U.S. goods abroad? Who buys what from whom is not purely a matter of price. My son will not buy anything from the most convenient furniture store in town because the manager was discourteous to his wife.]

One day during a conference in Athens, Greece, I showed those studies to a Middle Eastern professor. I asked him why such complaints were not conveyed more openly by foreign nationals to us Americans.

He answered:

There is a problem of pride or embarrassment that is not easy to understand. When we used to complain about the public insults of Americans, your ranking diplomats passed it off lightly with your old American saying that "sticks and stones may break my bones but words can never hurt us." Well, here in these austere lands, it is different; words hurt us. In fact, we have almost the exact opposite old proverb. We say, "The cut of a knife will heal quickly; but the cut of a word will last forever." And I have told your diplomats many times that when the cutting stops, the cost of keeping your military bases in these developing countries will go down rather than up. But they don't seem to believe me; that part, they don't understand.

I collected thousands of these questionnaire-responses during the 1950s, '60s, and '70s. Recently several professorial associates, some of my graduate students and I replicated the studies in Canada among Indians regarding their attitudes toward the dominant white population, among Mexicans toward Americans along the U.S./ Mexican border, and among high school dropouts toward society in two areas of the United States. Except for an additional element of rage among the teenage dropouts, nothing has changed since the earlier studies.

The thought, *Respect us as equal human beings!* I repeat, is probably the conscious (but seldom-spoken) value that controls the issue of peace or violence in all of human society.

Yet, in these Late Dark Ages of youth-gang violence and undeclared wars, the frustrated desire for equal respect is virtually unrecognized as one of the deepest causes of violence. A few observers pick it up. Read this report, February 11, 1988, about riots in the Middle East. It was written by the astute Ken Freed in the *Los Angeles Times.* From the violent streets of reality, Freed wrote:

> This area is... equal in squalor to the slums of Brazil, Indonesia and India. Poverty, filth and idleness are everywhere. A stench clings to every surface.... (The) residents... are considered essential to the... economy.... But in talks with dozens of [these] residents... the sentiment most heard was that humiliation and dehumanization are at the roots of the... discontent, even more so than the 20-year fact of occupation.... (Said) a 52-year-old woman.... We are also human beings, just like them.... [and] mockery boils the blood of the young people. They have feelings, and they won't forget.

UPSHOT AND TRANSITION

The most important words in this conflict-resolution work are words that ask questions. They ask, *Why?* and *How do you explain?*

By constantly asking those questions, eventually we learned the reason why the desire for respect remains unrecognized. The reason is embarrassment. I'll explain through the profile of an overseas situation in the Third World as seen by a newly arriving American Human Relations Officer. As you read it, ask these questions about your ability to solve the cross-cultural attitudes of disrespect—the roots of violence—involved:

- Are the issues here too embarrassing for me to discuss?

- Are they too embarrassing for the elitist leadership groups of the world to even consider discussing?

- If they are too embarrassing to be discussed, how difficult will that make it for me to eliminate the negative attitudes, the lack of respect, the resentment, the hostilities, and violence threatened from these issues?

Profile of a Third World Situation

Alias: The Old Bus Into Culture Shock (Copied from my field report to Washington)

During my first week in that country, I arranged to visit some distant ruins of an ancient city. It was a difficult, all-day trip with the rickety bus stopping at each of the few filling stations along the way for oil, water, or air. Of the thirty people on the bus, approximately two-thirds were host nationals and one-third were Americans. Seven or eight of the Americans were civilians and two or three were military personnel.

At the first stop, one American, a newcomer to the country, asked another how to find the restroom. A third American said quietly, "Don't." In response to an inquiry whether the latter had been to the place before, he answered, "No, but the toilets in this back country are all alike; best to take to the bushes."

There were no bushes. The man in need left the bus in search of the toilet. Most of the Americans and all of the nationals were already out of the bus to stretch themselves or purchase local soda pop. Soon the American returned, visibly shaken by his experience. "Gosh!" he exclaimed, "It was unbelievable; just a hole in the ground in the center of a little mud hut."

"Yeah, that's the way they do it," laughed the original adviser. "They just squat. And did you notice there wasn't any toilet paper; just a jug of water? That's the worst part. They just wipe on their hand, and then wash the hand."

As the fellow continued to laugh at his own remarks, another American described the toilet as a "small, dark, repulsive, windowless outhouse humming with flies." Americans backed away from it after one step inside; but the nationals, it was observed, were using it. "They wipe on their hand and then wash the hand." Memory of the comment rang in my ears during the entire trip.

By the time the bus broke down on the return journey, more real-life lessons of the cultural barriers between the developed and underdeveloped worlds had been well taught. For example, as the bus rocked to a stop on a blown tire, one young national shouted, "Well, that's one of our buses for you! My American professor says that this is the land where nothing works." The comment touched off a series of examples from other tourists. One described the newest apartment building for Americans in the capital city. The fireplace chimneys were so poorly designed that they acted only as downdrafts to suck smoke back into the rooms. Another told of the need to persuade an American carpenter to refinish all doors and windows in a new apartment building since none would close after the first rain. Plumbing difficulties were major contributions to the tales of humor and woe. Complaints included floor drains located in the highest area of the floors, water pipes that squirted more water beneath the sinks than into them, new toilets which either wouldn't work or else flushed some of the waste onto the floor, and one which flushed into the ceiling of the apartment below.

Talk turned to ethical standards throughout the country, especially the practices of money-conscious landlords and government officials.

Most of the latter, it was alleged, accepted bribes and to save face called them tips.

The tire was soon repaired and the tourists got back aboard; the mockery sessions lapsed. One sensitive American volunteered a compensatory compliment for the local nationals. He mentioned how friendly the peasants had been all along the way. No one could have escaped the image called forth by the comment. At every stop, as soon as the peasants learned that the bus carried Americans, their friendliness exploded into aggressive hospitality. Unfortunately, even the proffered hospitality was often rejected, especially when it included an invitation to eat the local sweets which were being shared indifferently with the swarming roadside flies.

By the end of the trip, I was well aware of a new set of facts in international relations. So-called culture-shock is actually *poverty-shock;* no one from the wealthy western world can escape it completely in areas of poverty. It includes too many phenomena that are disagreeable, repulsive, and downright dangerous.

TRANSITION

I presented that actual case not to shock you; I hope it didn't. I presented it for two reasons: so you will understand the *embarrassment barrier* that prevents us from, not simply solving our values-conflicts, but even discussing the issues; and second, so that you can understand what exactly is involved in this new, global (foreign and domestic), ideological struggle that Americans do not understand.

To eliminate most of the anti-Americanism abroad and considerable *militancy* and gang warfare at home, I submit that we must reduce that part of the bigotry and Ugly Americanism that derives from culture shock or poverty shock. The leader or change-agent must start that corrective process *ideologically*, that is, by revitalizing the 1776 American ideology of respect for human equality. Why? Because no other educational approach is effective. A purely intellectual, relativistic reaction (that says typically, simply, "you have to accept others' differences") usually makes the bigotry worse. Usually, it constitutes deceptive, insincere rhetoric that refuses to face the issues.

Since the necessary ideological approach is still not a part of official American policy, I had better relate that part·of my personal background that led to the development of the ideological approach for our seventeen years of crisis-oriented Cold War programs.

SOME NECESSARY PERSONAL BACKGROUND

After World War II the generous G.I. Bill for wounded vets granted me the privilege of attending the Harvard Law School. However, I soon discovered that I was not interested in reading legal cases for three years (and that is about all one does in law school). That lack of interest left a vacuum for me regarding my life's work. But from the time lost in the war, as a student I was older than others; and as a former boxer with a broken hand, I had no place else of interest to go. I decided to stay at the law school so I could join the FBI. I managed to pass the few law school exams (one per course per year) by reading commercially *canned briefs* of the cases and debating them with law-school friends. (Fortunately for me, debating cases is the other thing law students do.)

THE NATURAL LAW

As a result of my almost exclusive interest in philosophical issues, while browsing the law library for something to read, I encountered references to an obscure body of legal literature called the *Natural Law*. It was fascinating, a study not so much about the law as about justice. All through law school, through The Fletcher School of Diplomacy, during a Rotary scholarship in Mexico, and while teaching at MIT, the Natural Law became my private obsession. I gave serious attention to nothing else academically during that scholarly period of eight years.

The idea of a universal Natural Law probably started with the advent of serious human thought. It was pondered by the Stoics in ancient Greece, by Cicero in Rome, by the most famous scholastics of the medieval church, and by such recent revolutionary thinkers as Thomas Jefferson and John Locke. Jefferson, in our Declaration of Independence, called it the *Laws of Nature*. Its literature contains the persistent triangular search, through two thousand years, for the connections between three factors:

1. Nature,

2. The universal moral values of humankind, and

3. Man-made (so-called, positive) law.

Wearied by the search for those elusive connections modern lawyers, only a few generations back, gave up that search for humankind's connection to the rest of nature. They decided that our man-made, *positive*, laws were the only rules that were clear enough to try to recognize.

Until the Nuremberg war-crime trial, at least, this rejection of Natural Law cut loose the great *ships of state* from their ancient moral anchors; nations became completely free to establish their own principles of right and wrong in relation to other nations or peoples. All became morally independent, legitimately oblivious to the so-called international laws, which appeared too nebulous and unenforceable.

This deference to legal practicalities released us as individuals, also, from any objective morality. It set us free to rise (or fall) into the new flexible *ethical relativism in which there are no universal, natural laws or rules of right and wrong*. In response to my only question ever asked a professor at the law school regarding the Natural Law, he tried to guide me away from wasting my time: *"You don't study justice here,"* he advised, "you study the law. Such conceptions as the Natural Law or justice suffer from the unacceptable quality of vagueness. You will find that you win cases with precision. Forget the Natural Law."

At that time, I couldn't.

A REDISCOVERY IN THE COMMON FOLKS' ATTITUDES

The problem of making a living to support a large family eventually accomplished what the law professor couldn't: It forced those captivating ideological considerations into the back of my mind. But that old obsession with the Natural Law was rekindled when I read the hundreds of emotion-filled responses from those semi-literate, unwashed peasant folk. They were requesting recognition of their *human equality,* a fundamental concept of the Natural Law.

Those attitude studies were obviously politically sensitive—an indictment of U.S. State Department policies. They suggested that we Americans did not actively believe in our own founding principle announced to the world in our Declaration of Independence. Heavy stuff. But more important, those studies revealed an ideological weapon well within our grasp: Simply by *showing more respect* we could start to bridge that gap between us and the Third World's people whom we were alienating.

Conversely, our unspoken State Department/U.S. Information policy held that the only answer was for those poor nations to get rich, like us. In action, the official policy was dedicated to showing and describing our great wealth while attributing it to freedom and American know-how. With those two things plus our economic aid, all the underdeveloped nations of the world could *jump off into economic development.* That was our official message.

Since that policy ignored the comparative scarcity of local resources, it wasn't working (See *Attachment C*). And thirty years later, in 95% of the underdeveloped world, it still hasn't worked. Hence, the possibility of us overseas Americans learning to show more respect to the host nationals as equal human beings fostered not just a more enlightened policy, it might be more effective for promoting economic development. I was excited about showing this surprising, research-supported possibility to the embassy/USIS officials. Although I was one of the youngest and lowest-ranking officers, I scheduled a major staff-meeting.

THE IDEOLOGICAL WAR: TO FIGHT IT OR FORGET IT?

It was time for some careful preparation prior to the important presentation. Several times, almost unbelieving, I returned to the stack of questionnaires. Were the responses really as overwhelming as I recalled? They were of course; page after page, request after request, asked, in essence, for the same thing, respect for human equality:

- Respect us

- Respect us as equal human beings

- Don't laugh at us

- Don't cut us down

- Don't ignore us as nobodies

- View us as equals despite our poverty

- Don't call us names

- Etc.

I dug out a copy of the Declaration of Independence to check again the exact words of those towering thoughts that now, suddenly, held current, real meaning in a totally incongruous situation. I had always associated the expression of the sophisticated idea of human equality with Thomas Jefferson and other fine gentlemen in powdered hair and fancy robes. As an articulated idea, I thought it came only from the esoteric world of the mind for the people, but not *from* them in words.

Suddenly, out of the dirty streets, the idea was being reintroduced to me by masses of foreign peasants who allegedly wiped on their hands. Amazing!

I copied down the two key, related ideas from The Declaration, cutting them to the irreducible minimum for clarity:

WE HOLD THESE TRUTHS TO BE SELF-EVIDENT, THAT ALL MEN ARE CREATED EQUAL,... ENDOWED... WITH CERTAIN UNALIENABLE RIGHTS....

Pretty clear! But was the situation the same, or was it different? Could this 1776 American ideology be dismissed as irrelevant for our overseas situation there in an Asian nation two hundred years later? I pondered the ideas of the Declaration again, and tried to recall the details of its history.

Ah, yes, there was a significant distinction: Despite the protestations of Jefferson (as I recalled), the Declaration was aimed primarily at one nation's leaders, including a tyrannical king, by another (new) nation's leaders. Our modern case, there in a struggling Third World nation, was definitely different. Governments and leaders were not even involved, just common people in the streets, mainly American GIs and peasants, the latter asking the former for equal respect.

These questions followed, and filled my mind:

What is the meaning of the demand for human equality in grass-roots relations between two groups of peoples, totally aside from governments and kings?

If it has a meaning, how do we teach it to U.S. citizens who may honestly feel like superiors in relation to "smelly peasants" in a repugnant land?

Necessary questions—no answers.

The more I tried to prepare for the staff meeting, the more I feared the political sensitivity of the information in that huge bundle of questionnaire responses. In 1775, our nation was born in the blood of our patriots—mainly ragged, uneducated dirt farmers, who were fighting for equality through freedom from the wealthy British. Now, ironically, only two hundred years later, we Americans had become the wealthy ones. Now we were being confronted by the poor people of the world with the same type demand for equal human respect. Devastating!

From the magnitude of the request, unquestionably, I had stumbled onto something of monumental importance in the great unrecognized ideological struggle in the Third World. We Americans and respect for our form of democracy were being weakened unnecessarily. But what could I do? Would our wealthy, confident, self-satisfied Americans even be interested in those findings?

THE POSSIBILITIES OF UNDERSTANDING IDEOLOGICAL WARFARE

Thinking back to the home front, I estimated that upwards of 90% of all Americans had never lived abroad. So Americans at home could not even be expected to understand. And since most of those who were abroad were causing the problem, how could they possibly understand? I was especially uneasy about this question: Would our overseas leadership understand? (We Americans, always having had new physical frontiers to conquer, are notoriously adverse to philosophizing.) How about the hundreds of thousands of overseas GIs, a dominating force because of their numbers, would they understand?

There was an even more unsettling question: The year was 1957. The Russians had not yet launched Sputnik. America was still the unquestioned world leader, the only superpower. Believe me, we overseas Americans all felt that, and deeply. So even if our Americans did understand the philosophical issues, would they care? Or would they say: So what if the peoples of the world don't like our attitudes?

Is that really our problem or theirs? (Terrorism by the weak against the powerful was still a relatively unknown method of warfare.)

As my doubts increased about the possible reactions of our American officials, I decided to consult a few highly respected host-national scholars for their reactions to these studies. Might the local government want them censored?

Most of the upper-class host-nationals in those days were still exceedingly deferential to Americans. Hence, as I expected, most whom I consulted were ambivalent and equivocated. One, however, who was strongly pro-American but later became an equally strong anti-American Prime Minister of the country, advised me candidly: "Our people love you Americans. But as your studies show, we also fear that we are being deceived. All American leaders, in their speeches, say that Americans believe in equality, and that they respect us. But in personal relations, in the streets, *in scores of little ways too petty to mention,* they show that they don't; they believe in the superiority of the Americans. Our struggles against poverty and against our historic enemies are now, inexorably, tied to you to the end. Your lack of respect for us, we fear, could be our undoing."

THE DECLARATION OF INDEPENDENCE: HONESTY OR PROPAGANDA?

When the date arrived to present the studies to my State Department/Information Service associates (my bosses), my fear was that they would reject the importance of the ideological issue. It turned out to be worse: they rejected *its validity.*

At first, after my introductory summary, there was silence at the staff-meeting table—the silence of embarrassment at having to correct my apparent ignorance about the meaning of equality. The youngest officer, a recent college graduate, was the first to speak. He voiced what I later found to be a popular view of the *values-free* ideology in our American universities:

"There is no such thing as human equality," he declared confidently, *"Some men are stronger, some taller, some smarter, and that is it."*

Heads nodded all around the conference table in agreement. All eyes turned onto me. I tried to relieve the tension with a joke: "I can't accept that implication," I offered laughing, "I'm the shortest man present."

No one else laughed.

A mid-rank officer, a man of warmth and consideration, one who appreciated the new level of activity that I had brought to the Binational Center, tried to comfort me with an historical clarification: "You see, Bob," he asserted, "equality is just an old propaganda idea. Our Founding Fathers needed it to motivate the uneducated masses to fight the Revolution. Jefferson himself owned slaves."

I scanned faces to see if anyone caught the amusing elitism in his comments. (Regardless of Jefferson's possible views, the comment implied that the acceptance and active endorsement of the equality idea by the masses of American soldiers, who did the fighting and dying, was irrelevant, as if only the leaders' beliefs counted.) No one shared that little unspoken humor with me either. It was getting very lonely in that room, but not for long. The ranking officer was a huge, blustering man who managed his subordinates by intimidation. As he pushed his loud floor-crushing chair back from the table, he aborted the meeting with these growling words: "Let's stop wasting time, here; you can't have freedom and equality, too, and our cause is freedom! Let's get back to work."

I held up my hands to halt the group exodus. In that moment of spontaneous pause, I pushed the foot-high stack of questionnaires toward the boss and asked if he would not at least like to scan the responses.

He turned away, ignoring me, pretending not to hear the question. Everyone else scattered like scared chickens in the first show of urgency since their arrival abroad.

The shocking blow was yet to come. It was a message sent ostensibly by the ambassador (which I doubted). It did not order, but it strongly suggested, that I should destroy the questionnaire responses and never mention them again. It was a lightning bolt to me. Having been excited by the apparent breakthrough against the ominous, unfolding problem of Ugly Americanism, I had already withdrawn my resignation and signed-over for another two years.

Though I had feared some lack of understanding regarding the politically-sensitive message in those studies, I had not anticipated that unmitigated rejection of the equality concept. As a matter of (fuzzy) historical recollection, I would have challenged the view expressed about Jefferson, but I ascertained that an effort to do so, in that room at that time, would have been counterproductive. Those denunciations were emotionally charged. They were not arguments; they were declarations of faith. If I had challenged them abruptly I sensed that it would have simply stimulated anger and harden that faith. (At that time, I did not appreciate the ideological ignorance in many educated Americans that equated the Natural Law's human equality with modern communism's hated, government-forced economic equality.)

I still recall the psychic dissonance I experienced that day. I was virtually ordered to stop considering the human equality concept as an ideological weapon for use against our self-destructive malady, Ugly Americanism. Yet, these were not fascists or Nazis who were stopping me. It was a group of pleasant, attractive, generally liberal Americans who were absolutely open, sincere, and innocent in their *light bigotry.* Many had taken bus trips similar to the one I had taken and had succumbed to the deep, divisive shock of poverty.

I was struck by the comic nature of my predicament. In that distant Asian city, as I walked out of that meeting and into the streets, I was reminded of the man in the short story who stumbled onto a society of cave people who had no eyes. The eyeless people decided they had to blind the man so he could be normal. I actually felt a little head-spinning disorientation over my isolated ideological situation there among all the other officers in the mission.

For the next several days, in half-serious amusement, I kept picturing myself as the Connecticut Yankee in King Arthur's Court, but devoid of any phony magic to salvage the situation. I knew that I could not stop my search for an answer to those two closely related political time-bombs facing America: the American rejection of human equality in a respect-hungry world, and the Third World's reaction through anti-Americanism. But I also knew that I would have to exercise that search very carefully or get sent home. The next few months were, as my father used to say, character building.

SOME QUESTIONS

Did I actually have a promising breakthrough in those studies? Is the ideology expressed in the Declaration of Independence sound and worthwhile, or was it merely a propaganda trick used by Washington and Jefferson to raise cannon-fodder armies? Could the American *equality concept* have been activated overseas and employed effectively from the beginning in the Cold War? Could it have prevented the Ugly Americanism that caused the worldwide growth of anti-Americanism including some of the anti-American terrorism, not to mention, perhaps, the trade deficit? What would have been the effects in dollars, in happiness, *in lives?* More important, how will the issue affect America's future? Will the collapse of communism in Russia make us Americans more considerate of the Third World's people, or will it lull us into more dangerous indifference and self-defeating Ugly Americanism?

CHAPTER 3

THE BASIC IDEOLOGICAL PROPOSITION

After the excoriation experienced at the staff meeting, or because of it, I was compelled to stop all serious work in the American civilian community. It had been my intention to leave the highly vocal, harsh-talking military men until last, but this fiasco with my diplomatic associates compelled me to turn toward the military for a place to work. And pure chance introduced me into its most formidable rank-group: the older, conservative noncommissioned officers.

I can't say I succeeded with them; it was the opposite: They handed me success that I suspect I would never have found elsewhere. From their down-to-earth insights in relation to those attitude studies, denounced by the diplomats, we revitalized the equality concept to the point where we could activate it effectively in a large overseas binational community *anywhere*.

Our results were of historic importance. Within three months we had salvaged one of the most vital NATO missions ever undertaken: The installation of our first missile system in the Mediterranean. Part of it apparently became a significant bargaining weapon on the day the whole world held its breath, during the Cuban missile crisis. Our work was given credit for saving the United States millions of dollars every week on that project for more than a year. And it led to ten million dollars worth of tightly financed (nonprofit) contracts in several countries. So even if the bottom line is only economic efficiency and inspiring employment, teaching *respect for human equality* is worthwhile.

In addition to those bottom-line answers, I will immediately correct the fallacious ideological assertion mentioned in the previous chapter: *that equality and freedom are competing values. Actually, the two are politically inseparable.* Closely related, this is also the time and place to identify the basic proposition for proper and successful ideological warfare; this, whether it is waged against dictatorship abroad, or our divisive enemy within: bigotry.

THE HUMAN-EQUALITY/POLITICAL-FREEDOM CONNECTION

Human equality, a universal (Natural Law) concept, is the only unshakable justification for political freedom. Because we are equal as human beings, each of us is entitled to an equal voice (political freedom) in the government over us. If humans are not equal, then a dictatorship of the superior persons over the inferiors (fascism) is justifiable. Hence, the human equality principle cannot be rejected consistently with an averred belief in democracy. Those who plead the cause of freedom but reject human equality actually plead a different cause; consciously or unconsciously, they defend preferential status and a license to exploit others. As we saw in the peasants' questionnaire-responses, equality is something deeper than logic, it is an irrepressible *feeling* in each person.

America's serious social problems, domestic and foreign, can be solved only through respect-in-action for the equality/freedom principle so that the domestic and global social situation fits human nature. The disregard or denial of the human-equality/political-freedom principle on any grounds, anywhere, will cause problems, just as it did in 1776.

TRANSITION–THE NEXT STEP IN THE SEARCH

Please flashback to that failed effort of mine with my State Department bosses to foster recognition of the human equality principle. You know how it is when your job is not going well, not well at all, as mine was not after my studies were denounced. At such times, it would be nice if one could just go fishing every evening. I could. I did. No one cared. Also, I hunted on weekends, and I started playing nine holes of golf, noons, with some military officers. I was disgusted and wondering what to do next. Eventually, in defense against the needling of some military men about my apparent semi-retired status, I described my official relegation, in my work, to a status of uselessness.

To my amazement, I was invited to a lunch with the local military commander the next day. He virtually commandeered me for community-relations duty with the troops. To my further delight, he granted me carte blanche freedom to work on troop-community relations and encouraged me to teach the equality concept as much as I liked.

CLARIFYING THE IDEOLOGICAL QUESTION

I visited various embassies in the capital to ask if anyone else had a clue about how to teach and activate the *equal human respect concept:* the English, the French, the German, the Pakistani, even the Russian (since an even more unattainable form of equality—economic—was supposed to be their forte). At best, some expressed sympathy for me in such a search; others just laughed. I wrote back to my scholarly colleagues around Harvard, MIT, and The Fletcher School of Diplomacy. Those who responded sent comments on *equality of opportunity and equality under the law.* The American GIs, not to mention the host-nationals on my planning committees, laughed at those ideas as "intellectual suicide" under the (alleged) local circumstances of mocking inequality under the law, and even less equality of opportunity.

These initial disappointing results gave me no answers, but they clarified for me the two crucial questions:

1. How does one teach equality?

2. What, exactly, does human equality mean?

Days went by, then months, searching, talking, trying everything. Again, to escape, I began to go on a few hunting trips. It was on one of these that I was treated to the fundamental breakthrough leading to our eventual success. It came from an unexpected source: an old army sergeant who always had tobacco juice running down the corner of his mouth; he spoke with a Tennessee drawl; no one suspected he had a thought in his head. Still, his common-folk wisdom provided us with the understanding to improve grass-roots relations for almost two decades in the hottest spots of the Cold War. It helped us reduce racial conflict under the lawless conditions of combat; it helped us stop atrocities; it saved lives.

Here is the story; it is the account of an amazing hunting trip deep in Asia Minor:

THE HUNTING TRIP—DON'T TREAD ON US

On weekends, the Americans would form parties to hunt the wild boar that were destroying many villagers' crops. As a party would arrive in a remote village, the more curious peasants would crowd up behind the truck carrying the American hunters.

The sight of those peasants in the poorer villages was often depressing. Many of the villages were only a few miles off the highways which connected the larger cities, but they were hundreds of years behind the cities in economic and cultural development. When the rains came, the mud spread like wall-to-wall carpeting in the streets throughout the villages.

As usual, on this trip, the sight of the ragged, destitute villagers drew comments from one or another American. A young airman proclaimed: "Look at them; they are like a bunch of animals. What have they got to live for? They might just as well be dead."

What can anyone say against those comments? They seemed true enough.

I sat in chagrined silence, but this day, in response to those familiar words, the old sergeant drawled out his answer between spits of tobacco juice. He said, "You better believe they got something to live for, Jack. If you doubt it, let me see you jump down there and try to kill one of them with your hunting knife. They'll fight you like no one ever heard of. I have fought beside them in heavy combat, and I don't know either, why they seem to value their lives so much. Maybe it's them women in them pantaloons, or maybe it's them dirty-faced kids; whatever it is, they seem to value their lives just as much as we do ours, even with all of our money. In fact, both in combat and in freezing prison camps, they hung in there after a lot of Americans was yelling quit."

After the grizzled sergeant spoke, all the whispering stopped on the truck; everything went silent. I still recall hearing the villagers' campfire crack in the sudden stillness of the early morning dusk; I heard the old sergeant suck and spit. I am sure my mouth dropped open. I was both embarrassed and excited. I thought to myself: *Good God, he is talking about the equality of life and all of these rich Americans are buying it.*

I stashed my rifle in the truck cab and lost interest in the hunt. I stayed close to the sergeant so I could talk with him during the stakeout. Two of my questions brought forth additional deep feelings and insights.

He told (or lectured) me that while we were looking down on those peasants and insulting them, it really embarrassed him because even though the villagers didn't speak any English, they understood exactly what we were saying. They could tell from our tone, and had given him almost exact translations on previous occasions when he had stayed with them overnight. He added, "You know, when we are making fun of them, they are looking back up at us there on the truck and saying, 'Laugh, you bastards in your fancy clothes, but we don't care how sweet you smell, or how rich you are, or where you come from. We value our lives and the lives of our loved ones just as much as you do yours. And if you don't give us that, you have got to go.'"

I asked the sergeant how we could *prove* a belief in equality despite our striking differences in wealth. He answered easily:

"You got to be able to jump down off the truck into the sheep manure, go over there into that village of mud huts, walk down those narrow streets, and pick the dirtiest, stinkin'est village-peasant that you meet; and as you walk past him, you got to be able to make him know, just with your eyes, that *you* know that he is a man who hurts like we do, and hopes like we do, and wants for his kids just like we *all* do. That's how you got to be able to do it. Nothin' else ain't going to work."

I didn't shoot any pork that trip; I didn't try. I sat scratching out notes with a broken pen on what the sergeant was saying. I kept thinking about his *equality-of-life* concept and wondering out loud if Jefferson had also sensed this hard-core, basic life-defense meaning. I persuaded our interpreter to help me interview several of the villagers. One thing was sure: the more I got the peasants to level with me, the more strongly I realized that it *was* their meaning. Basically, they *all* said independently, *We are the friendliest people in the world; but no one can tread on us.*

Notice emphatically that this life-value, as it was expressed by that old sergeant and those uneducated peasants, is not a selfish "me" value. The value was always stated in terms of *me-and-my-loved-ones or me-and-my-group.* Functionally, this means it is a *self-and-species* value. Some of our original American flags, that spoke appropriately for an entire colony said, *Don't tread on me.*

Expressing the same irreducible *right of life-defense,* but speaking for destitute, humble people rather than a great political state, these peasants warned, *Don't tread on us.* Actually, I had known about the awe-inspiring selfless dualism of the life value from what I had seen in combat. I had written versions of the concept years earlier in the scholarly journals. But I had not persisted. Until this experience, I had not had the full coverage of my own convictions.

This new experience with the peasants was absolutely conclusive. As a result, I kept comparing the wisdom of the uneducated old sergeant to my own, with all my twelve years of college, and to my best law school professors' and just kept shaking my head. It was some hunting trip! I returned to urbanized civilization with a precise, common-folk, down-to-earth meaning of human equality clean and clear in my head.

Obviously, it does not mean that people are not different in almost all measurable ways. You may be bigger than I, smarter than I, better built, stronger, faster in mind and body, better looking, possess a more popular skin color, etc. Nonetheless, in one way, in a way that eclipses all others in controlling importance, *I AM YOUR EQUAL: MY LIFE AND THE LIVES OF MY LOVED ONES ARE AS IMPORTANT TO ME AS YOURS ARE TO YOU.*

Analyze Figure 1, next page.

In other words, human equality is almost synonymous with the basic life value in the natural order of values. Isn't this why our Founding Fathers in 1775 named the right to life as the first characteristic of human equality? Isn't this why they wrote on their flags, DON'T TREAD ON ME—don't tread on me because I will not be ground down as if I were inferior to you, to your king, or to anyone—I am an equal human being!

On returning from that memorable trip, I strongly suspected that I had learned how to teach the equality concept: Just teach the equality-of-life meaning voiced by the old sergeant, and use his down-to-earth words to do the teaching.

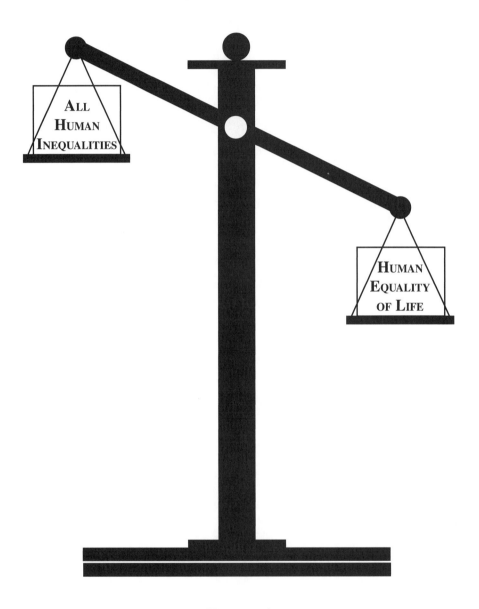

FIGURE 1
THE IMPORTANCE OF LIFE'S EQUALITY
VS. ALL OUR INEQUALITIES

CHAPTER 4

DISCOVERING THE SOURCE OF HUMANKIND'S NATURAL LAW

During all my years of reading about the Natural Law, its rules had always seemed to hover overhead somewhere out in space—out in Nature, above humankind—to be perceived and articulated by the great philosophers. Suddenly, as a result of my emotional experience in the village on that boar hunt, my understanding changed; reversed itself. *The Natural Law, I saw, came from inside humankind*, from inside those peasants. The nature that it expresses is *human* nature. Of course it has a *self side* but also a strong altruistic or, functionally, *species-preserving side*.

As I recalled, vaguely, the little-known Scottish philosopher, Francis Hutcheson, had seemed to see the Natural Law this way. I had discounted his view because such giant intellects as Locke, Hobbes, and Rousseau had seen it differently. Now, however, this interpretation derived from association with illiterate peasants, living on the edge of survival, eclipsed in my mind every book on the matter from the elite world I had ever read. Along with the earlier massive questionnaire responses, I was certain that finally we had decisive, living, convincing, anthropological evidence *that I could use* regarding the meaning of equality.

A TIME OF TESTING

I couldn't wait to test this old sergeant's approach with our masses of notoriously anti-intellectual common-folk—especially GIs. When I found the peasants' basic and dual (me and my loved ones) life-value meaning of equality to be persuasive with my wife and friends,

I tried it informally on larger and larger groups in party conversations. Finally, the military community-relations officer, a captain, agreed to fill the theater with a thousand enlisted men. It was the first of several crucial *times of testing* for me in trying to develop effective weapons for modern ideological warfare (or mass diplomacy, if you prefer). Now, as I write this many years later, I still get butterflies thinking about that first great test. More than all the other heavy challenges that followed, it was truly a crossroads in life for me, professionally.

The men, and a few women, poured grumbling into the barn-like theater. I stood at the door and listened to their comments. We had announced that this was a "human-relations meeting." Because the troops hated such meetings, the announcement was included to add to the *testing factor.* I mingled-in as the crowd entered. My nervousness increased. These young soldiers are so boisterous, so cynical, and so unconscionably vulgar. Their talk would embarrass an X-rated movie maker. "More of this crap," was the sanitized version of the thought expressed by most who spoke. They added all of the profane and vulgar variations of protest possible in the GI vernacular, and they are endless.

I introduced myself. Some in the crowd already knew me as a former Marine and boxer. Word spread through whispers; that helped. Against their fears of "another boring hour," and in deference to my own last moment of stage jitters, I placated them with a promise to take less than thirty minutes.

I began my substantive comments by referring to the growing official concern that we might be kicked out of the country. It backfired; the men cheered. Damn! I tried to recover with the spoken thought that I, too, wanted to take my family home. But I wanted to be able to go on my own terms and not as an unwanted failure. It worked; they started to listen.

I confided that I had conducted attitude studies among the host-nationals asking:

1. What they (the locals) did not like about us Americans, and

2. What they wanted us to do or stop doing in order to improve relations.

I advised the men that most of the locals had given the same answer. I told them what the embassy official had guessed: that we should give more money or go home. I cautioned them that he had been wrong, and asked them to try to guess the answer in little discussion groups with the persons seated around them.

No one obliged; they did not believe I was serious. I tried again, and persisted by waiting matter-of-factly. (It was touchy; one shouted putdown might have sunk me.) I continued to wait, nonchalantly looking through my notes there at the podium. The men started talking quietly, thoughtfully. I relaxed. The discussion quickly built up into a friendly, involved, roaring discussion.

After two or three minutes, I placed a viewgraph on the overhead that projected large on the movie screen:

RESPECT US AS EQUALS

There were dozens of both loud and physical reactions through the audience: some of surprise and disbelief; others of recognition, approval, and confirmation. One black GI jumped to his feet with a shout of delight and outstretched hands to collect several odds-on bets that he had won.

The moment was exciting. "Good grief!" I mumbled to myself, "The theater is full of lay philosophers." Confiding further, I told them of my search through the embassy, and back to Harvard and MIT for the meaning of equality, and of the empty answers that had followed.

Then, to the heart of the test, I told them the story of the hunting trip and the old sergeant's words. The entire theater went as silent as the truck had been when the sergeant first uttered the challenge. It choked me up; I knew we had the basic weapon needed to win the war, *ideologically*, for democracy. (Do you understand why it was such a long—70 year—war against communism? Certainly not because Communist dictatorship had any appeal; it was because communism's *economic* equality has tremendous appeal. We defeated it, by 1989, because economic equality does not fit human nature; *human equality* does. Human equality is more subtle; it is an ethical, not an economic, concept. Its demands in action are less materialistic and more general than economic equality.) I closed the address to the GIs with the sergeant's declared formula for the irreducible minimum demonstration of respect for human equality in action:

> If you want to stay here until we can leave by choice rather than by rejection as Ugly Americans, if you want to take the leadership in making the military a life-force for peace, if you want to help start the movement that will change the world so that your kid-brothers and possibly sisters won't have to die in war, then you have got to be able to do what that sergeant said: You have got to be able to get up from those seats, walk out of this American theater, go out into those foreign streets and down into the narrow byways of this unfamiliar town; once there, you've got to be able to meet the dirtiest, smelliest beggar-peasant, and as you walk past him, you've got to be able to speak to him, and make him know, just with your eyes, as you exchange glances, that you know he is a man who hurts like we do and hopes like we do and wants for his kids just like all of us Americans do. If you can do that, if most of us can do that, we can stay here until we want to leave. And we can win the worldwide ideological war, peacefully.

It had been barely fifteen minutes. I left the podium in the dim light of the theater that had been darkened for the viewgraph. As I walked across the stage, the theater had grown deathly silent. I didn't know what to think. The captain met me at the stage stairs, grabbed my arm in the dark, and whispered: "Tremendous."

The lights went on as I started up the aisle. Suddenly, the young men realized that the meeting had ended. They rose to their feet.

Some near the aisle where I was passing started to clap. Then it exploded into a standing ovation. I was overwhelmed with delight; couldn't look up. Do you know the feeling?

I hurried out of the theater and into a local bar; ordered a beer, needing to *get back down*. Even though I was a nondrinker at the time, the heavy bock beer didn't work. I knew for certain I was now committed to this new field of ideological warfare for a long time to come. I talked with the local bartender, who did not understand one English word. It was better that he didn't because I advised him that, "The Connecticut Yankees can succeed now. We don't need an eclipse of the sun. Sound ideas and sincere speakers will do it. The Declaration of Independence has the ideas needed to win."

TESTS WITH THE INTELLECTUALS

I could not help but wonder how American intellectuals, strongly conditioned to the individualistic *me syndrome* in America, would react to a *universal dual-life value*. I recalled the tests in college psychology used to substantiate the belief in ethical relativism. Classrooms of students were asked to select their top value from a list such as this:

LOVE	FREEDOM
HONOR	LEISURE
BEAUTY	STATUS
TRUTH	COMPASSION
DIGNITY	POWER
	(OTHER)____

Responses were always so predictably varied, that it was offered as evidence that *all is relative.*

I wondered what would happen if we included the life-value choices on such a test. Would the college educated select the life values, or would they think them too mundane (animal-like) when measured against such lofty ideals as truth and beauty.

I increased the list to read as follows:

LOVE	FREEDOM
HONOR	LEISURE
BEAUTY	STATUS
TRUTH	COMPASSION
DIGNITY	POWER
MY LIFE	THE LIVES OF MY LOVED ONES
	(OTHER)____

Now, conduct the test for the top value anywhere in the world and watch what happens. I have conducted that study scores of times with thousands of respondents, military and civilian, in over a dozen cultures. The results from every large cross-section of citizens always agree: Life is humankind's strongest earthly value. And species-preservation (*the lives of my loved ones*) is the top half of the value. Self is only a close second, *even in strongly individualistic America.*

One day while visiting my thesis adviser, the scholarly giant, Harold Lasswell, at Yale, he mentioned that freedom might be man's first value. I asked him, *How about the lives of our loved-ones?* He pondered the question for a moment and observed, *Well, yes, I guess we all take that for granted.*

TAKING NOTHING FOR GRANTED

As a result of these experiences with our most basic values, I learned that when working in the field of values, one dare not take anything for granted or there will be unnoticed misunderstandings. Hence, when you are teaching (or actually, reinforcing) our basic human values, it is wise, early-on, to draw an illustration showing clearly the relationship between our conscious values of freedom and equality and our more basic—and therefore, taken for granted—life value.

Freedom and equality, respectively, protect life from tyranny and bigotry. That explains their derivation and function. If anyone questions this, as some will, by suggesting that freedom is more important than life itself, you can help them clarify their thinking by asking this question: If freedom (democracy) is more important to humankind than life itself, why don't military organizations vote (exercise political freedom) in combat?

Analyze Figure 2, next page.

THE FORMULA FOR UNDERSTANDING CULTURAL DIFFERENCES

With this equal life value identified as the basic, universal value, we can see the formula for understanding *cultural* differences: Once we can explain to the members of one group the life-supporting reasons for another's hated (misunderstood) differences, the hatred begins to subside. The differences become reasonable after they are seen to be life protectors. The formula is:

THE LIFE VALUE + ENVIRONMENTAL = HUMAN DIFFERENCES
    (a given)   Differences   (genetic & cultural)
                      (a variable)

Here are two obvious examples:

1. Life's Body Temperature + Arctic Cold = Much Clothing

2. Life's Body Temperature + Equatorial Heat = Few Clothes

Of course we are working in the difficult social sciences here, not the more stable and predictable hard sciences of inanimate objects.

FIGURE 2
OUR POLITICAL VALUE SYSTEM:
A LIFE-PROTECTING SYSTEM

So we are faced with a greater degree of instability or a maximum likelihood of encountering exceptions to the rules. *But, in general, the natural laws of human behavior, that emanate from the life value, work with a degree of predictability that you can rely on for your problem-solving actions.* AND THAT IS ALL YOU NEED FOR ANY SCIENCE. It is all you need to work successfully toward peace (conflict resolution and violence reduction).

The formula works for cultural differences such as the clothing example, and for genetic differences, such as skin color. The challenging problem is to find the environmental differences (natural or cultural) that explain—or harder, the environmental differences that *once* explained—the origin of the differences that otherwise don't seem to make sense to outsiders. To search out the explanations you must become an astute cultural detective, as you shall see. Fortunately it is fun, once you get over your own culture shock.

Scientific Reliability of the New Problem-Solving Method

The real test for a new scientific method is replication by others. At one time, we had close to one-hundred GI orientation officers lecturing thousands of Americans in four countries. Anyone who did not get a standing ovation from a large audience of fellow GIs was disappointed. Unfortunately, because of the transient nature of the populations plus the semi-secrecy of the program, it was never publicized and institutionalized anywhere.

Simultaneously, in the troubled American universities, the philosophical thinking was moving in the opposite direction: into militant ethical relativism. This movement, I ascertained later, was political more than intellectual. Ethical relativism (the view that there are no universal values) was taught (understandably) to protect us from the foolishness of national chauvinism and from genocidal ideologies such as Nazism. Ironically, ethical relativism (the rejection of the Natural Law) in which led to Nazism, which is again not without its *true believers*, including present-day Americans. In that vein, it has been said that the failure of dictatorial communism in Russia ended history. The observation sounded somewhat true but also absurd. It is both.

The final defeat, possibly, of both right-wing (fascist) and left-wing (Communist) dictatorships probably ended a two-thousand-year-old period of history. It was the history of brainwashed masses fighting and killing one another in the millions to determine what would be the prevailing form of government for leading nations. Democracy won. Among the educated, industrialized countries we are now moving into a more rational, less mob-like, *individualized* stage of world history. It will be written in terms of individual rights and duties, or that is, in terms of the struggle for justice; justice for equal human beings despite artificial geographic boundaries. For example, inevitably, some of the strongest political voices in America, soon, will be for the veiled women in Eurasia, and for the hungry peasants of the world. The most exciting stage of history—for true individual life-respecting civilization—has just begun.

Our job now in the struggle for international understanding and peace in our streets, against many little revolutionary wars and much frustrated fanatical terrorism, is to clarify further, *and activate*, the individualized human-equality/political-freedom ideology. In so doing, we must endeavor to abide by the wisdom expressed some years ago by Daniel Bell (paraphrased): *No word nor line of any ideology (philosophy in action) should be endorsed unless we can explain satisfactorily how, precisely, it serves humankind.* I would add that *humankind* must always be interpreted carefully to mean the *balanced* individual-and-species' well-being.

SUMMARY AND TRANSITION

In the field we had been searching for the universal (culture-transcendent) values that could be activated to reduce disrespect, Ugly Americanism, anti-Americanism, and resulting violence. We had identified the most basic conscious value—*human equality*—and a means of teaching it effectively. And though our ideological programs were impressively effective temporarily, more was needed for greater and longer lasting effectiveness. For example, in the case of the ride on the old bus described earlier, the embarrassing (almost unmentionable) toilet-habit remained a whispered, mocking, seriously divisive issue. There were several questions:

1) Did we dare face those embarrassing issues openly?

2) If we did dare, would we improve relationships or just make things worse?

3) How does one manage the issue; what can one say?

4) Where do you start?

Only the answer to this last question was clear: Start with more research.

CHAPTER 5

THE UNMENTIONABLE CAUSES OF VIOLENCE

During the darkest of ages, religious communities practiced human sacrifice to placate their gods and foster successful growing seasons. The cause of those tragic killings was ignorance. Conditions are similar in these Late Dark Ages of extensive violence. The most basic and general foundation for violence and war is still ignorance. This is why the worldwide violence can be stopped. Good values-based education can provide a reliable long-term solution.

Incidentally, it is helpful to consider the roots of violence, initially, from the overseas perspective, rather than the domestic, for two reasons: 1) that is where we first clearly perceived the deep, somewhat innocent nature of those roots as ignorance, and 2) it is easier for us rational/emotional human beings to maintain objectivity while discussing our foreign, rather than our domestic (for instance, racial) troubles, because most of us are less emotionally involved in the overseas issues.

Since the foundation of the violence is innocent ignorance, that makes it easier to solve than if the basic problem were intentional wrongdoing, but it does not make it easy; easier, but still very difficult. Why so difficult? Because the ignorance at the foundation of the problem is shielded against correction by what we call the truth-resisting *embarrassment syndrome*. Often *neither* side of a social conflict wants the true underlying reason for the trouble admitted. Both insist on attributing the problem to more respectable, surface causes (if not, most naively of all, to intentional evil itself).

Here is a small but typical illustration: a few years ago, I was asked to solve a cross-group problem in the U.S. between two white groups. The children in a grammar school from the hilly, wealthy area were discriminating against comparatively poor children from the low country. There was some fighting among the children. The complaining parents of the poor children believed that the reason for the discrimination was bigotry among the wealthy children. It took me less than a day of interviewing among the wealthy children to find out the real reason: (as one child stated) "the skin diseases that all the gully kids have and are giving to us (highland) kids."

The facts proved to be that a few, and only a very few, of the lowland children occasionally brought the itch to school, and over the past three years, possibly two of the wealthy children had picked up the annoying skin irritation.

I presented these findings to an informal committee and advised that it would be an easy problem to solve. But guess who did not want to have the problem discussed any further if we had to reveal a few cases of the itch? Would you guess: the school administration? The parents of the wealthy children? Or the parents of the poor children?

The answer: all three groups. Why? Because a little fighting over alleged bigotry was more acceptable than facing that actual problem of a *dirty skin disease* no matter how minor. Too embarrassing!

The indispensable purpose of this short chapter is to establish strongly the fact that there are hidden, unmentionable roots of violence. Being unmentionable because of embarrassment, these basic reasons—such as a skin disease—can be almost impossible to surface and cure.

A TIME OF TESTING FOR THE READER

So we have come to the time of testing for the reader. This test will determine whether or not *you* can proceed with us to solve our deepest social problems including violence, drug misuse, and war. Perhaps you will be unwilling to face the issues that must be faced. They may be considered too repulsive, too ungentlemanly, too unladylike, and you'll turn away. (If so, maybe the police will stop the violence in the streets for us and perhaps the terrorists will come to the conference table. Or maybe you can isolate your family so it can escape the growing violence in the world.)

If you can laugh properly at that parenthetical, facetious challenge above, then we are on our way. We can have peace. But it does require a grass-roots movement of tough-minded persons facing issues that most would prefer to evade.

To break through the *embarrassment barriers* on the way to peace, first one has to expose and discard many euphemisms and myths so that the actual barriers can be considered. Before we attack the unmentionable issues that divide human groups and spawn violence, it is worth citing, for an example, a misleading euphemism. It is the worst one of all. (No reasonable effort should be neglected to persuade readers to face the relevant issues with tough-minded maturity. Is it worth all this preparation? You'll see.) The example exists in a familiar description of war.

PARALLEL: THE NATURE OF WAR

When great warriors are asked what war is like, if they answer, they often deceive (unintentionally or otherwise) with a tone of seriousness to reveal their own disapproval, "War is hell," they say.

That is a romantic deception that actually tends to create images of daring exploits through *Dante's Inferno*. What adventurous boy can resist the desire to test himself in such a challenge? The statement, *War is Hell,* is such an understatement that it amounts to a deception.

The two wars that I have participated in were not horribly fascinating like the devil-protected, fiery gates at all. Rather, war is unspeakably disgusting. War is seeing poorly trained American boys committing atrocities—savagely cutting the ears off of injured enemy soldiers. It is stopping them and then wondering about being shot in the back. War is a young husband with his privates blown away and begging you for a grenade and you are tempted to give him one. War is the elderly, half-crazed peasant suffering from "interrogation wounds" lying in the mud beside his dead wife who had been sexually assaulted because he would not tell secrets that he probably did not possess. War is to see an American Marine cut in two by machine gun bullets; seeing him writhing in the dirt, trying to pull his own intestines out of the black, gritty sand and shove them back into the cavity that was his abdomen while pleading with his eyes for you to come out in front of the lines and help him; war is seeing that tortured silent plea just after seeing two of his buddies try, but be killed immediately by sinister, hissing sniper fire from nowhere. War is a young man, your own brother (say), with half his face shot away, while he is choking and drowning in his own vomit as it pulsates out of his throat. This is war. To veil it with the word, "hell," is a manipulative lie, like calling it "heaven." Face it; be able to discuss it for what it is—horrible death over and over—so that we are truly motivated to stop it.

CULTURE SHOCK VERSUS HUMAN EQUALITY

You must be exposed to culture shock in *depth* before we can dig deeper toward a better understanding of the surprisingly controversial concept of *respect for human equality*. That is, in order for most persons to develop unshakable equal respect for all human beings, usually they must proceed through three ideological steps:

1. Learn to appreciate, emotionally, the feeling of life's equality in all of us;

2. Be able to avoid a show of revulsion when exposed to the unattractive poor of the world. (Do you understand? I reiterate, poverty tends to be dirty, smelly, loud, unsanitary, and often dangerous.);

3. But be able to remain understanding and respectful of the wealthy who suffer from culture shock even to the extent of having become haters of, or bigoted toward, the shunned persons. Violent revolution against them will continue to some degree, but it is foolish; too many innocent persons will be killed.

Culture-shocked persons are not bad persons per se, they have suffered psychological shock much the same as, but in a way worse than, an accident victim. *Worse*, because they tend to deny that they are in shock. Most culture-shocked persons honestly believe that their hatred and superior attitudes are justified. Because of values-free education, they do not understand that we are all born with and retain the violence-controlling human equality feeling for our balanced life value. (Denial of this equality threatens lives and stimulates life-protecting violence; it is the Natural Law in action.) Rather, culture-shocked persons—innocent bigots—insist with deep conviction and tortured frustration that respect for human equality is something that others must earn by the observer's standards.

Ranging from a strong conviction to a fuzzy uncertainty, this perspective persists among the overwhelming majority of us modern Americans (and other Westerners as well as among other highly accomplished cultural groups such as the Chinese and Japanese).

THE CULTURE-SHOCKING STIMULI

American college textbooks usually advise that culture shock occurs due to disorientation caused by the absence of familiar stimuli. That's nice; like saying, "War is hell."

It is not the unfamiliar that shocks us; it is the entirely familiar stimuli that are, to the observer, disgusting or frightening. You were exposed during the trip on the old bus but we did not pursue it. Now we must. For we cannot possibly solve problems that we will not face.

CHAPTER 6

THE TRICKY CLEANLINESS-AND-SANITATION VALUE

This chapter moves us from what might be called pure theory to applied theory. Human beings' basic life-protecting equality or behavior-controlling sameness allows us to understand others' cultural differences that had previously caused us to show disrespect.

[Why have we jumped to this step rather than first completing the theory as we would in a traditional academic approach? Because this is the way the conflict-resolution method was developed in response to field problems and the way it must be applied in order to be most successful. Strong culture-shock issues are so unnerving that they must be managed the moment you get the ideological equality/sameness foundation established. Otherwise there will be backsliding as the initial effect of the ideological insight begins to wane.]

POPULAR NEGATIVE TALK

In our bathroom habit case, almost a year of research turned up little that was promising. I found only four items of information that seemed important: One was good; one was great; one was bad, and one was terrible.

First the bad: Research soon revealed that the issue was broader than the mere toilet custom. Many Americans, both military and civilians, in response to general questions regarding their dislikes about the host-nationals, asserted: "They are dirty, smelly people who wipe on their hand."

So the entire issue of a *dirty people* was involved (as is common in the poor countries that are not tropical, *water cultures*). In the latter, many persons bathe several times a day, and may regard Americans, who generally bathe only once or twice a day, as less than clean.

Now the terrible: Someone advised that I should attend one of the military troop orientations for new personnel so that I would know what I was "up against."

All new Air Force personnel were required to attend an orientation within 48 hours after their arrival. I attended the next one scheduled. After an hour or so of lecturers on *creature comforts:* where to buy toothpaste, catch the buses, purchase hamburgers, etc., the *medic* appeared smiling and waving. He was a US Air Force full-colonel with those big birds on his shoulders; that kind of rank impresses the troops. He also happened to be a new friend of mine and a good sport. I had taken more than his pocket change the Saturday before in an enjoyable golf game.

He walked to the center-front of the stage and said candidly:

> My job is to look after your health, so I must be brutally frank. There are seven cases of hepatitis over there in our hospital... (He did not mention an equal number of cases in several of our comparative U.S. cities nor the fact that his forthcoming medical analysis was pure conjecture.) He continued: Now I apologize to you female personnel for my straight talk, but this is your health we are talking about. So I must make certain that everyone understands. He paused for effect, then said, while slowly acting out his message: Hepatitis is an ass-to-hand-to-mouth disease. (Another pause.) Maybe some of you don't know it yet, but the local people don't use toilet paper. They just use their hand, and then maybe twiddle their hand in water. So here is my warning: Do not shake hands with the local people. Hepatitis is a killer.

Culture shock swept across that audience of 400 airmen like a death sentence for jaywalking.

The doctor finished his brief comments, referred to his bundles of handouts at the exits, and asked if there were any questions or comments.

I felt I had to say something in rebuttal so I raised my hand, stood up, got his recognition, and asked if I might make some closing comments. (I did not know exactly what I was going to say other than try to soften his warning a bit.) I stepped to the center-front of the theater just beneath the doctor who was still standing up on the stage. He introduced me:

"All right, ladies and gentlemen," he said, "this is Bob Humphrey, director of the local binational association. I'm sure he is going to invite you into the war for the minds of men." (His tone was fairly serious; I was surprised and pleased. Then he continued in a lighter vein.) "He'll also invite you over to the binational association. So don't forget my warning: Don't shake hands with the local people. And now one more thing: Humphrey DOES shake their hands; so don't shake hands with him either!"

After the explosion of laughter died down, I raised my arms and hands, shook my head in apparent disbelief, and followed the doctor with my eyes smiling disdainfully as he made his departure from the stage. It got some friendly laughter. I then tried these words, hoping for the best:

I'll detain you only one minute or less. The doctor pretty much said it all regarding my invitations. I'll add only three things: One, I give free boxing lessons on Saturday afternoons over at the center. (Pause; good muffled reaction.) Two, we have plenty of places over there where you can wash your hands. (Good laughter.) And three, don't come if you are afraid. (Better laughter.) Hope to see you soon. (Good reaction with some shouts of "Okay," "Right on," and a scattering of hand clapping.)

It seemed that my comments had relieved the tension from the doctor's scare orientation. By the time I walked out of the side door, down front, there was the normal commotion of a departing audience that had seen a jolly movie rather than a somber one. Nonetheless, my mind was still reeling from that devastating medical orientation. Under my breath, I cursed and said: "No wonder we have a relations problem; it's official."

Now the good and the great findings: First, I went to the doctor and complained, nicely. He was friendly but adamant. Then, I went to the local support-detachment commander, also a colonel. He was more than friendly, assuring me that my work had already helped him considerably. But he advised that he was not prepared to tackle a doctor who really did not answer to him but rather had his own chain of command back to the Surgeon General in Washington. Finally, he cautioned me realistically that the ideological war I spoke of was not official and was seldom mentioned.

He did, however, agree to let me conduct a 100% survey among his troops. From that came the first encouraging factor. Again it was a set of responses to only two of my several questions.

One question asked:

Do you like the host-nationals?

A surprisingly high 80% answered *YES*.
Now think about the answer to this second question. It asked:

Do your friends like the host-nationals?

80% answered *NO*.

Explain that inconsistency. (The surveys were always anonymous and confidential.)

Another month of attitude sampling and in-depth interviews revealed the answer conclusively: Only approximately 10% of the Americans in the community felt a strong, prevailing dislike for the local nationals. But that 10% was very vocal. Their loud voices intimidated the other Americans, in general, and they totally controlled the public talk or social atmosphere. (Very good news; possibly great.)

THE IDEOLOGICAL IMPACT OF THE SANITATION/CLEANLINESS BARRIER

The colonel's comments on official disinterest in the ideological war calls for a few words of clarification.

In one of the first countries where I worked, the following question, asked continuously by the host-nationals at our binational functions, was my single biggest nightmare. They always asked: *Where are all the Americans?*

In the community there were at least ten thousand Americans who received our advertising. Yet, at our widely publicized functions in the Center, prior to solving the equality issue, after a hundred or more host-nationals had already arrived, it was customary for me to have to call one or another of my hunting buddies and beg him to drop in *just this one more time* so we could have at least two Americans present.

Can you understand the depth of this problem and its connection to our unfortunate relationships in the Middle East, Asia, Central and South America, and even Germany? Our government organized these Binational Centers or America Houses in order to foster social relations and demonstrate the mutual respect that exists between our two peoples. By Americanizing the functions it makes it easier for us isolationist Americans to participate. However, when we still won't even attend these Americanized functions, these institutions highlight the very problem that they were intended to solve: American indifference, or worse.

To maximize the effectiveness of this institution, obviously I had to find means to reduce the American isolationism caused by the expressions of this negative double whammy: 1) *they are dirty,* and 2) *they wipe on their hand.*

That year became my "interview-everybody stage" because the scholarly literature provided nothing helpful. This lack of a scientific approach to attitude improvement constitutes the absence of the ABC's for global violence reduction.

One day I encountered a small lead. It was like a fishing nibble (or was it just the wind?). It turned-up during a public bath. You may know that all over the world where economies cannot afford a private bath in every home (which is most of the world) there are public baths such as the Finnish or Japanese sauna, the Turkish bath or American-Indian *sweat*.

After you take the steam or hot-water soak, in many you can get the rough-cloth rubdown. The men (for men) and the women (for women) who give these rubdowns or scrub-downs are experts on body cleanliness. During one such rubdown I asked the scrub-boy if he thought the local people were clean. This young man was somewhat objective because he was a Spanish-speaking, Sephardic Jewish lad with whom I could converse a little in my Mexican Spanish. He responded with a surprisingly definite affirmative:

"Oh yes! Very clean," he said.

Surprised at the assertiveness of his answer, I asked, "Why are you so definite?"

He responded: "Well, you see, the village people come in here once a week for this scrub-down. And even though they may be covered from head to toe with dust or mud, it all comes right off. They are very clean underneath, unlike some others." He laughed, and shook his head.

Embarrassed but interested, somehow I knew he was talking about us Americans.

"What others?" I asked, and then, tentatively, went to the crucial question: "How about us Americans?" He shrugged some kind of an affirmative.

I asked again.

"Well," he said, "the first American who ever came in here, the first one I had ever seen, wanted the scrub-down.

But he had that golden hair and that white skin that looked transparent to me. I didn't think he needed the scrub. He insisted. I gave it to him and was astonished to find that the dirt was ingrained in his elbows, knees, and heels. This cloth is like soft sandpaper as you know. The first thing I knew I had rubbed through to little specks of blood on his heel just trying to get it clean.

"I soon found that it is like that with many other Americans. You take your little showers every day, but you don't always get clean. One American doctor tried to tell me the dirt in his elbows was pigmentation. I won a bet off him by making just one of his elbows clean."

I was impressed enough to ask the young man to make certain my elbows were clean. In other words, this new information *was working* on me in the ideological warfare effort to cancel out the idea that they are dirty—and therefore dumb or subhuman—compared to us "clean, superior" Americans.

I told the story the next day in my Language and Culture Course for some sergeants. It worked. They began to pull their elbows down off the arms of their chairs so the persons behind them could not see if they were dirty. There was the nibble I mentioned for fighting against the idea that, *They are dirty.* It turned out to catch a whopper regarding the more difficult issue of wiping on the hand which I'll soon explain.

It also made an important point that I'll not dwell on but should mention. Cultures are different. Human behavior patterns in all cultures are all relative, that is, all relative to *the basic life value, or to human survival.* It, the dual-life value (of self and species), is the basic, universal value to which all else is relative. I'll cover this in detail later. But, it means in general that *cultural relativism,* to a degree, is a sound concept. Different cultures achieve the *same goal* in different ways. Since their environments are different, they are compelled to use different ways. But *ethical relativism* is not a sound concept.

The basic standard of good and bad or right and wrong in all cultures is the same; it is balanced life support. For an example of both points, again, persons in the tropics and persons in the arctic seek the same life-sustaining body temperature. But one group puts on clothes while the other takes them off to achieve that sameness.

CULTURE SHOCK, BREAKING IT OPEN

My closest friend among the host-nationals was a businessman/scholar who had earned his college degree in America.

I telephoned him and reported my little nibble of success with the sergeants, regarding the cleanliness issue. He received the news in silence rather than with the expression of surprise and pleasure that I expected. I repeated the account, adding details.

"Bob," he said, "could you come down to my office this afternoon." It was more like an order than a question. I agreed. When I entered the store, he placed the CLOSED sign in the window and pulled the blinds. Not unlike the typical elderly host-national, he was a taciturn fellow, serious and silent. I was concerned. I was in Asia, after all. He took me into the back room which was a sort of living quarters. Uneasily, I sat down. Finally, he spoke: "Bob," he declared, "I spent some time in our capital city last week. There is considerable talk that maybe we would be better off if the American forces were not stationed here. The ostensible issues are military bases, relations with third countries, and the like. But I can tell you that those are just surface issues, excuses. It's like the woman who shot her husband for wearing his shoes in the house. The shoes were not the problem. He had a second woman. It's the same here. Our people are far too proud to endlessly tolerate the whispering and sometimes loud drunken denunciations which allege that we are dirty. This bathroom habit issue seems to be at the seat of the problem."

With that comment, he laughed and paused. Finally, I saw the humor and laughed, too, in great relief. I was not going to be stabbed or shot or whatever.

Perceiving my reaction, he said, "Yes, relax, Bob; this is not going to be a complaining session against Ugly Americans, but an intellectual discussion. Your sensitivity to the dirty elbow issue convinces me that you can handle a supersensitive discussion of differences in the toilet customs. Quite frankly, I have been working on our relations since the American soldiers first arrived. It has been terribly frustrating. Now, I suspect that your cultural-detective approach has revolutionary promise."

He stood up and went to the stove to check the water. Yes, it was boiling; time for tea, a matter of considerable social importance where there are still traditional cultures rather than merely modern economies. Slowly, we sipped two cups of tea through much friendly banter about hunting, fishing, and the weather. Finally, he set his empty cup down definitively and returned to his serious mood.

"You see, Bob, we all know that Americans say we are dirty because we do not use toilet paper. We hear them making jokes about wiping on the hand. Well... we view it differently. (Long pause.) We believe a person should take a little bath... (pause) after a trip to the toilet. It is inconceivable to us that anyone can get clean by just using dry paper. (Long pause.) You know that I speak not as an ignorant Asian peasant. I attended one of your greatest universities. There I tried not to be an Ugly Asian. I tried to conform to your bathroom habit—just using the dry paper. I almost had to try because your toilets are not equipped with handy 'little bath' water facilities. But after about six weeks of a determined effort, I finally realized that I had to find some way to take the little bath. I could not get accustomed to the itchy feeling of dirtiness from just using dry paper. What I learned to do was find a way to take water with me into the toilet and wet the paper. I used to laugh about it to myself thinking what Rudyard Kipling would say if he learned that someday East and West would meet merely through the use of wet toilet paper."

It took him a long, long time to tell me that little story. As he talked, he watched my face closely, observing my reactions. Each of those few thoughts was softened carefully through an interspersion of reassurances about the greatness of America, and his memorable experiences there. Apparently pleased with my silent, open-minded attentiveness, after a second session of tea, he concluded with these thoughts:

I am telling you all this, Bob, not confidentially, but hoping that you might be able to use it constructively as you did that marvelous hunting story, and now the dirty elbows. I am convinced that if our government changes, your military, on some excuse, will be asked to leave. But, still, your work, the work of the Center in this city, might be able to keep things more friendly in this province. In closing, let me admit that even though we don't say critical things in public about Americans as the Americans do about us, we do have a joke about the American bathroom habit that you might consider using. We ask if that is the way they wash their dishes. Do they just take a dry piece of paper and wipe them out?

He smiled cautiously; I laughed. It worked on me. (He was prophetic; American forces did get asked out of the country eventually. But the leading citizens in his province spoke against the expulsion and were among the most vocal in rescinding the repudiation.)

Of course his explanation created for me another *time for testing*. I was not looking forward to this one. Having been a part-time teenage vagabond (*bum* to the unromantic) during the Great Depression as well as a member of the CMTCs, the CCCs, the Marines, and the merchant marines, profanity and vulgarity did not bother me. Talk of personal toilet habits did. For a test of *these* new materials, I did not ask the military community relations officer for a theater full of men; I asked for just one small group. I did dare to request the toughest group: the top NCOs.

To these twenty men I summarized our overseas situation as I saw it, and then gave an account of my session with the local scholar regarding the bathroom habit. The men were not embarrassed, but there was pin-dropping silence. So I knew they were listening. I finished the account quickly and waited for reactions.

Silence.

I needed comments. "What do you think," I asked.

An older staff sergeant spoke: "Okay," he said, "I'll comment. As many of you know, despite the Moslem religion here, I am one of the lucky few who found a woman to live with. She is a dancer from (the next city over). When I first brought some American toilet paper into the house, she was interested. In fact, she liked it. You know, it is nice to squeeze, like the Charmin. Then a few days later, she threw it all out. She said it left her itchy and dirty. She said I had to get out too unless I could change to cleaner ways. "Well," he smiled big, "I became a big LITTLE-BATH-MAN, myself, after that!" Everyone laughed.

A top sergeant stood up. He was not only a top sergeant, older than most, but also an imposing man who spoke with a fatherly tone. He said: "I am pleased that this finally has all come out. I have lived here since Americans first came after the war. I married a local girl and have three children. I don't want to embarrass anyone but this is something I have always wanted to tell all Americans. These local ways are cleaner. At least be up front with your kids. Teach them to wet the paper."

Open surprise and laughing agreement prevailed in the classroom. A couple of men joked about wanting to excuse themselves to go and take a *little bath* before we continued the lesson.

I had a visit the next day from an American teacher from the local girls' school. She advised that her boyfriend, a sergeant, had told her about the bathroom habit discussion. She said she was the daughter of a missionary. She was born and had lived much of her life in the East Indies. Her parents had taught her the *little bath* method. She said when she first visited the U.S. and found out about the dry paper method, she viewed it as the filthiest habit on the face of the earth, and still felt that way. She advised me irrefutably, as only missionaries can, that it was my duty to share the information with the local American women, as the more appropriate and *"psychologically tougher"* recipients (she used the term) than the men.

I asked her why she thought that the women were tougher psychologically. She advised that in her experience with these grim patterns of life in the suffering underdeveloped world, the women are more likely to accept them for what they are, or else conceal them quietly, whereas the men make them worse by making dirty jokes about them.

"You know," she added firmly, "regarding the little bath, there is not as much difference here as is obviously imagined. All Americans also take the little bath of the unmentionable anatomy when they do take a bath. Does it not make sense then, to take it more frequently and every time it might be needed? You watch, she said prophetically, some day, when America grows up, there will be wet bathroom paper. Meanwhile, tell Sergeant Smith they don't have to spit on the paper as he has suggested; just keep a little glass or bowl of diluted mouthwash in the bathroom for wetting the paper for the final nice, clean wash. Cleanliness is truly next to Godliness," she concluded.

Together with the hunting story, we used these new culture-shock materials to construct a very high-impact orientation. Soon we had covered the ten thousand or more military personnel in the area through their own opinion leaders. It was so successful that I could send a new man, as a shill, to a table of men in any of the military clubs and ask him to complain about the apparent dirtiness of the host nationals. It became a rare event when such a shill was not treated to a hard-talking GI lecture on the comparative cleanliness of the local people.

Now, these many years later, I am approached occasionally by one of the many thousands of Americans stationed at that post during my days on that assignment. The words are rewarding. He will say (usually laughing). "I was with you at so-and-so where we learned the cleaner little bath habit. I still wet the paper-spit on it if necessary. I taught it to all my children."

WINNING THE PEOPLE

The host-nationals that we hired there on that job in the huge multinational defense corporation became very strongly pro-American. Local people would quit higher-paying jobs at other American firms just to be with our Attractive Americans.

The local government did not allow their citizens to keep many weapons. But it was clear to me that our GIs, properly trained to win the people, could safely arm the local civilians, there, to stand with them in defense of democracy against an invader. Unfortunately, it is too late to discuss that possibility for democracy versus the Killing Fields in Lower East Asia, but it is not too late for the rest of the Third World where oppressive forces are still strong and threatening—especially in Latin America and Africa. The day of that need is coming.

Friendship of the kind that our GIs could develop but do not now enjoy even in Western Europe could change decisively the likelihood of recurrent dictatorships anywhere. We could establish a deep love and respect for democracy and Americans worldwide. Of even more immediate importance, host-nationals such as the people of Spain, Greece, and the Philippines would strongly insist that our GIs remain in their countries, even if it meant (as a far-out example) the retention of missiles. In fact, on the three cases I worked that involved local people's ostensible opposition to our missiles, it was our *people* they wanted out. Opposition to the missiles was a subterfuge. How do I know? Because after we improved the person-to-person relations, the opposition to the missiles disappeared.

CULTURE SHOCK, RECENT FOLLOW-ON

Recently, I was teaching this culture-shock lesson to a group of business-school graduate students who were hoping to work overseas. Of the thirty students, about ten were from the Near East. One of the young Americans asked if this old lesson on culture shock and bathroom habits was still relevant. The laughter from the Asians and some of the military officers in the class more or less answered his question just as the class ended. So I advised that he should talk with some of his classmates who had been abroad in the past few years. Instead, he, several other Americans, and some Asian students gathered at my desk.

The first to speak was a Near Easterner who laughed about the problems he and some of his friends were having while trying to keep clean with our *limited American bathroom facilities.* Their modern toilet stools, *back home,* he explained, have a little faucet inside them somewhat like a bidet (or sit bath).

His current problem here in America was that he lived in a private home where the toilet was inside a little closet inside the larger bathroom. So to keep from being embarrassed and to keep from embarrassing his landlord, he had bought some kind of a green plant that he kept in the toilet closet on the grounds that he loved to have some kind of green growth in all his rooms. This allowed him to keep a small sprinkler of water in the toilet closet. He said that all of his Asian friends had nicknamed him *The Closet Gardener.*

Another student explained that in order to accommodate Americans back in his home (Near Eastern) country, his father had installed American bathroom facilities in their huge bathroom right next to their own traditional facilities. The traditional toilet in much of Asia does not have a chair-like toilet stool. You do not sit; you squat or hunker down. There are places for your feet straddling a toilet hole in the porcelain, or cement, floor. The water faucet and soap dish for the little bath are adjacent.

The young man laughed that American military men who visit his home have given special names to all of the facilities. He said they call the American seat, *the throne,* and the local facility either *the squatter,* or *the bombsight.* His point was that these terms had added light humor, in the place of criticism, to the entire issue and made them much easier to discuss. He insisted that some place between two-thirds and three-quarters of the world's people use the squatters; that all Americans should learn about them because they are not only cleaner but better; better facilitators of bodily functions; much better than the tons of laxatives purchased by Americans.

The young American who had started the discussion was by this time in a bit of culture shock; red necked and defensive. Almost angrily he said, "Well, I have always been taught that a man's home is his castle. So for me, as king at my house, I prefer a throne to a bombsight." The only female in the conversation, a diminutive Asian girl, tweaked by the castle-king talk and the implicit putdown of the squatter facility, spoke softly: "Homes should be castles with thrones for both the king and the queen, but the thrones should not be something you put in the toilet room."

CHAPTER 7

UNDERSTANDING CROSS-GROUP LOVE AND HATE

You've got to be taught to hate....
You've got to be taught before it's too late.

Are those the lines of the marvelous South Pacific song? They certainly teach the first lesson we learn in school about the cause of bigotry. And, in that human beings possess huge freethinking brains rather than uncontrollable instincts, the lesson is, to a degree, true. However, according to my overseas experiences in this work, it is only about half-true. One learns to hate easily from one's own ignorance and natural fears. One does not have to be taught by bigots.

In the early 1970s, the U.S. Navy began transporting entire families overseas to live in attractive foreign *homeports* for morale purposes. This was at a time when the U.S. Navy, under the compulsory Race Relations programs of the Pentagon, had introduced the *touch-feel* approach to human relations. It included the removal of rank designators from uniforms; then encouraged cross-rank fraternization—hugging (normally violations of regulations).

Bad as that program was for military discipline, it did not teach persons to hate. On the contrary, one of the most interesting aspects of its inclusion in military training was how aggressively it taught touch-feel *love*. Occasionally, stories leaked out about little cross-rank, male-female *love-ins* that occurred spontaneously at the edge of one of those mandatory human relations sessions. Here is the point again: Unabashedly, that program taught love, not hate. Nonetheless, it was totally ineffective against culture shock, or, that is, poverty shock.

For example, a huge contingent of American families was shipped into one allied country that was already regarded favorably by most

Americans. That contingent was given this special love-oriented touch-feel love-training during its trip across the ocean (as well as the traditional language and culture training). As a result of the comprehensive indoctrination, more than 95% of the Americans in the entire contingent committed themselves to becoming *Attractive Americans* in the new homeport.

A few months later, I was dispatched to the country to try to salvage American/host-national relations which *had gone sour.* Some local newspapers were already suggesting that the Americans should go home.

I conducted questionnaires on both sides. The host-nationals complained about our Ugly Americanism *in general terms.* (There it was again. I realized the local people were embarrassed to say, *specifically*, what it was the Americans were doing or saying that was offensive.)

Questionnaires also revealed how long it had taken for the high expectations on both sides to turn to disillusionment. Guess how long.

Approximately twenty-four hours.

Here is a typical explanation from an American officer, husband and father:

> We came down that gangplank meaning to love this country and these people. After all that unique orientation and training, that determination was foremost in all of our minds. No shipload of people has ever been more filled with love for one's fellow human beings. But by the time I got my three children and all the bags off the ship, there were no taxies left. Then, of course, my little daughter needed to go to the restroom. I had to take her back aboard ship. Susan, my wife, stayed with the two small boys.
>
> When I returned, Susan was crying. Robbie, my eight-year-old, said they had moved over closer to the ship to escape the sight of some men around the dock who were taking leaks in the streets. During that time, my wife's suitcase was stolen.

We finally got two cabs for the trip to the designated quarters; the rides were just too dangerous. I couldn't control both cabs, so I decided to let mine keep up with my wife's. Combat was less frightening. Then after we got to the quarters, the plumbing immediately got stopped up. The local people who promised to come right out and help did not come. Meanwhile, I had a job to do at the office. Shall I go on? You asked me about feelings of love and hate. I'll tell you for sure, before I got through that first night, hatred had set in.

I did not seek an extended contract in this country because, simultaneously, I had an offer from the U.S. Navy to try to solve a more interesting problem in the fascinating island of La Maddalena, Italy. But I mentioned this single case from another country because it illustrated so well the point that you don't have to be taught to hate. You learn on your own.

Hatred comes easily to humans. In fact, most of us have had occasions to hold someone else's new baby child. Remember that unflattering experience? Human infants are not just uncertain about strangers, many will screech enraged rejections of every person except that wonderful woman with the familiar smell, voice, and loving face—not to mention the friendly flowing nipples.

We humans with our big flexible brains have to nurture or have nurtured our natural inclinations to love as well as to hate. But it does not always take third parties to do the nurturing. Customs of others that seem unsanitary or dangerous will tend to cause us to fear. Hate follows easily. Universal values education is required to overcome the customary disrespect for, or hatred of, foreign, frightening cultural patterns.

Remember: The glib approach of the modern relativistic intellectual who says simply, *Everyone is different and you have to respect those differences,* is just talk. Seriously culture-shocked persons, on hearing those idealistic shibboleths in reference to some other groups' differences (apparent filth or casual vulgarity, for examples) merely say to themselves: *Yes they certainly are different, but I don't have to accept them. And I don't, because those differences are dangerous or harmful, and the people who practice them are stupid... (dumb, dirty, dishonest, lazy, unsanitary, immoral, cruel, crazy, and downright subhuman.)*

GENERAL REVIEW

To overcome the natural human inclination to be culture-shocked and start avoiding, and in extreme cases, hating, others over their strange differences, the irreducible minimum is this:

1. Teach convincingly humankind's equality of the life value. *This respect for human equality* rather easily expands into the scientifically-supported proposition that humans enjoy a certain sameness regarding general intellectual ability, and especially, life-supporting common sense.

2. This new, ideologically based acceptance of equal, basic intelligence is a primary proposition you must reinforce with your cultural detective work. That is, find the original and hidden rationale beneath cultural differences that are shocking to newcomers.

3. Remember that because of the normally exaggerated negative public impressions, it helps to ascertain from attitude studies, and publicize, how many persons from both, or all, conflicting cultures are persons of goodwill who would like more amicable relations. It is usually around 80%. During my last studies a few years ago, it was that high in U.S. black/white relations. And even though the following two sets of studies were necessarily casual and oral—without keeping records—the figures were quite high in South Ireland regarding peace with the North, and also in Greek/Turk relations in several of their cities.

TRANSITION

After the equality concept is established and the cultural misunderstandings are reduced, a deeper block to peaceful attitudes will still cause violence-threatening hostilities in a considerable number of minds. That phenomenon is physical fear of others, of society, and of life. Can it be solved? I think that question asks this: Are we willing and wise enough to arrange for its solution in our own children despite our sedentary, softening cultures?

CHAPTER 8

WALKING THROUGH LIFE WITHOUT FEAR

Despite our need to avoid publicity, word spread through American diplomatic and military channels about our successes in overcoming massive anti-Americanism. One day my assistant hurried into my office and asked if I recognized the name, von Braun. I did. The von Brauns were brothers, two of America's leading missile experts. My assistant was excited:

"Well, one of them is in town with some other high-ranking civilians and military officers. They want to see you about using our program to help install the Jupiter missile system in the Mediterranean. The work apparently has slowed to a standstill in southern Italy over bad relations. Billions of dollars in losses are involved. It sounds like you can name your price."

I named a price and returned to the U.S. to give the offer serious consideration. During that time the troublesome *fear issue* arose noticeably. It is time to discuss it. I'll do so in terms of this case and two others that are otherwise unrelated. One was in the military; the other, in the Peace Corps regarding a job that I was considering as an alternative to this missile assignment.

FEAR OF NEW IDEAS

During a brief contract with our Foreign Aid program in three Latin American countries, I was told by prominent local businessmen that our Peace Corps, in those Catholic countries, was being discounted or ignored. Why? Because of the members' liberal attitudes (and practices) regarding *free sex*. The Corps, instead of being translated, in Spanish, to *A Body for Peace,* was being called sarcastically, *Bodies for Pieces.*

I discussed this and similar *ideological* problems with a traveling Peace Corps representative and was asked to come back to Washington and go through their employment procedure. I went, and asked for Indonesia where the Corps contingent was likely to face ideological arguments from Communists.

I was advised that the Corps was *preclusively fearful* of ideological issues and would not even discuss my suggestion. Rather, I was offered a *politically safe* country.

In the *individual rights* atmosphere of the 1960s, it was futile to try to explain just how deeply the young Corps members were already involved in ideological issues such as the socially defiant sexual attitudes, so I gave up that Peace Corps possibility. (That is no reflection on the more responsible Peace Corps personnel of today.)

Most interesting, during this interlude, was a possible opportunity to brief the President on the new ideological warfare program.

If I accepted the Jupiter missile contract, the ideological character of my work was certain to become a little more high-profile than it was in any of my previous situations. So while in Washington, I decided to give a few low-level briefings. I speculated that the politically acceptable nature of my work would be seen. Then word of that assessment would spread casually up through the talk-oriented Washington scene. The project would then be politically safe, I ascertained.

Those lectures stimulated considerably more interest than I expected. I was asked to make a presentation before the huge so-called *USIA Noon Forum* which I was told included all the USIA personnel in the Capital. It was a head-spinning success.

There was a dynamic young psychologist, Dr. Leo Crespi, in USIA who grasped the values-based educational program's worldwide possibilities. In conjunction with an Assistant Director of the International Section of the Bureau of the Budget, Dr. Robert McNeill, Dr. Crespi encouraged me to give some higher-level briefings. I agreed. We proceeded through the necessary levels and were finally asked to give a formal briefing to the powerful, behind-the-scenes combined organization called the Operations Coordination Board and National Security Council.

After the presentations, the members of that NSC/OCB committee sat silent and pensive, clearly surprised by, and interested in, what they had heard on overseas culture shock and ideological education. *However, the first to speak expressed fear about its ideological warfare nature. Remember now, this was at the height of the Cold War.*

The members looked at one another with raised eyebrows and questioning glances. Eventually, one suggested that I should make a presentation to the chief training officer of the CIA. I declined in disgust toward that implication that emphasizing America's belief in human *equality* was in any way requisite of covert action. Granted, our overseas, people-to-people networks that developed incidentally from our win the people efforts were retrieving considerably better *intelligence* than our CIA's small covert operations; but that *intelligence* gathering was *entirely* coincidental.

Finally, I was asked if I would be willing to make the presentation to the President and Vice President. The intellectual fear represented by that suggestion made me feel a little sick. I had been told these NSC men were among the most powerful in the government. Yet, obviously they were afraid to trust their own judgments and support open ideological warfare against bigotry overseas.

The Administration, at the time, was *lame duck,* so my own advisers in the room smelled a (political) rat. The brightest among them whispered at once: *Don't touch it, Bob; they are all obviously scared. They will pre-brief the President with that fear. And what, really, is there to gain? If the President says yes, you will still be asked to take the missile assignment for the next year. It is about the most important overseas task in the world today. You already have that. But if he says no, this vital program is dead.*

I requested a day's delay to consider the decision.

I did not conduct an attitude study, but quietly investigated the reason for the obvious fear. Reminiscent of the McCarthy days, it was a fear that endorsement of *human* equality might be mistaken for support of communism's *economic* equality. Amazing!

Meanwhile, do *not* think that this uncertainty about human equality prevails at America's grass-roots. The equality idea still rules the actions of our common folk, and it is being carried solidly in our legal system through our common law or case law. (See the book, *Fairness and Justice, Law in the Service of Equality* by the Harvard and UC Davis professors, Charles Haar and Daniel Fessler, respectively.)

I declined the Presidential briefing opportunity and headed back overseas to tackle the challenge of the failing missile installation. The site was southern Italy, down in the heel of the boot. My only weapons were the old ideas from 1776 that our top-level presidential advisers were afraid to discuss. That fear meant I had to continue to keep the ideological content (the human equality/freedom principle) as secret as possible.

"Whom They Fear They Hate" —Cicero

I mentioned earlier an approximate 80% *silent majority* of Americans who are basically constructive persons. They don't want to dislike nor criticize foreigners nor anyone, but they get intimidated by the loud 10% *hater* group. In that potentially constructive but silent 80% group, a small number (about 10%) are highly positive persons who are daring enough to try new policies or programs until most are crushed by tradition or other forces.

In that hopeful 10% group, there are smaller subcategories. There is a tiny faction, maybe 1%, whose members are so opposed to the *industrialized rat race* that, overseas, they go native. That is, they join completely into the slower-moving, foreign cultures. Often these are sweet, loving, apolitical persons who sincerely become devotees of the traditional cultures.

You can't employ them actively in your programs because they will alienate all other Americans. But you can learn much from them about the constructive aspects of the shunned cultures.

Another one of these tiny 1% groups consists of persons who have learned to compete and excel in our own culture, yet are enlightened enough and daring enough to glean out the promising new ideas from among all the fuzzy stuff. Perhaps most important, they are intelligent enough to know how to try these new ideas without destroying themselves. The rare combination of talents in this unusual group seems to run in families. I am sure you can think of examples.

The Krulaks of Marine fame constitute one such family whose members I have met on crucial occasions in this change-agent (nation-building) business. The father became a three star general in time of war; (that is the supreme test in a military career). One of his sons, of all unexpected professions, became a Marine chaplain; another, a Marine officer, who served in Vietnam, is now also a general. The unusual qualities they possess that kill off most would-be leaders are, 1) the daring to try new methods that are questioned by other leaders, and 2) even more hazardous, the courage to change their minds publicly on major policy. I'll cite one example as an introduction to the next example of the enemy to social progress: fear.

At a time when my ideological (*win the people*) approach was being attacked at the top, the young combat officer, Charles Krulak, dared to put one of the programs into a Marine unit to stop cross-cultural difficulties. As polished as Marine brass, he led a program of hard-punching unarmed self-defense skills (tied appropriately to the ideology of protecting others) just as smoothly as if the new training were a part of the Old Corps.

It is this new American martial art, called STRIKE, that we must now consider. As another somewhat lucky discovery, it gave us the means to overcome *personal physical fear,* the third major cause of hatred and violence in the world. The first two major causes, recall, are *ideological* (the superiority complex), and *cultural* (cross-group misunderstandings).

TEACHING MEN HOW TO FIGHT
IN ORDER TO STOP THEIR FIGHTING

The leader of a small (thirty-man) overseas contingent of Americans tasked me with building good relations between his men and a small community of Asians on a Pacific Island. These local citizens demonstrated neither open friendliness nor unfriendliness. They were passively polite. They advised me that the previous American military contingent had shot up their city a year or so earlier. No one was killed. The incident, they said, had been settled and officially forgotten.

The new, small American unit represented one of the most respected organizations of fighting men in the world. I talked to every man. They seemed to be typically nice, friendly Americans. Attitude studies among them did not turn up the customary attitude that, *these (foreign) people are subhuman.* So the case seemed to be a mild one. The allegations were merely that 1) *these people are stupid, immoral, and dangerous to the American cause.* And 2) *they are also unfriendly; their women won't talk to us or date us even though they are adequately Westernized that they date, to a limited degree, with their own men.*

I persuaded the young Americans that we should win the local people over to a position of mutual respect for two reasons: so we could place machine guns in their second-story windows if needed, and (obviously) so we could date their available, respectable women. I took the men through the ideological and culture-shock-cure materials, and tasked them with winning back the town.

To my surprise, it did not work. These men continued to start fights quickly with the local men over trivial incidents.

For a couple of weeks, *I worked the town.* I watched the areas that the Americans frequented at night and on weekends. These young Americans, self-appraised toughest of the tough, swaggered excessively, pugnaciously inviting trouble in public. Some fought well before anyone ever dropped a hat. They knew they were going into combat soon, and were nervous about it. I arranged to accompany them on a camping trip, a bivouac. There, I talked with each man extensively. Campfires at night tend to loosen the tongue. My findings were surprising at first; then, on second thought, understandable.

These robust, young fighting men were brave. It was one of their most conscious and cherished qualities. But brave men are not fearless. Fearlessness, obviously, is a much more unusual quality than bravery. Fearless persons are not afraid even when they should be. (I once saw such a man in combat on Iwo Jima. His name was Taylor—a corporal who was leading a platoon. Because of his fearlessness, described in *Attachment A,* he could not possibly have lived through that conflagration uninjured.) Brave men, on the other hand, are willing to do what they should do despite their fear. And men who pride themselves on their bravery, especially young ones, seem to feel compelled to do what they are afraid to do. That, of course, involves street-fighting over insignificant incidents.

Suddenly, research, again, had clarified the problem for me. These men were a little afraid of the local nationals. They were simply too young and confused to deal with the combination of factors involved: bravery, high pride, their own close-knit social-group pressures to fight quickly, and finally, a surrounding foreign population of men *who frightened them.* They had to fight or else someone, especially themselves, might think they were cowards. These specific thoughts, in those long talks by the campfire, were expressed. The possible answer was also clear: Teach the young men to fight well enough so that they did not feel afraid of the local nationals. I did. The excessive swaggering stopped, so did the fighting. It worked like the proverbial charm; friendly dating started with the local women. To teach them to fight, we used the modified boxing training called STRIKE for decisive reasons: With well-trained supervision, it can be taught quickly and safely, yet raises self-confidence significantly. (In subsequent years, seeking something safer, we tried most of the other martial arts. Even though they have superior qualities for other purposes, we found that none of those can be taught effectively enough to get a lift in self-confidence for large numbers quickly).

In addition to STRIKE'S experimental (confidence-building) use with a few friends in Italy, we have now used the STRIKE component in several major programs and in one long, field experiment, all while working to stop or preclude violence among young clients of unusually high pride:

1. In a program between American military men and young Turks in which both groups got the training,

2. With Marines in a California Guard Detachment under Major Charles Krulak in Coronado, California,

3. With Green Beret troops in Okinawa under two other outstanding leaders both, also, (as I recall) by the name of Taylor: one, a colonel and the other, a top sergeant, and

4. During eight years of experiments with different groups of troubled teenagers: (a) with white *children at risk* in the Chicago area, (b) with Mexican/American hard-core dropouts in trouble with the law on the California-Mexican border, and (c) with Native (Indian) dropouts in northern Alberta, Canada. The success rates (with over 90% retained in school, including advancement of several into college and into the military services) would have been impossible without the STRIKE-motivator.

OVERCOMING FEAR FOR A MODERN MILITARY

Transition: Continuing the topic of fear, (1) Do you know what happens when a boxer gets hit and hurt in the boxing ring? Answer: *If he is an amateur,* fear and anger are likely to overwhelm him, and he will quickly fight himself into exhaustion. (2) Do you know what happens when a soldier in combat suddenly sees many of his buddies blown to pieces? Answer: *If he is an amateur (inexperienced with physical fear),* fear and rage are likely to overwhelm him, allowing irrational acts to the extreme of committing atrocities.

EXPERIENCED, TRULY PROFESSIONAL FIGHTERS DO NOT LET ANYTHING MAKE THEM UNCONTROLLABLY *MAD.* ANGER IS USUALLY SELF-DEFEATING; PHYSIOLOGICALLY, IT SHUTS DOWN THE THINKING PROCESSES.

As the result of Marine Commandant Chapman's earlier endorsement, and another innovative experiment by another outstanding Marine officer, Major Jan Rider, the commander of Camp Pendleton, the late General Wilcox, studied the new military training approach. He let me give him the values lessons including the STRIKE for a month in his office and then decided to put the entire program into all of the 1st Marine Division.

Tragedy struck the week after he announced that significant decision. The wonderful man and daring leader suffered a fatal heart attack after a tennis game. Had he lived, I speculate that many years ago we would have upgraded our infantry military training appropriately for the current age of ideological (low-intensity) warfare.

Here is the key point: In Camp Pendleton at the time when General Wilcox was considering the use of STRIKE, our attitude studies showed that almost 100% of the enlisted men in any group questioned wanted the semi-boxing training. However, most of the officers and senior NCOs were reluctant about adopting the program *out of the definite, expressed fear that they could not learn nor teach even the modified boxing.* Numerous experiments, properly coached, have always proven that this self-doubting fear is unfounded.

Nonetheless, the fear is very, very strong. Think about this: That fear of boxing is not strong among most of the many young women's groups we have taught, including Catholic nuns. But it is almost *stunning* among young men in groups *who are already supposed to be fighters but are only amateurs.* The fear of looking bad, of course, is the explanation. The most commonly expressed reason for rejecting participation in the hitting-skills training is somewhat as follows: *I boxed once against a bigger boy and got hit so hard that I hurt for a week. That was the last of boxing for me, forever.*

In this coming age of low-intensity (win the people) warfare, that fear of the hitting skills, like the fear of foreign cultures, must be overcome. The fast self-confidence that STRIKE (the hitting skill) builds among young men is now of decisive importance to America. It allows young military men in strange and foreign lands to walk calmly as friends and protectors in any civilian society, no matter how frightening. But as of right now, despite lip-service to the contrary, our troops are trained (or untrained) more to alienate foreign citizens than to win their respect. (Our younger enlisted men are not even always welcome in all U.S. neighborhoods.) It could be otherwise, and needs to be.

Our military forces could easily be upgraded into more professional fighting forces whose men would never degrade themselves to the point of committing atrocities as has occurred in all past wars considerably more than anyone likes to admit. I'll mention one injury-depleted rifle platoon of seven men that I took over temporarily on Iwo; three *proudly* showed me the gold teeth they had been tromping out of Japanese mouths for their own personal spoils of war. I stopped it of course, but learned that three lieutenants before me had not.

Through a full, fast, values-teaching program, that necessarily includes STRIKE, our GIs could also be made into much better soldiers; men who, for example, could be relied on to overcome heavy combat stress and fire their weapons almost unanimously. (According to my observations of several front-line platoons in combat, only too few men fired, sometimes none.) Simultaneously, these values-trained men would be the type who would make all civilians feel safer in any situation, just by their presence.

SUMMARY AND CONCLUSION

Fear is a mighty culprit, especially if it is not reduced to a minimum in men who are trained to kill. The only known way to reduce it rapidly and safely that we can find is through very, very carefully controlled training in the unarmed fist-fighting skills; this, despite my opposition to boxing as a profession.

When we have had to teach hard-core dropout boys to get out of crime and back into school, we found that we had to start with STRIKE in order to overcome their fear of society, their under-confidence, and their generally dangerous rage.

When we have had to build up the confidence of teenage girls who have dropped out of school and allegedly lost their way in life, in order to teach them to read, we learned to start with this confidence-building and self-respect-building hitting-skills training.

[Initially, when we objected to teaching STRIKE to girls from the street-gangs, they protested on two grounds: Men no longer protect them in the streets. Second, they thought it might also help them to resist frequently encountered efforts at rape (including incest). A few later reported that they were right. It did help.]

The reason, it seems, that STRIKE, uniquely, prepares men to overcome the debilitating stress (uncontrolled fear) in *armed* combat is that it forces practice under conditions of close-in, *sustained battering* where you must learn to calm yourself during the battery and fight back coolly (or else get clobbered). In the other martial arts there is too much distance between contestants most of the time to provide this sustained stress training. As a *proven* self-confidence builder for overcoming debilitating and dangerous fear, *safely,* STRIKE has no rival.

In the Iraq war, the horrible factor called "friendly fire" became a major cause of fatalities. In my combat experience, the dreaded "friendly fire casualties" were primarily the result of uncontrolled fear from inadequate training.

CHAPTER 9

THE SECRET TO TEACHING VALUES

So what is the best *formula* for solving human conflicts? As you know, we have been discussing its key factor, the basic life value, all through this document. But during all of our early field programs, which uncovered and employed this basic concept (the life value that demands equal respect), there were serious elements of uncertainty in our minds:

1. How does one explain briefly the *dual* aspect, especially the species-preserving side, of the life value, and do so decisively? The values-selection-list introduced in Chapter Four is helpful but a bit too intellectual for many groups.

2. How does the species-preserving side of the value operate *exactly*?

3. Closely related, how do the great spiritual values such as love, charity, honor, and loyalty tie in objectively to the total system? Is there really a science of human nature that includes our earthly, *horizontal* (person-to-person) spiritual values? Of course in these educational courses you cannot get involved formally with the students' religious or *vertical*, spiritual (person-to-God) values.

4. What precisely are the dictates of the Natural Law so that they might be followed more effectively thereby reducing global tensions and violence?

We knew for a long time that if our search uncovered exact answers to those questions, we could not only reconcile the great disagreements between human groups including Communists and capitalists, but also upgrade the nebulous field of ethics into humankind's most important science—an active science for developing peaceful human relations.

As these answers ever so slowly were forthcoming over the years, we could see why they had defied perception so persistently: They are extremely subtle despite their simplicity. In my judgment, they have eluded the great philosophers because those brainy scholars relied mainly on their thinking ability rather than on scientific observation of human behavior. Since several were so cerebral that I could hardly read their literature, I knew better than to trust my intuition. I constantly repressed those internal whispers to a irreducible minimum, and used, in their place, the patient, year after year scientific method: observation.

For half a lifetime I moved from country to country, state to state, city to city, village to village, observing and studying how the human being behaves *consistently* (that is, according to species-specific genetic tendencies), despite major environmental differences. We then rechecked these findings in action programs in widely diverse cultures designed to test the strength or weakness of these apparent behavioral tendencies. How else, really, can one determine the nature of any living species?

We spent considerable time in at least twenty-five countries and lived from one to eight years, each, in nine. Of course, field conditions seldom allow for completely valid and reliable studies. Consequently, as I present the additional ideological findings of the past three decades, I'll also flesh out the methodology in enough detail that you can see where the research needs replication. Of course, as it is with any scientist, I worked under the influence of my personal experiences. I'll present that part of my background that most influenced my early hypothesis regarding the life value.

RELEVANT PERSONAL BACKGROUND

The catastrophic Great Depression loosened the family ties for my generation of children. It allowed me, as it did many, a Tom Sawyer/Huck Finn childhood. Parents were too busy making ends meet to control our lives. My parents, luckily, were there when needed. But my somewhat wild-boyhood included the repulsive but exciting task of helper on a wild animal trap-line, adolescent exposure to lawless hobos (other bums) in the railroad jungles, a few teenage trips in the harsh (unionless) foreign merchant marines, travels through the series of semi-military organizations mentioned earlier, and, finally, the indescribable slaughter on Iwo Jima during World War II.

From those experiences, I have been exposed more vividly than most to the workings of the self-preservation inclinations and the species-preservation inclinations that express the total, Balanced Life Value. It is closely balanced between its two, usually mutually supporting, inclinations. But its primary subtlety is that the species-half of the drive has a slight edge in healthy human beings when choices are necessary. This, I suggest, is necessarily so in all of the few species of life that have managed to survive on earth (possibly not more than one percent of all that ever lived).

The species-preservation inclination is not an altruistic compulsion that triggers only in crisis situations; it operates as a daily socializing force in almost all human relations. Constantly, in scores of little ways, daily, individuals are, inclined to risk, give, and work themselves to early deaths, if necessary, for others of their species (for loved-ones and the recognized in-groups). Obviously we humans possess an almost equally strong self-preservation side in our nature.

In my first academic foray on this topic (the Balanced Life Value), as a young college instructor, I was able to challenge successfully some of the leading scholars who were teaching that human nature was either basically profit-motivated or else, closely associated, freedom-motivated. I submitted of course that the most basic drive of human nature is the dual (self and species) life value. The decisive encouragement came when I was able to register the challenge successfully in the prestigious *Political Science Quarterly* and, as I mentioned, persuade the scholarly giant, Harold Lasswell, that freedom is not humankind's basic earthly value, life is.

BACK TO THE RECENT FIELD-FINDINGS ON THE LIFE VALUE

Recall in *The Hunting Story,* the old sergeant's insistence on the equal importance of the life value to the humble peasants compared to us wealthy Americans. His gripping words articulated for us the meaning of human equality and identified equality's biological roots in the basic life value. Recall his punch line: (If you think they don't value their lives as much as you do yours) *try to kill one.* Now, here is a key question regarding the problem of teaching the life value: Would you think you could stop the story there and get the full, desired effect?

Why or why not?

The first answer is no. In order to inspire enthusiastic acceptance and instill a lasting effect from the account, you have to add the sergeant's points of elaboration. In essence, he said:

1. I don't know what it is that makes them value their lives so much; *maybe it's those women, or maybe it's those kids.*

2. You have got to realize that while we are up there in the back of that truck in our fancy shirts looking down on those peasants and mocking them, they are looking back up at us and saying to themselves, We value our lives and *the lives of our loved ones just as much as you do yours,* (and finally)

3. You have got to be able to look the dirtiest peasant in the eyes and realize that he is a man who hurts like we do, and hopes like we do, *and wants for his kids just like we do,* or you lose him.

(I have quoted those comments of the sergeant slightly differently because he repeated himself, that day, in response to my constant questioning. He stated the same ideas in slightly different words in responses to my repetitive questions designed to see if he held the ideas firmly. He did to the point of anger.)

As I said, you have to add one or two of those ideas, and preferably all three, in order to convey the full impact of the account. Why?

We ascertained that it was not only to make sure the life value, normally an unarticulated, taken-for-granted value, gets the necessary conscious attention, but also to make certain the audience not only realizes, but will be able to articulate the idea that the life value is *more than just self*. It includes, as a minimum, at least loved-ones and close in-groups.

But here is another interesting nuance. *If we devoted extensive time to talking about the species-preservation side of the life value, we also lost impact.* Such intellectualizing seemed to turn the common-folk civilians and GIs off a bit. Why?

I could not understand; I could not explain why minor changes in presentations made the difference between success and failure when reinforcing the behavior-changing values. That is, I did not understand what, exactly, it was that made for the effective activation of values.

I did not care enough to find out. I was satisfied when I found the version that worked as long as it was honorable. Giant mistake! Out of that little carelessness (or laziness) I neglected to do the experimental research needed to discover a way to state the species-side of the life value more succinctly and persuasively. That failure was the most torturing mistake that I made over the past thirty years. I'll explain.

CONTINENT-WIDE COMMITMENTS

Outstanding successes in our first two countries catapulted our program into four more countries for a combined four to six contracts. I had strong, dedicated civilian assistants or military counterparts in all four countries. But soon, I realized, *we were spread too thin* because the assistants and counterparts did not understand the basic theory—the Natural Law concepts—well enough to react effectively to program threatening challenges in the field. How could they since I was never sure myself?

So I roamed all four countries to *put out fires* and gradually add program facets or components. Here is the rub: Those four contracts were in countries surrounding the Communist block during the Cold War *military containment.* Our projects, of course, were directed at the most vital *mass diplomacy* issues in each country. One was to stop the theft of copper wire (the military communication system) in one huge country-wide international military command. Another was to keep the lid on ripples of violence among the civilian population during the international transfer of command over an entire island province. The third was to stop or preclude the *sapper* (saboteur) attacks on our air bases in an international command in a third country. The fourth was the one that put me into my brief one-martini-every-evening phase: It was in Vietnam.

EMOTIONAL INVOLVEMENT IN VIETNAM

My youngest brother, Galen, was a peaceful accountant with four small children. He volunteered for navigational duty on a Marine air transport plane with constant runs into Vietnam. His older brothers, his father, and all his uncles had already served in Korea or World War II. Like almost every other young, naive American who went into Vietnam, he went for patriotic reasons. As he told me, "It is my turn." Soon after a few trips into Danang, in early 1965, he called me on inter-country radio and told me, "Rob, you won't believe it, but we are going to lose this war. You must try to bring the values program in. Every American I encounter in Vietnam refers to our Asian allies as 'gooks' or some other similar derogatory term. We cannot possibly win this war." I dismissed his *make-believe war* as one we could not lose. A month later he was killed.

That absurd death, the first in my close family of seven, took much of the verve out of life for me and started me thinking seriously about *losing the war or winning the people* as my younger brother had put it. My despondency deepened as my father back in Missouri began receiving anonymous calls that "Galen deserved to die."

One day during the succeeding months of debilitating depression while I was working a project in Korea, an apparent Marine major approached me in the field and said he had flown up to see me from Vietnam. He turned out to be a U.S. Navy chaplain assigned to the Marines. He told me about a daring program started by General Walt to win the people through a new so-called Combined Action Platoon program (CAP). It had been a small volunteers-only operation because these CAP Marines, unlike any other combatants in the country, were staying all night in the villages rather than leaving those villages for Viet Cong control by night.

General Krulak, commander of all Marine forces in the Pacific, had seen the program's war-changing potential and wanted to expand it. This meant taking men who were not *naturals* for this people-to-people work and trying to re-educate them in a special training program sponsored by the Navy Chaplains called Personal Response. It concentrated on teaching an understanding of the Buddist religion. As a representative of General Krulak, the chaplain asked that I come to Vietnam to introduce my approach.

It was a staggering offer. Besides the physical danger involved, it meant *reversing* the ideology of the chaplains' Personal Response program. Their written program materials were teaching that the Vietnamese were *AS DIFFERENT ON THE INSIDE* as they appear to be on the outside. In mid-program, I would have to reverse that theme to the EQUALITY/SAMENESS ideology. Similarly, it meant reversing the essence of the participating Marines' recent combat training from its boot camp and General Patton informal philosophy that says, *you are killers* into a true professional fighting man's philosophy (such as a good professional boxer is taught). The latter teaches, *don't let anyone make you mad.* It meant trying to upgrade the *men's behavior in combat* to the religious-like standards of actually abiding by their military oath and Constitutional obligations which hold in essence: *You are a defender of equal human life and all that is right and just, NOT A RECKLESS KILLER.*

That high moral message, I had found, was easy to teach in peaceful or even in COLD WAR situations. But if, for some unknown reason, the educational materials were not effective, one could add the clincher by teaching the physical unarmed combat skills. The heightened self-confidence that this gave the men made it almost easy to inspire them up to the warrior-knight self-image. This attitude would hold indefinitely, barring a turnover of personnel, when the anti-culture shock education was added.

However, under the excessively harassed combat conditions of Vietnam, I knew that the absence of command-understanding would not allow me to include the *unarmed* combat training. I had used it with a few Marine replacements (through slap fighting) on Iwo Jima to counter-shock them out of their combat stress. This was to enable them to fire their weapons despite the sight of blood-gushing death all around them and the mind-shocking stress of their own impending death. It had worked; I had cut our platoon's terrible daily casualties to almost zero for two weeks this way; this, because I got them all to start putting out highly effective suppressive fire as others moved into the open. But many other front-line platoon leaders had not been able to deal with the stress among their men. Most of these young leaders on Iwo were soon killed. I was certain that military leadership in Vietnam would not understand any of this. I would cause trouble; it added another doubt about accepting the opportunity in Vietnam.

To my surprise, I found in Vietnam that the inability to teach the unarmed combat skills was only a minor problem. Interviews with the CAP Marines and River Patrol Boat sailors revealed clearly why the unarmed combat training, STRIKE (the modified boxing), was not indispensable inside the Vietnam scene. It is interesting; there are several related reasons:

1. The STRIKE is effective in non-combat combined-action (or cross-race integration) situations because *it*, the STRIKE training itself, feels so dangerous that the men derive the *band-of-brothers* camaraderie from it—the band of brothers camaraderie felt by those who suspect that they are about to die together. Obviously, the combat

situation, itself, in Vietnam took care of that emotional bonding experience.

2. Understand that the combat stress in Vietnam was not at all similar to that experience on Iwo Jima; the stress in Vietnam was not sustained every second all night and all day. Nonetheless, the emotional experience of facing death together, to any degree, is so strong that it tends to cut through and evaporates the artificial barriers of culture-shock and racial differences, so

3. Most of the Americans in the combined action programs got emotionally involved in a Platonic, or brotherly, love and protective relationship with specific Vietnamese people. They knew a few in each other's group by name and mutually depended on one another for safety and friendship.

4. Finally, these men carried weapons which tend to be physical-fear reducers in a low-intensity combat situation. In other words, they did not fear the local men in the villages as one might fear the men, unarmed, on the side streets of a place like Manila, when unarmed.

In addition to requesting the use of our materials for a Platoon Leader's Notebook on Vietnamese/American relations, the chaplain and his successor asked that I fly in and out of Vietnam to serve in an advisory role and to motivate officers and NCOs through our high-impact orientation speeches.

Despite my serious doubts, I saw the offer as an outside possibility to unify the American/Vietnamese effort and still win so that my brother's death might not have been in vain. I gave a qualified affirmative and started investigating the details.

Soon I learned that for good reasons, there were some serious *catches*. For my own safety as well as some political considerations, my intellectual role would have to remain secret. I had to go into the country without a contract (on loan from the Army Research Office). This meant *no blame* but *no credit* for the program. Most *character-building* of all, it meant going into Vietnam *uninsured*; I had five children.

The clincher that finally persuaded me to make the reckless effort came through Admiral Zumwalt, America's Naval commander in Vietnam. He asked that I try something similar in his special U.S. Navy operation. The Navy was tasked with integrating their large River Patrol Fleet (Brownwater Navy) with Vietnamese sailors for ownership-transfer of the boats to the Vietnamese. Under the Navy's religiously oriented Personal Response program, things had not gone well. On the first boat, the *Cato Parish*, it was reported to me that one or more Vietnamese had been thrown overboard by our own men.

THE LOST WAR FOR THE MINDS OF MEN, WOMEN, AND EVERYONE

By the time of my first trip into the country, I had conjured up a cautious optimism. I hoped and suspected that my brother had been overly pessimistic because he associated mainly with Air Force personnel. A little arrogance from them toward the Vietnamese was to be expected since they seem to look down in a joking, friendly way even on other American military personnel who are not Air Force. But after a few hours in the country, I fully appreciated the near hopelessness of the situation. The *gook syndrome* was not simply an American attitude toward the Vietnamese, it also had become a means of expressing the frustrated rage toward our own country for sending us into that war and then denouncing us for going. The *gook syndrome* stifled the American effort in that land worse than the tropical heat. More important than anything else, the derogatory *gook syndrome* in reference to *all Orientals* revealed an American ignorance about the behavior-controlling equal life value among all people. Most Americans whom I interviewed on the use of the term did not know that our Vietnamese allies were taking offense. Amazing.

For an example of a related ignorance, the young airman who met me with a jeep at the airport near Saigon was a bright, jolly lad; married, he soon told me, to a Vietnamese girl. Yet, he drove so wildly through the crowded Saigon streets that Vietnamese pedestrians had to scatter like wing-flapping chickens to avoid death under his wheels. When I objected, he informed me, infallibly, that the Vietnamese did not mind dying.

During my first eighteen hours of interviews, I talked to only one American who did not refer to all Vietnamese—enemies or allies—as gooks, zips, dinks, or slopes. That one exception was the chaplain.

During that first night, feeling absurd in VIP quarters in the midst of a war, my thoughts no longer vacillated between optimism and cautiousness; they had been reduced to a state of utter amusement over the fix I had got myself into (again). It was that old sinking Connecticut Yankee feeling; still no tricks available to get myself out of a scary situation, but this time the bad guys had guns. I remember dropping that Connecticut Yankee parallel for myself while lying awake that night thinking about the possible briefing for Admiral Zumwalt the next morning. I decided that more so than the Connecticut Yankee, an innocent victim, I resembled the clowns Laurel and Hardy, both of them together, in a *pretty fix* of my own making.

The pessimism and resulting *nothing-to-lose* feeling probably helped. In my early-morning briefing for the Admiral, the futility allowed me to admit candidly that we could not possibly win unless we went all the way, ideologically, and stopped the *gook syndrome.* That brilliant military man repeated the ideology more clearly than I had stated it, and approved it for the river boat program (ACTOV) training without reservation. I was allowed to recommend a delivery system; I chose the revision of the ongoing Personal Response Program under a chaplain who was clearly a very bright social scientist.

MY LONG-RANGE AGENDA IN VIETNAM

My personal plan had three goals:

1. Try to stop the *gook syndrome* which is actually a low-intensity anti-Asian racism. (Could we admit that?)

2. Change the military measure of success in Vietnam from the atrocious body count method to a civilized *maximum land pacification with minimum deaths;* this, through the Marine CAP leadership, and

3. Spread the program beyond the Marine CAP and Navy river boat operations to all forces in Vietnam.

Unlike in the other countries where I was the most active teacher, success in Vietnam depended more on my military counterparts. It was not encouraging that these two counterparts in Vietnam were *do-gooder* types in military eyes, that is, chaplains. On the other hand, they were, indeed, unusual chaplains. Both had agreed to assume the professional risks of leaving their pulpits to work unarmed with the men in the combat areas. Their names were Dick McGonigal with the Marines and Earl Fedge in the Navy.

Both chaplains turned out to be dynamic teachers and bold, brave men. From day one, both programs became increasingly successful. I had been able to introduce the ideological (equality & freedom) concepts and the culture-shock materials without limitations. Not many weeks had passed until a Chief Petty Officer, a teacher on one of the river boats, told me: *"Humphrey, the new materials are powerful. Today we stopped the reconnaissance by fire for the first time."* (What that means in terms of fear and risk is this: The Americans on the boats, for the first time, did not fire machine guns into the high foliage along the river banks where innocent villagers with their livestock might be hiding. That is highly admirable. But it also meant not firing into the cover where enemy ambushes also at times *would* be hiding. No matter how routine that might have become, that little exercise in self-risking self-discipline approached heroic behavior.)

SURPRISING SUCCESS, WIDELY NOTICED

Soon, I was being asked into the country more and more for special briefings, leader training sessions, and even to develop a similar course for integration of illiterate hill tribesmen into the Vietnamese Navy. Eventually, when I learned that our materials had been bootlegged (the term was used) into the U.S. Army training for incoming *advisers*, I knew it was time to broach the two big issues of stopping the *body count* insanity and of trying to expand the program as a pacifying effort among all U.S. military forces in Vietnam. I submitted the body count proposition to the new Marine commander, General Nickerson, a deeply religious man, and the *program expansion* idea to Admiral Zumwalt.

General Nickerson agreed to consult his top combat colonels and allowed me to name the one to ask first. Admiral Zumwalt's recommendation had to go back through the two top Navy men in the Pentagon. Consequently, my own necessary task involved the most difficult program component of all: *Institutional change.* It was similar to putting a new bill through Congress. I would have to contact and educate all the key recipients of the forthcoming suggestions so they could exercise a well-informed judgment. Both of these war-changing policies, I knew, would encounter heated opposition.

I went to my strongest communication center in Asia, my headquarters in Thailand, to organize that major educational task. It meant more trips into the field in Vietnam and one back to Washington to see the Chief of Naval Operations and the Navy Secretary.

I never made those indispensable trips. They were stopped by the explosion in my face of that little ideological bomb I had left smoldering by procrastinating in finding a way to teach the species-preservation side of the life value more effectively—the philosophical foundation of the entire program.

When I arrived in Thailand, I was met by my permanent counterpart there, Pat Marr, a scholarly former Green Beret combat officer in Lower East Asia. He was married to a Thai general's daughter and enjoyed top-level contacts in both Thai and American society. He notified me with a laugh that according to Thai Intelligence, the Communists had suddenly placed sizable prices on our heads. (Troubling.) Also, I learned that two special briefings for leadership groups had been requested: one in Bangkok, and another in Okinawa. Also troubling: such requests, other than through direct, *inside* contacts with me, were most unusual. My secret involvement was growing quite public. I was annoyed because it delayed the beginning of those all-important institutional-change trips into Vietnam and Washington.

SUDDEN ALARMING OPPOSITION

The next day, at my strangely-scheduled orientation, there was a heckler present. That was only the second time in ten years. He was a pretty nice heckler, the type who only coughs, shuffles his feet, and whispers too loud during your speech. (The bad ones shout while you are speaking.) His main effort came the second I finished my comments. He jumped to his feet and shouted before anyone could applaud:

"Your human-equality story does not make sense!"

Absolutely bewildered, the only response my shocked brain could produce was the expression: "What!"

His answer cut right to the heart of the actual weakness of the presentation. My orientation implied, but did not establish with overwhelming persuasiveness, the proposition that species-preservation constitutes a genetic half of the individual's *that controls one's own happiness.* In brief, he said this:

You are asserting that the equality concept is based on the fact that the peasants say they feel equal to us. Well, just because they feel that way does not mean that we have to respect that feeling. A snake or bear, if they could talk, would say the same thing. We would still not consider them equal.

Hence, he was asserting that actually there is no Natural Law reason, or no Natural Duty reason, why we should protect others *for our own satisfaction or greater feeling of spiritual well-being.*

Fortunately, for me, the crowd shouted him down; because I knew that, logically, he had a point. He had opened grounds for a rational argument. And when you are reinforcing values (attitudes) to inspire immediate changes of behavior, you cannot be effective if your words leave the audience in doubt. Your audience must experience a finger-snapping conviction. This heckler had tried to create a defeating doubt. He saw that he had failed and slipped out; but he left me shaken. Was it a happenstance attack? Or was it tied to the news about the price on our heads? We were working in four crucial countries, and enjoying impressive effectiveness everywhere, especially in Vietnam.

I was deeply shaken. The ideological foundation of the entire program was under a noteworthy attack.

I reported the situation to military intelligence. The officer advised me to move my living quarters for the family to a protected area. I did. I also reported the new developments to my headquarters in Washington. A message came back from my Contract Officer, who had never lived abroad, advising me not to be "paranoid." That was especially character building.

PHYSICAL ATTACKS AND MORE HECKLING

A week later, my oldest son, Rob, was assaulted by two thugs in a downtown street. A good boxer, Rob knocked down the lead attacker, who dropped his knife and fled. Spinning to take the rush of the second culprit, he was delighted to see the rascal being dispatched by Rob's taxi driver with a jack handle. Rob's flashing thoughts after the incident were, he reported: "Thank goodness Dad and Mom always encouraged us to learn a little of the local language. The taxi drivers were always the most delighted. I think that taxi driver may have saved my life. I bet Mom and Dad's big tips helped too. (And) Maybe I should not go around in town under Dad's first name."

Real fear did not strike me until later when a car-bombing was apparently aimed at a second son. There have been four such incidents in the past thirty years, all during emotionally heated projects involving either anti-Communist or race-relations programs. But all could have been coincidental. Remember the Washington Contract Officer's admonition, "Don't be paranoid." Our family inside-joke has been to maintain a *healthy paranoia*.

A few days later, I gave the second strangely-scheduled presentation to an audience thousands of miles away in Okinawa. I was stunned to encounter the same heckling on the same point I had faced in Thailand. *It was the same heckler.* At least there was no longer any doubt. The program had a problem. It was under some kind of an organized, well-financed attack.

My main concern was for Vietnam. If there was any danger that the presentations there could spark any public controversy, the presentations, meaning the program, would have to be stopped.

I contacted my offices in all four countries. None of our other teachers was being heckled. I quit giving presentations, myself, and spent full time trying to find a means to teach more decisively the species-preserving characteristic—the idea under attack.

What was at stake was the most important intellectual point of this work: humankind's species-preserving nature. It is the concept that allowed us to recognize, exactly, human nature's life-sustaining base of the Natural Law, and the grounds for resolving conflict, not causing it.

For most persons, *law*, to be worthy of the name, must include a penalty or sanction for violations. Through the list of great Natural Law thinkers from ancient Greece until serious consideration of Natural Law ceased, a brief hundred years ago, most Natural Law scholars concluded that the penalties for its violations came through divine channels. So when the world's leading philosophers declared that God was dead, that pretty much rescinded the Natural Law in the minds of scholars. Our field-observations had seen the mistake in that rescission.

Human nature has a strong *self*-preservation drive, so strong in fact that we consider its various expressions to constitute *natural rights*.

Equally strong though, and probably with a slight edge, human nature contains a species-preservation drive as a felt set of *natural duties*. Many parents feel these natural duties toward their children so strongly that many cannot resist their compulsions even when the children on any logical grounds don't deserve the continuing loyalty and sacrifice.

Similarly, if our nation (in-group) is attacked, we feel a duty to risk ourselves defending it if absolutely necessary. This inclination is so strong that when avowed pacifists in pacifistic (Buddhist and Hindu) nations are questioned (needled) about their willingness to fight if their families or religious groups are attacked, they answer simply, *"Well sure, that is only natural."*

In fact, these natural duties of the Natural Law are felt so strongly, I have found, that men who consider themselves cowards cannot rely on their own avowed self-protecting cowardice when their loved ones or in-groups are threatened.

The scholarly Abraham Maslow identified the altruistic [species-preserving] tendencies or feelings as an *intrinsic conscience,* or if neglected, as an *intrinsic guilt.* Consequently, the punishments for violations of the Natural Law do not come from outside or not (just) from divine forces; they come from inside the human psyche. Also one's natural duties are not just the other side of others' natural rights. They exist independently of others' rights. The duties, similar to rights, are felt expressions of one's own natural drives. That is, if we do not show proper respect for other persons, it makes us sick. It gives us tensions, ulcers, cancer, or less happiness than we could have enjoyed from being considerate and respectful.

You will hear a few *values-free* psychologists glibly voice the cliché, "We humans do not possess a *good* gene." Or, "to search for such a gene," others say, "would be like looking for the needle in the haystack." Actually, what confronts us in those clichés involves another old adage: *failing to see the forest for the trees.* The altruistic genes in human nature do not compare to the proverbial lost needle, *they constitute half of the entire life-supporting stack of hay.*

If you agree with those thoughts, you have endorsed the Natural Law. It is stronger than positive law because it is inescapable. And it is no longer just the priests and preachers who are saying it, more and more medical doctors agree: hating makes one sick; love can help make us well again. (Just the act of *smiling*, apparently helps.)

Incidentally, if you have ulcers, don't feel guilty. The penalty from the Natural Law works from both sides. If your altruistic tendencies run out of control (from the control of your equally natural reasoning powers), that too, it appears, can make you sick. That is, if you try too hard, worry too much, or blame yourself excessively, for that wayward child or the failings of another loved one, despite your respectable efforts, that too can make you sick.

Back to the heckler problem—the ideological question (attack) on the species-preserving tendency (or felt duty)—as I analyzed it, was this: The heckler probably represented an anti-war group inside the military. Such groups were well-organized and well-financed in the Pacific area during the Vietnam conflict. Usually they attracted disgruntled, college-educated American soldiers who had been drafted—one that I met openly admitted that he carried a Communist membership card. These men, who quite generally had been indoctrinated in college to the philosophy of ethical relativism, would be receptive to the argument that the species-preserving concept was merely a mask to promote unwarranted patriotism. Two or three loud hecklers on the edges of a GI audience, I knew, could render our programs ineffective in all four countries. This was certainly true in Vietnam where confusion about the validity of the cause was already prevalent.

THE NECESSARY IDEOLOGICAL SOLUTION

As the first priority, I had to find a way to teach the species-preservation characteristic of life very briefly and unassailably to an audience or possibly sacrifice the entire program in Vietnam. The task was confounded by the fact that the oral presentation to the troops could not be allowed more than a few more minutes, or else many, fatigued as they always were, would start dozing off. So the new insert had to be not only decisive in effect, but also succinct. I was not optimistic.

After weeks of futile searching, dispirited, I trekked back to Vietnam to warn the Marine and Navy commanders about the newly revealed ideological weakness in the program. They would have to decide if they wanted to proceed unabated despite the politically sensitive booby trap. We were truly involved in an ideological war.

The Navy headquarters in Saigon was the easiest to reach. I went there first. While waiting to see Admiral Zumwalt, I reviewed the problem with a Lt. Commander Joe Purcel in the Admiral's outer office. Purcel was an ongoing, down-to-earth, rough-cut person. He reminded me more of an army sergeant than a typical white-dressed Navy officer.

Few military men understand that they epitomize the human inclination to risk, or if necessary sacrifice, one's life for the group. Purcel, despite his *commoner* appearance, was an intellectual. He understood my problem. Later I learned that he was also a voracious reader. Under the doldrums of his Saigon curfew, he was reading three to five books a week.

As I explained my ideological plight, he suddenly stopped his office flurry and demanded my attention with his stare. It was one of those stares that causes you to stop your own actions and ask: "What did I say?"

Purcel stood up, pointed his finger at me, and said with the certainty of a drill sergeant, "That lesson is available; it's in the literature. I read it recently." (He thought for a moment.) "You'll find it in Robert Ardrey's *African Genesis*. It reveals that even monkeys possess the self-sacrificing species-preserving trait. *And Ardrey's account delivers the lesson with the brevity and punch that you want.*"

"You seem certain," I mulled out loud.

"Absolutely certain," he said, "it carries the same emotional punch as that delivered by your hunting story on human equality."

"Wow! do you suppose?" was my brilliant response.

"No, I don't s'pose," he mocked, "I know. At least cancel your appointment with the Old Man (the Admiral) until you can check it out."

I did. I found the brief account and tried it on some Navy personnel that afternoon and twice the next day. It worked all three times.

Military men in combat zones for some reason don't thank one another extensively. They communicate the signals of gratitude without saying much. I went back to thank Purcel. I poked my head into his office; he looked up and stopped his work.

"Did you find it?" he asked.

I nodded yes.

"It worked," he asserted, smiling.

I didn't answer directly but asked him how he got his commission: "Did you come up through the ranks, or through a college program?"

Quizzically, he answered, "Mustang, up through the ranks; why do you ask?"

As I backed out of his office I responded: "I was wondering about the source of your common sense in recognizing the relevance of that story. But don't gloat; I've met semiliterate old army sergeants with equally as much wisdom."

Because of his confidence, competence, and his own mischievous needling personality, I was pleased to see he was a little non-plussed. As I walked out into the empty, ominous, bunkered Saigon street, I felt a little guilty for that low-key thanks. It really didn't fit my style. But it was considerably better than what I felt like doing: kissing him.

As I hurried watchfully along that street, unarmed and a little uneasy, for some reason the key words Purcel had used the day before, came to mind, *emotional punch.* The answer to the riddle, *how one teaches (actually, reinforces) values,* finally dawned on me: *It requires an experience or story with emotional impact.*

LOVE AND SACRIFICE

Robert Ardrey's account describes one of those grim life-and-death incidents that occur constantly in nature. This particular incident involved a troop of baboons and a leopard. Leopards eat baboons. It is said that baby baboons are leopards' favorite dessert. However, the big cats won't attack a baboon troop that is foraging in formation with five or six males tactically situated for a united defense. For a kill, a leopard awaits one of the disorganized moments in the baboons' pattern of life. Ardrey's account describes one of those terrible moments. A naturalist, Professor Marais, was the observer:

It was still dusk. The troop [of baboons] had only just returned from the feeding grounds and had barely time to reach its scattered places in the high piled rocks behind the fig tree. Now it shrilled its terror and Marais could see the leopard. It appeared from the bush and took its insolent time. So vulnerable were the baboons that the leopard seemed to recognize no need for hurry. He crouched just below a little jutting cliff observing his prey and the problems of the terrain and Marais saw two male baboons edging along the cliff above him.

The two males moved cautiously; the leopard, if he saw them, ignored them. His attention was fixed on the swarming, screeching, defenseless horde scrambling among the rocks. The two males dropped. They dropped on him from the height of twelve feet. One bit at the leopard's spine. The other struck at his throat while clinging to his neck from below. In an instant the leopard disemboweled with his hind claws the baboon hanging to this neck and caught in his jaws the baboon on his back. But it was too late. The dying disemboweled baboon had hung on just long enough and had reached the leopard's jugular vein with his canines.

Marais watched while movement stilled beneath the little jutting cliff. Night fell. Death, hidden from all but the impartial stars, enveloped prey and predator alike and in the hollow places in the rocky, looming krans, a society of animals settled down to sleep.

[Robert Ardry, *African Genesis* (N.Y., Atheneum Publishers, 1961) p. 81.]

For my first experiment with this story, to give it a hard test, I walked into a Navy training room in Saigon and approached a group of sailors who were on a smoking break. Speaking above their casual conversations, I interrupted: "Hey fellows, let me read you something. I want to know what you say it represents."

I read the account slowly, with emphasis, looking up after each line or two observing their reactions. It was working as far as capturing their attention was concerned. There was that wonderful rapt attention when something is captivating. They had even stopped their cigarette puffing. When I finished reading, I looked up, observed their expressions, which remained attentive, and asked, "What is the moral of that story?"

There were a few seconds of thoughtful silence but no bewilderment. Finally, a young man, in his own picturesque words, confidently stated the account's self-sacrificing species-preserving meaning.

The next two formal trials, the next day, were equally rewarding.

The only little drawback I saw in teaching the point was the considerable delay required for the members of an audience to process the meaning of the story and state it. A few weeks later, while working with some poorly educated men who were assigned to a hard-labor task, I read the account and again asked: "What is the moral of that story?"

To my surprise, there was no hesitancy this time. One young fellow shot his hand right out to speak and exclaimed: "The moral of that story is clear; don't screw around with those baboons."

After the laughter, I realized that I was not asking quite the right question. I changed it from then on to ask: "What basic characteristic of all life, animal and human, does that story illustrate?"

To complete the lesson, we learned, one must add and ask: "Of course, those were animals, acting out of instinct. Do we human beings possess a similar self-risking instinct-like inclination even though it is ultimately controllable by reason?" (There are always quick head-nodding approvals.)

We add, Answer in your own mind these questions:

- Would you risk or give your life to save your loved ones or members of your group?

- Further, do you think the religious leaders are right in asserting that we humans could develop an empathy that would include other races and all of humankind in our circle of loved ones or in our emotionally protected human groups?

- If your answers are 'yes,' would those decisions make you a worse or better soldier—willing to kill an aggressor if necessary in order to protect innocent human lives?

- Can we average citizens responsibly decide who is which, the good guys or the bad?

- Can we handle these ultimate life-or-death ideological questions: when to kill? and whom to defend?

Fortunately for human survival, formally uneducated, illiterate human beings, for all of their genetic history, managed these issues successfully. And despite the objections of an occasional GI self-styled *killer*, every group of GIs that I have ever addressed has seemed pleased to be referred to as *defenders* of life versus *trained killers*.

The expressed desires in these sentiments project reliably the possible role of the military as a constructive peace force if we intellectuals could upgrade our educational institutions into values-reinforcing centers rather than mere fact-collecting organizations. The military academies and training programs would stay abreast.

In summary, the species-preserving drive, according to the evidence that we have observed among most animal species and all observed races of humankind, expresses itself stronger than any other drive including self-preservation. Here is the key intellectual point reviewed, regarding acceptance of the dual life value: The fact that most animals possess the species-preserving drive destroys the assertion of some psychologists that such a natural inclination in humans would be impossible. In fact, an argument that human beings possess only self-preserving tendencies with no self-giving species-protecting tendencies at all, would rate us among the most reprehensible animals on earth; even rats and alligators will risk themselves for their young.

TRANSITION

How effective is the story and those follow-up materials when presented sincerely and orally?

Through the last twenty-two years, in half a dozen countries, with scores of different speakers, and hundreds of thousands in the total audience, the lesson is so matter-of-factly accepted that it is anti-climatic after all of my fears of failure. I still do not know how generally representative they are, but more than once, philosophy students with Masters degrees and Ph.D.s have advised me after conferences that the description of the balanced-life value clarified human values for them more than all their years of study.

But how valid is the concept in scientific fact?

At this point in the total presentation, that question leaves us realistically (as it did in the field) with three parallel tracks of partly unanswered questions:

1. Do we humans possess a species-preserving half in our life-drive as a scientific fact?

2. If so, does it allow us to perceive the factual (scientific) relationship of our detailed earthly spiritual values to our basic balanced life-protecting nature?

3. And incidentally, what happened to the institutional-change efforts (a) to stop the body-count barbarism, in Vietnam, and (b) to expand the win the people approach to all of Vietnam (both of which obviously failed)?

CHAPTER 10

COUNTING DEAD BODIES AND MAKING INSTITUTIONAL CHANGES

When I started this search thirty-five years ago, you will recall the goal: It was a means to stop the development of anti-Americanism, especially in the Third World. It looked easy. Remember? I estimated it would require one, maybe two years. I had no idea that it would be so baffling, requiring 1) a search for the deepest values that come out of human nature and control human happiness, plus 2) the means of activating those values for the promotion of peaceful relations. You have seen that there are four major components: the ideological, the culture-shock detective work, the individual development (to build self-confidence and reduce fear), and the institutional-change component, meaning the method for institutionalizing the new conflict-resolution methodology.

All of my projects were crisis oriented, that is, designed to solve pressing field-problems. I never set out to solve those problems in order to change institutions; rather, I always tried to change institutions only to the degree necessary to solve my assigned problems. Very different.

Seeing the Natural Law ideology and teaching it was most important; the cultural detective work was the most interesting and time-consuming; individual development was the easiest until we encountered the dropouts in the high school programs; and institutional change was the least important on my limited projects. To change institutions to the degree necessary, sometimes I defied the *powers-that-be* by working at the grass-roots level; sometimes *won the leaders* over to support the reform after they saw its introductory successes; sometimes I confronted those who were open bigots and got them removed from power, and twice such persons got me fired.

If I had it all to do again, I would devote more care to this institutional-change component. Because now I know for certain that the values-based conflict-resolution method provides a strategy for world peace and significant domestic violence reduction. But a successful method for institutional change, on a major scale, remains the weak factor in the formula. I am going to spell out the details of one of my most egregious institutional-change failures where, with a little more care, success was possible. Many of my past students have advised that such accounts have been helpful. In fact, whoever it was who said that we learn best from our failures was the sage of all sages. Also, I would advise you to consult the literature on *networking*.

I will not *dwell* on the institutional-change failures. They came among more important successes with the other three components. I will present the anatomy of an institutional-change failure conveniently in the context of a more important lesson: the significant but neglected evidence from Vietnam that a superior strategy for world peace is within reach. It must be able to stop and defuse cross-group violence. If the Cold War is ending, a world of little wars, global street violence and fanatical terrorism remains. Hence a strategy for low-intensity warfare or conflict resolution is much needed.

The East/West struggle to determine which form of government, dictatorship or democracy, is the more powerful—which one can bury the other—is now settled. The North/South issue—a question of justice or just relationships between rich nations and poor—will now grow in importance. The new, relatively easy to use, but powerful and horrible weapon of terrorism will likely continue to play a certain equalizing role for the weak nations against the strong. A new, likely source of dangerous conflict between the larger (financially competitive) nations will turn on the fuzzy issue of *meaningful* versus token democracy in the Third World nations.

America, if good judgment prevails, will build a strong military even if considerably reduced in size. If we learned the lessons of Vietnam, our military forces will be developed into high-type organizations that the entire world will learn to trust as responsible protectors of peace and democracy (life) with justice. That total military force, its training, and its global strategy will be patterned along the lines of the lessons learned from our win the people, unsung successes in Vietnam. In view of the life-or-death importance of oil, let us be excused from belaboring the morality question in the Iraq war. After reminding foreign critics that, initially, about fifty percent of all Americans opposed the use of force, suffice it to admit that it was not exactly a war for democracy or "the people," especially not for my old hunting buddies, the wonderful, tough, and tortured Kurds. They, along with the ignored, starving thousands in East Africa, and others, now constitute the conscience of any new world order that claims a degree of morality.

COUNTING DEAD BODIES

Was the body-count in Vietnam the most barbaric policy ever devised in these Late Dark Ages? Did it, or did it not, alienate the Americans back home and help turn them against the effort to stop communism (dictatorship)? Which did it promote: more atrocities (killing civilians), or more false reporting?

Whichever, it became the measure of success for all combat outfits. My recommendation, recall, made to General Nickerson, was to substitute for that measure of success, this one: Maximum acquisition of land with minimum deaths on both sides. The outstanding colonel whom I named for General Nickerson to consult, unknown to me, had one of the best body-count records in Vietnam. He rejected my suggestion for stopping the body-count as a measure of success. That delayed the effort long enough to defeat it.

Of course, it was my fault that the idea was not given a chance. That is the lesson I am stressing on institutional change: I repeat, one cannot request, responsibly, a major policy change without doing one's homework and proper lobbying (educating).

I was compelled to forgo those necessary (homework and lobbying) tasks because of my previous carelessness in not perfecting, when I had time, that known gap in the Balanced Life Value theory (how to teach the species-preservation concept effectively). So, after the appearance of the heckler, I had to deal with that crisis rather than make the indispensable trips back to the U.S. and into Vietnam.

Admiral Zumwalt's effort turned out to be even more responsive than I had requested. He had written an official request to the Chief of Naval Operations in Washington laying out in considerable detail the success of our river boat integration program. He had not asked merely for the program's consideration for expansion among all the U.S. troops in Vietnam but rather among all U.S. forces worldwide. Because of the strong, insightful John Chafee, in the position of Secretary of Navy at the time, had I gone back as planned, the idea would have been assured at least a responsible consideration. But due to my digression, to fill in that gap in the basic theory, the idea was given no chance.

Six months too late, I learned that Admiral Zumwalt's message had been sidetracked politically, or pigeonholed, in the Navy Annex (by the Personal Response Naval Chaplains' Headquarters Group) without being delivered as addressed to the Chief of Naval Operations. A couple of years later, when the competitive atmosphere had lifted, I asked one of the chaplains why they had risked that act— sidetracking a top level message? He answered that "Christians have tried two thousand years to bring peace through an ideological approach; it has not worked."

Had I been properly attentive to the institutional-change needs, that message would have at least reached its addressee.

Even though it is unpleasant to discuss these mistakes, some provide magnificent lessons. Often it is indeed the little things that cause the major failures. In this case, simply not asking to hand-carry that message back to Washington was possibly a war-changing (war losing) catastrophe.

Ben Franklin warned: A little neglect may breed great mischief... for want of a nail the shoe was lost; for want of a shoe the horse was lost; and for want of a horse the rider was lost.

He could have added, and the battle was lost, and then the war.

No-Fault Failures

A social-change program such as this inevitably encounters so many failures along the way, that one dares not look back to agonize. Fortunately, in the Vietnam failures, there were always plenty of comforting rationalizations. For example, by the time I *really* got into the war, it was late in 1966. At home, in America, the nation was turning hard against the war. As well, racial troubles were dividing our population. In Vietnam, itself, murderous ramifications from the *gook syndrome,* possibly, had made it too late to turn things around with any program. There had already been too many blanket bombing raids on villages, too much Agent Orange, too much napalm.

In fact, by that time, my Vietnam confidants implored me not to get my program associated with the otherwise centralized *pacification program.* They believed, rightly or wrongly, that the official country-wide pacification program included a policy of reckless assassinations. They also insisted that the CAP Marines who lived in the villages were the only Americans in all of Vietnam with activated, official policies *against* sexually misusing destitute Vietnamese women. Even if I had escaped my own blunders, I was possibly too late. Anyway such rationalizations allow me to laugh philosophically about the good fight that we made, and lost (but the truth still is that I blew it). The only real satisfaction that I can take in my more serious moments is that you can learn from those failures of mine and succeed the next time around.

The Reason (again and again) For America's Vietnam Loss

Much postwar military literature now insists that we could have won the war during its final phases, or anytime after TET, had we been allowed to attack enemy sanctuaries in neighboring countries. Maybe so, but I doubt it. Judging from the views expressed to me by Vietnamese civilians, by many disillusioned American GIs, and by some young officers, winning the war with more massive killing, anywhere, was and remains an unrealistic thought. Even if our U.S. population would have tolerated more massive killing, on television, what would we have done after the victorious devastation? Replaced the French as an army of occupation? Would the guerrilla warfare against us not have continued to this day?

In answer, contemplate this assertion; it should be called The Vietnam Lesson: In this modern world of low-intensity warfare, American forces can never again voice or practice anything like the gook syndrome or Ugly Americanism and also avoid a defeating level of anti-American terrorism. Human nature, in this age of embryonic civilization, will never again tolerate such insulting arrogance.

I will say this in defense of those who wanted to stay and win for democracy in Vietnam: Anyone who knew the desperate thinking inside communism at the time and also in Southeast Asia, had to know also that if we left, the bloodbath was coming. It came.

WE LOST THE PEOPLE

After the French were driven out of Vietnam, there was only one possible way for democracy to have prevailed meaningfully through our involvement there. That was to win the people. Something similar is true in the rest of the Third World now—in Asia, Africa, the Middle East, and Latin America. This is especially true in such wavering countries as El Salvador and the Philippines. To win the people, our forces must have values training similar to that contained in these materials unless something else new and even better can be found.

The Rambo/Chuck Norris screen portrayals are not just inadequate for the new era of low-intensity warfare, they are fallacious Hollywood fantasies. However, in their place, we do have real-life fighting role-models: Sergeant York and Audie Murphy for two examples. Single-handed, they did in fact take entire companies of enemy soldiers. But they did not accentuate fighting. Their heroics were momentary, last-resort details in their lives. They did not kill in anger—more likely in sadness, if not in prayer. As youngsters, they were considerate, humble, physically unimpressive men. They were excellent hunters and fistfighters—qualities which they developed as mere sidelines to normal lives in rough and robust areas of the U.S.

When the license to kill is involved, fight-training is more wisely associated with self-discipline than it is with bravado. History's most devastating fighter ever to grace a boxing ring, Joe Louis, was a humble, soft-spoken man. This is the healthy role-model image of a fighting man for our armies of fighting men.

Let us consider the evidence from Vietnam that this type personality can represent a new world strategy serving both the trust-winning, and the fighting, roles for America. First, let me implore those who are still hungover from the '60s to open your minds to the reality of the world. It is filled with oppressive violence that cannot be stopped by talking, demonstrating, and hoping; at times murderous violence must be met and stopped by force. The only responsible issue is how to exercise that force while limiting it to the minimum amount necessary.

THE MILITARY MISSION IN THE AGE OF VALUES

In Professor Allan Bloom's insightful book, *The Closing of the American Mind,* he probes the primitive intellectual shortcoming that still persists in the human species in these Late Dark Ages: immaturity—the immature inclination to close our minds. That is why wiser persons warn us, "Don't try to discuss religion or politics with anyone." What a childish characteristic! For those of us whom it describes, it means we are finished with learning in those fields that we cannot discuss. Are you one of those with this childish closed mind regarding the topics of either peace or the military? Let us investigate.

Since Vietnam, America has been polarized and weakened by a close-minded immaturity among many educated Americans regarding *the peace movement* on one hand, and our *military establishment* on the other. Some of my *hawkish* friends are solidly rational on all other topics. They are typically *great guys* who literally hit you on the arm with a friendly hello every morning. (I call them *the hitters*.) Then one day you happen to mention the peace movement with a tone of objectivity. Their minds close like the slamming of prison doors to a conjured specter of your imagined unilateral disarmament policies. If you confront their misapprehension, they express their willingness to die for your right to say anything, just as long as you never again mention that fuzzy-minded word, *peace*.

Similarly, some of my *dovish* friends will hug you hello every morning until they fit your ribs (*the huggers*). Then one day you commit the sin of referring objectively to *the military*. They go glassy-eyed, drop their heads, and quiver in a little emotional trauma. They give you one last patronizing hug of farewell in the absurd conviction that you must believe in nuclear war because you mentioned that evil institution, the military.

These two immature groups for too long have cut off rational discussion regarding the topics of world peace, on the one side, and the possibility of a responsible military on the other. By remaining fanatically closed in their minds, unable to think about and discuss either one of these two topics, each childish group increases the possibility that we will lose our cherished democracy.

The closed minds portend increasingly polarized inabilities to discuss and reconcile confused values. This is dangerous childishness indeed; the stuff from which dictatorships develop, from which revolutions are made, and from which national decline begins. When open-minded discussions stop, clandestine efforts start. Already three national administrations out of the last five have tried to slip around the U.S. Constitution. We humans all hold to a higher law of right and justice than that which can be put down in detail on paper. To be respected, and willingly obeyed, written laws must be consistent with those higher principles. To maintain that consistency requires constant open discussion—not closed minds that refuse to listen.

Honorable men and women will always attempt to rise above laws and constitutions that they perceive to be unjust and deadly dangerous. That is what happened in 1775 and in most revolutions.

If you have, from in-group conditioning, fallen into one of those two nation-dividing, long-range, violence-causing polarizations where you cannot discuss either the peace movement or the virtues of a strong (not huge, but strong) military at the grass-roots level, open your mind for the good of everyone. The greater danger now, after the collapse of militant communism, is to let our military become second class. Consider the following materials that reconcile the dual need of a continuing search for peace but also the maintenance of a strong military. We want peace, but not through weakness which must accept injustices, rather, through strength and more equitable democracies.

A U.S. MILITARY PEACE FORCE

Is there any hard evidence that our American teenage fighting men could actually be trained to be true defenders of life? Could they ever be taught to show respect for, to blend in with, to protect and defend the peasants of the world? Could they be taught to win illiterate, unwashed peasants to the side of democracy? Then, on the other side, could such tactful soldiers still be tough enough to stay in the villages of the world, *at night,* and fight against organized drug dealers if that is what the villagers ask? You would have to admit that this would certainly be an admirable role if our men could ever be trained to accomplish that high-type combined mission.

The fact is that some of our young American military men (teenagers)—*uniquely in the modern world*—have already demonstrated their ability to take on that world-changing role for the sake of justice, humanity, and democracy.

Certainly no one would ever suggest that Marine General Walt of Vietnam fame could be called a "softy" or "do-gooder." Here is his account of how some of his men, on their own, developed the Combined Action Platoons in Vietnam, long before they ever heard of my program.

First, he described the way the war was fought in most of the thousands of villages in Vietnam, that is, he described the way the war was lost despite our overwhelming military superiority. We alienated and lost the people. This was the village of Binh Nghia. It was typical:

> General Walt: (It) contained about five thousand people. It was guarded by a (Vietnamese) Popular Force platoon of twenty-eight men. There were two companies of (enemy) Viet Cong generally operating in the area from nearby mountain and jungle camps. The Popular Force unit was frightened. The Viet Cong moved in and out of the village at will during the night, taking money from the villagers, conscripting new men, confiscating rice. Only the day belonged to the legitimate government. [The Popular Force in Vietnam was a weak National Guard organization.]

Then, taking no credit for himself for development of the Combined Action Platoons (CAPs), General Walt explains how some of his Marines developed a successful (but now substantially ignored) answer to the modern challenge of *low-intensity warfare*.

The names I heard in the field (where accuracy is subject to my spelling) who (I was told) developed this approach were Marines Cullen Zimmerman, John Mullin, Bill Taylor, and Paul Ek. (I didn't get their ranks, but none was high. All were fighting field officers.) The transformation that their approach allowed, eventually, in a majority of the hundred or so CAP villages was described in the following way by General Walt. [About three-fourths of the CAP villages, it seemed to me, resembled this description]:

> Sergeant Sullivan and his men lived no better and no worse than the Popular Force platoon. No PXs, movies, or cold beer, but tension and constant danger. Sergeant Sullivan and his men began to patrol at night... with the Popular Force troops through the long, dark hours. During the day, instead of sleeping, they taught the Popular Force troopers the proper use of weapons, how to fight as a team.... the Viet Cong knew what was going

on—there were more than a hundred families in the village with some ties to the guerrillas in the hills.... The people of (the village) began to respect their little local soldiers.... began to show their natural warmth toward the Marines as well, instead of fearful restraint under the all-seeing eyes of the Viet Cong. Information welled up from the people.... information on the goings and comings of the Viet Cong, their food and arms, their local hiding places. Sergeant Sullivan and his men grew thinner, and the fatigue lines on their young faces deepened, as the prosperity, health, and well-being of the villagers improved. They were winning this war at the rice-roots level, and they knew it. So did the Viet Cong.

(You might ask, could these Marines have accomplished something like this in a village as tough as Binh Nghia, described earlier? The answer is yes. This was Binh Nghia.)

PEACE-ORIENTED LOW-INTENSITY WARFARE

With values training, could most of our fighting men be educated quickly to fight this kind of low-intensity war for the minds of men (and equally important, women) in the Third World? Success with that type effort is a key theme of these materials. It is what our programs accomplished in numerous countries for twenty years. Even though our work ranged from *in-the-woodwork* secret, to informally confidential, here is the way General Krulak described the program's application when he increased the number of Combined Action Platoons and Companies in Vietnam:

(In) Vietnam.... the Marines became persuaded early in the conflict that the key to victory lay... in establishing a nexus of mutual respect and understanding with the native population.

As a means of achieving this end the Marines created a mechanism called a Combined Action Platoon where our men became integrated into the structure of the native militia, living with them and sharing mutually in the hazards.

It was a fine concept and, even though many of the Marines involved were not adequately grounded, it achieved some early success.

At this point, Mr. Humphrey was brought on the scene to attempt an organized educational effort for the Marines, to equip them more effectively to deal with their indigenous counterparts.

He created lessons, textbooks and outlines to support a very broad educational program which generated an extraordinary level of patriotic dedication among the many who took part. In addition to performing more effectively with the natives they, as a result, performed more effectively with each other....

V. H. Krulak
Lieutenant General,
USMC (Retired)

To close this chapter with the assertion that, through our overseas military forces, we can lead the world out of the Late Dark Ages, I included that letter from General Krulak for several reasons. First, General Krulak is known to be one of the tougher Marines. Yet, you can see, if we educators provide our fighting men with better ways to *win the peace*, they will use them, and not resort to killing (and being killed). Many general officers have sons in the military. They are not interested in dying or seeing their sons die in combat.

Second, those USMC Combined Action Platoons, as you might not have suspected, were among the most effective fighting outfits in Vietnam, not just friend-winners. Despite the fact that a quarter or so of these revolutionary efforts with the CAP villages, in my judgment, did not really make the grade, I heard of only one that lost a village. Generally speaking, the Marines and the Vietnamese from the CAP villages had good things to say about one another, as distinguished from the widely expressed gook syndrome and its whispered anti-American reactions so persistent everywhere else. All was not sweetness and light in the CAP villages. But it crossed the line from a prevailing losing approach to a winner.

It did not take many Marines for a sizable village. The units were called platoons and companies, but frankly I never saw more than a squad of Marines (a dozen or so) in any village, and I saw no heavy weapons. The idea that obsessed most American military men in Vietnam was the number of days they had left before returning home. Not so in the dangerous but effective CAPs. Almost every Marine that I talked with in those friend-winning outfits in the jungles talked of signing over in Vietnam.

Finally, military history of this highly successful aspect of the Vietnam war is now being lost or concealed. It does not fit in with the two major themes that have come out of that tragedy: One, the unspoken neurosis—mental block—of many good people who forced America's withdrawal in a way that was irresponsible; those persons have developed closed minds about discussing the war since it forces them to face their possible indirect responsibility for the Cambodian Killing Fields. Millions, it appears, were executed. So it is painful for many to admit that democracy might have won and avoided those deaths.

Two, the Hawkish *big bomb* military version requires the rewriting of the military history to state that we could have won with, and only with, more big bombs and more killing. It requires the denial and a washing-out of the records, Orwellian, *1984* communist-style, of what actually occurred in those Combined Action Platoon villages and on the river boats. It was in those two unique operations that a few daring, innovative American military men learned and proved how to win the people and win modern low-intensity conflicts with minimum killing. What my materials gave them mainly was the human equality concept, the foundation of democracy, EFFECTIVELY TAUGHT, plus good research-guided, cross-cultural conflict resolution.

From the U.S. President down to the lowest ranking military man and from the draft dodger in Canada to the men who committed the atrocities at My Lai, anyone who says we could not have won for democracy and the people in Vietnam, almost without killing, if our men had been properly trained, ideologically, is simply ignorant of the facts as I observed them for three years during continuous periodic trips into Vietnam from Thailand and Korea.

Why do I insist? I repeat, and will do so again, because, most likely, we will again be called to protect innocent lives in Latin America, Africa, the Middle East, Greece, Turkey, Spain, the Philippines, and so on. Those situations will resemble Vietnam more than Iraq. For the sake of the U.S. future and world history, no lesson as costly as Vietnam should be lost, distorted, or denied. How many chances does a great nation get to learn the lessons that will let it avoid decline?

A FALL-BACK POSITION FOR PEACETIME

During the Vietnamese struggle, the chaplains and other strongly religious members among my advisers were also my strongest supporters. However, a few warned occasionally that after the desperate need to stop violence and save lives in combat was past, it might not be wise to use the animal incidents as the introductory evidence of the species-preservation drive. Rather, they advised, we should find impressive accounts of human beings giving their lives to save others as the primary evidence, and then add the accounts from the animal world; this, to avoid the mistaken judgment that we might be teaching Darwinism. I agree. See especially Robert Heinlein's true account of the heroic hobo in *Attachment A*.

CHAPTER 11

THE NATURAL (SCIENTIFIC) FOUNDATION OF MORALITY

Science is described variously as: *The study and explanation of anything that can be perceived by the senses, or knowledge gained from experience.* So do not be awed nor deceived by the word, science, or scientist. I have known scientists who were terribly superstitious and others who would cheat you blind in tennis and golf. They are just people like us who try to work under the above definitions. We common folk also employ a scientific method. We call it, humbly, *learning from experience.*

According to these dictionary definitions of science, can the behavior of living creatures such as white mice, or chimpanzees, or human beings be studied scientifically?

Which do you think makes for the more reliable scientific knowledge of natural behavior: the study of white mice in cages, or the study of chimpanzees in the wild?

What do you think is the best scientific method for studying human behavior or human nature?

SCIENTIFIC OBSERVATION ON THE FIELD OF BATTLE

In my observation of human behavior, the study of the species-preservation inclination has been the most fascinating. To observe its operation continuously, at the most basic level, and reliably in its full expression—where individuals choose to live personally or else die for others—one needs to participate in a situation where such choosing of life or death to save others is fairly common. The battle for Iwo Jima was one of those horrifying situations. It is often cited as the USMC's most costly battle. There, the species-preserving versus self-preserving choices were routine matters, daily, hourly, for hundreds, maybe thousands, of men.

In that cesspool of blood and vomit, as a replacement lieutenant I took over a front-line rifle platoon where the record of daily death is documented in these figures and similar official statistics: My platoon, originally of forty men, by the sixth day on the island when I took over, was down to seven men, and I was their sixth lieutenant. In four weeks the platoon suffered almost 200% casualties; the entire regiment including rear areas, almost 90%. Similar figures were coming in from all over the island. From my relatively safe, Beach Party job (unloading boats), before I assumed command of a front-line outfit, it was clear to me that I would unquestionably be called forward soon. The original rifle platoon leaders, lieutenants, were lasting only hours. Consequently, for three days prior to my call, I crawled up into front-line units hoping to learn the best ways to lead and also keep my men alive.

It was on the first such trip that I encountered a Corporal Taylor, mentioned earlier. In the absolute chaos of a deafening firefight, one of our tanks had turned the wrong way and was firing into our own men on the flank. When we saw the hill-shaking explosion of a cannon round on those American positions, Taylor stood up as if it were not certain death, ran out thirty yards or so, and grabbed a communication phone from the back of the tank. I saw him trying to yell into the mouthpiece, holding one hand over one ear, yelling hard, obviously having trouble being heard. He pounded the phone on the back of the tank; tried yelling into it again, and finally slammed it down in disgust.

Feeling weak over the anticipation of seeing him shot to pieces, I flushed with hope as I saw him discard the phone. I crowded over to the side of the shallow foxhole so that he could come diving back in. Then the absurd happened. Taylor stopped hurrying. Despite the earsplitting noise and the ongoing firefight, he just calmly walked out in front of the tank, held up his two hands while looking back over his shoulders so as not to stumble, and started giving arm and hand signals to the tank driver just as casually as if he were guiding a truck-driver, back home, in some parking lot.

The only way I can think that he did what he did, and lived, was that the Japanese soldiers who were watching were just as dumbfounded as I was. Some of them must have yelled to the others, "Hey wait! Don't shoot! Look at this crazy guy!" laughed at his audacity, and let him off. It *had* to be that way. He was an easy target; and some of the Japanese Iwo Jima fighters were like that. They had that type of respect for unbelievable fearlessness or bravery. Despite the usual take-no-prisoners viciousness on both sides, the starving Japanese in several caves let one of our interpreters with a white flag walk into their caves and offer them a chance to surrender rather than be burned out with flame throwers. They refused, but they let our Marine interpreter walk back out and live. (Incidentally, one of our interpreters advised that the Japanese soldiers did not choose to die in those caves in order to go the heaven as is often reported. They said it was their way of sending us Marines a message about how hard it would be for us to take their homeland.)

The point of the Taylor story is what he said when he came back. I told him who I was—an observing lieutenant—and admonished him, as a needed leader, for risking his life so recklessly. He overruled me confidently before he crawled away to conduct the firefight: "No lieutenant," he said, "you'll see that that is not the way you keep score out here."

I knew I had been told something profound that I did not understand.

The next day the lesson was clarified. I crawled up into a platoon-sized company that was pinned down behind a rock wall. Crawling up, I had seen that the most dangerous fire was coming from a cave above and to the right of those at which our men were firing. When I called attention to the flanking fire, a bazooka round was decided on for that cave. The isolated platoon had only one bazooka round left. This posed the problem of making sure that the one shot was a hit because time was of the essence. The platoon was pinned down flat and taking casualties. Terrain was a deadly problem. To get a decent shot into that cave, someone had to go over the rock wall with the clumsy bazooka, crawl out some fifteen feet only partly protected by a log about eight inches high, lift his head enough to get off a shot, then try to get back. And this was not Hollywood; it was a suicide mission for someone, but necessary to protect the rest of the platoon. No one was really dug in.

Immediately there was a volunteer. He took the bazooka, crawled over to a corporal beside me and asked privately and hurriedly about how to fire the bazooka alone. In that tight little circle of our three heads with our chins in the dirt, I saw an exchange of glanced communications between the two boys. The volunteer winced slightly in shame that he did not know the weapon. The corporal gritted his teeth, shook his head minutely once, and took the bazooka. This time I saw more clearly the way the better men kept score out there: one takes his turn to die if he is the one who can do the job to save others. *Good Lord! He was going, voluntarily, to pay the price of his life for superior competence; whereas incompetence was saving the other lad. I could hardly stand it.*

As the corporal slipped across the low wall, the first Marine who had volunteered but knew he could not perform, peeked through the rocks with me for a second but then dropped his face into his dusty, grimy hand, unable to watch.

"What's his name?" I yelled.

"McCorco," I thought he answered.

I watched the corporal inch out dredging the black sand in front of him with his chest. I noticed the correct spelling of the young unsung hero's name on his back: McCorkel.

McCorkel got the bazooka in place up on the half-buried log. He exposed his head in hopeless danger to the crack Japanese snipers. He took quick but careful aim, and fired.

Direct hit! McCorkel glanced over at us and smiled and died without moving again as the return fire from a sniper's bullet tore through his head.

Soon after that, I heard that my brother, Calvin, had been killed over in the next regiment, the 27th. Although only a tiny, hundred-twenty-pound, eighteen-year-old PFC, he was an outstanding Marine who won a Silver Star taking a machine gun nest. I wanted to give him a proper burial rather than have him pushed into a mass grave. When I found his platoon, as was typical, it was only of squad size. It was on the front line, but all was quiet. In fact, the little clutch of men was out on the ground, lying low, but not dug in. I asked, "Is this Humphrey's outfit?" Someone looked over and nodded.

"Was he hit," I asked.

Everyone looked up and laughed a little as one said pointing: "He's over there in his hotel."

I crawled over and found him with only minor injuries but down deep in a well-dug foxhole. He looked up, recognized me, and yelled with no other greeting: "Get down in here! And keep your head down; there is sniper-fire out there."

I did, but by then concerned about his mental state, I asked, "What's the matter, Calvin? All the rest of your squad is out on top of the ground laughing because you are dug in."

"Okay, Rob," he said impatiently, "let me teach you something. Peek your shavetail head up there and count them; but just peek."

Ecstatic that he was still alive, to humor him, I peeked up and counted.

"Seven," I reported.

"Well, you see what I said about the sniper fire; there were eleven of the damn fools out there laughing at me yesterday."

After my grim laughter at the lesson illustrated, he made the point I am after. "Everyone gets too casual and careless about death when it is all around; especially you shavetails (lieutenants). Ours haven't lasted five minutes. As soon as they get responsibility for other men's lives, it just seems like they automatically take chances that cost them theirs. Don't do it. Lead quietly from inside like in a bunch of ants where you can't tell who the leader is."

When I took over my own platoon, it was in a protected area. Men were up walking around. It was a confident, experienced group that had helped with the fighting at the top of Mt. Suribachi during the famous flag raising. One young man was especially noticeable, carrying an unusual Thompson submachine gun. He oozed self-confidence and independence. After chow that first evening, as he perfected his foxhole, he started declaring to himself but out loud: "I don't volunteer for nothin' else! Fuck the Marine Corps! Fuck Mt. Suribachi. Fuck everything except ol' Number One! That's all that counts: gettin' off this island alive! I don't volunteer for nothin'!"

He shouted this so repeatedly that a couple of the other men picked it up. "Yeh! Right! We don't volunteer for nothing!" Suddenly, it dawned on me that the declarations were trying to tell me something as their new platoon leader. I felt the chill of having my leadership threatened.

The next morning as we edged out of our foxholes, as luck would have it, a radio message came in for me to send a volunteer out onto a hill up front on an almost sure-death scouting mission. Hesitant to ask for a volunteer after those warnings the previous night, I decided to go myself on the excuse that, as a new lieutenant, I wanted to see the terrain. As soon as I told the men of the radio message and my decision, the *same* Marine who had made the declarations said, "I'll go, lieutenant."

"What!" I exclaimed. "You were the man with the big voice last night about not volunteering for nothing. Now why this?"

Almost sheepishly trying to cover his willingness to take my place, he answered, "Well I can't trust any of these other jarheads on such a mission."

During my experience in that black-sand slaughterhouse, it was always that way. Every time someone had to die to protect the others, there was always a casual volunteer, as if the man were simply volunteering to go get the coffee for everyone. Yet each time, to me, it was absolutely awe-inspiring. Each time, I would not expect it. Then it would happen. Each time it would almost tear my heart out. My mind would go to the boy's family back in the states who would be crushed by the staggering news of their loved one's death and would probably not even know of his supreme greatness. Each time I knew I was experiencing something spiritual. The strange, disturbing thing was that no one else seemed to recognize the heroic, sacred, monumental nature of those acts unless they involved a lot of flashy action, several enemy killed, or many Americans saved.

Even then, most of the time, there were no officers around keeping score on sacrifice, to recommend medals. Everyone was too busy staying alive. The general self-sacrificing was appreciated but considered routine (only natural). A story came in of a man who had smothered a grenade with his body to protect his friends. The grenade had not gone off. When asked about it later, the man laughed and said he had not realized what he had done. (Maybe so; maybe not.)

One night, some Japanese soldiers had crawled between two of our foxholes into our small defensive circle before one of my only two good shooters, Mercer, shot them. The next morning, I warned the others that while they were on guard at night unless they kept their heads up far enough to peek out, the Japanese would get into their foxholes and kill them. It did not work. The same thing happened the next night. I warned them again the same way. My best man, a Texan by the name of Clyde Jackson, pulled me aside and advised: "You are saying the wrong thing, lieutenant. Don't tell them that they will get themselves killed. You have to tell them that the Japanese will crawl by them and *kill us others*."

That worked.

SPECIES-PRESERVATION: LOVE AND GROUP-BELONGING

Twenty-five years later, in Vietnam, I began to hear identical stories about the same species-preserving phenomenon. It is strange but strong. It does not take individually targeted love to trigger it as most persons believe, and it does not work only for kinfolk (as in the sociobiology of communal insects). In combat, at least, according to my careful and persistent observations, it works among persons who hardly know one another's names, it works cross-racially, it is triggered just from *group belonging*. This innate or instinct-like protective bonding is so powerful that "old hands" in combat tend to resist association with, or even learning the names of, new replacements in order to avoid suffering felt when the new combat-incompetents are killed.

SUMMARY: LIFE, A SELF-AND-OTHERS VALUE

In summary, life is humankind's most basic natural, earthly value. But this is not primarily a selfish value. Species-preservation is the stronger half of the drive. For practical guidance from this fact of universal human nature, if you wish to travel the globe and avoid serious trouble, here are the two top rules:

1. You can get yourself into the second-most dangerous position anywhere in the world by threatening a person's life.

2. If that is second, what is the most dangerous action? The answer is obvious isn't it? By threatening someone's loved ones. *That describes the most basic nature of the human animal.*

This balanced—self and species—life value, as the basic value in human nature, may not as yet be recognized as an acceptable scientific fact. That may require more scientific observation to establish it conclusively, especially in our excessively competitive (individualistic) society heavily conditioned toward the self.

Nonetheless, the Balanced Life Value is definitely a respectable scientific proposition for your consideration. Most important, have confidence in your own judgment.

You do not have to wait for experiences similar to mine on Iwo Jima for equally credible evidence. Talk with other observers who were in comparable realistic testing situations such as the Anzio beachhead or the battle for Tarawa, or Stalingrad, and listen to them.

Please do not place any credence at all in any intuitive contradiction from the Ivory Towers of institutionalized education. Comparatively comfortable persons who make up our educationally elite, even the brilliant ones, in general, are out of touch with the common people and the controlling survival values of the world. They have allowed the values of materialism, relativism, and elitism to dominate their detailed daily lives and, therefore, saturate their thinking. This causes them to overlook the deepest causes of our modern problems and even to denounce such issues as "boring." At least a few of the more unusual scholarly elite, themselves, including a few college presidents, have admitted that our universities are overly-specialized anachronisms that produce cultural barbarism. Please stop ignoring the fact that our colleges train our high school teachers and administrators. That training is failing us and our children.

CRITIQUE

Other credible evidence of the human species-preserving nature comes out of the Nazi prison camps. Read for example, *Survivor*, by Terrence Des Pres, (Oxford University Press, 1976). He advises: "...the best of us did not live through that abomination; the best gave their lives so others could live."

The most interesting (apparent) contradiction to these field-findings (on the dual nature of the life value with its edge given to species-preservation) came to me a few years back out of Africa. An outstanding Australian scholar had studied a tribe of Africans, the Ik, who had been driven out of their homelands onto a barren area where they had to forage as scavengers for survival. He advised on national television that these people in their starving condition "had lost all feelings of love and belonging." This evidence from the field, presented a respectable challenge to the Balanced Life Value theory.

I read his book and found the passage with the key contention about *the loss of all love and belonging*. Submitted as his strongest evidence of this *loss of all love* were these facts: The parents who foraged for survival in adult groups forced their own children out of the home to scrounge for their own food in children's groups at the tenderest of ages, almost as soon as the children could walk.

Do you see the fallacy of the reasoning? Starving adults who had actually lost all love and belonging would not have kept those little ones through their most troublesome, loud-screaming years. Rather, most likely, they would have killed (and perhaps eaten) them.

Later I noticed that the Australian scholar had corrected his own mistake. He returned to Africa a few years later and found that the scavenger system in different age groups, contrary to his prediction, was a successful survival system even for the little ones.

Occasionally, in Buddhist countries, I encountered mild challenges to the dual, or balanced, life value on the grounds that I was reading it *too narrowly* rather *than too broadly*. Buddhists have argued that our species-preservation half of the life value includes not just other humans, but all life. They mean it. My little barefooted golf caddie in Thailand stepped on a sick cobra and jumped away with a yell. I raised my golf club to kill the snake. The caddie jumped back in, over the snake, and grabbed my arm to save the deadly reptile. (The life-protecting action of the child impressed me, but spoiled my golf game.)

Recently, I read a beautifully written and strongly reasoned apparent agreement with the Balanced Life Value concept by the notable modern biologist, Lewis Thomas. See his chapter entitled, *Altruism*, in his book, *Late Night Thoughts on Listening to Mahler's Ninth Symphony* (Viking Press, 1983).

Summarizing in legal terms, the Natural Law works not, as the scholars have speculated, indirectly in response to rationally perceived natural rights in general. Rather, it operates directly through psychic penalty or reward, respectively, for one's personal rejection of, or deference to, one's own natural (emotional) duties. The late, great Professor Maslow saw something similar in human nature's intrinsic conscience and intrinsic guilt.

CHAPTER 12

THE SCIENCE OF TEACHING VALUES

[A Note on Religious Values: The spiritual values being discussed are the earthly spiritual values, that is, the horizontal (man-to-man) spiritual values as distinguished from the vertical (mankind-to-God) spiritual values. The latter are the bailiwick of religion in a realm considerably beyond what we are discussing here.]

By 1970, America had given up in Vietnam, and I returned to the States to develop the Marine Corps Race/Human Relations Program. We had the basic inputs we needed to develop a Science of Values. It astounds me that I still could not put those pieces together until after another fifteen years of teaching and help from my sons as they applied the lessons in further experimental Marine training and for upgrading high school education. Now it is all fairly clear:

1. There is a science of values that describes, and emanates from, human nature.

2. There is an embryonic, scientific methodology for teaching, that is, *activating*, ethical, moral, and earthly spiritual (self-sacrificing, species-preserving) values. We have submitted an overview of the substantive content of a total program, omitting only the artistic component. (Two of my sons' experiments clarified this artistic component in the high school projects. In fact they, and two other sons in the Marines, also filled in details of much more complete mental and physical individual-development training packages, briefly discussed in the attachments.)

Until recently, there was still one major, troubling question regarding the basic Balanced Life Value theory of human nature: What is the exact tie-in of the *detailed* earthly spiritual values to the total life-sustaining system?

THE SCIENTIFIC CONNECTION OF THE DETAILED EARTHLY SPIRITUAL VALUES TO HUMAN NATURE

Of all the factors of human nature that we pieced together over the years, it was this relatively small feature that gave me the most personal satisfaction. This feature is the direct connection of the detailed earthly spiritual values to the rest of the system, that is, to life-protecting human nature. That specific feature came the closest to being my own perception rather than the mere result of endless observation or someone else's insight. Also it was the last piece to come, so it provided that satisfaction of filling-in that last little empty spot in the great puzzle. Here is a description of human nature with an explanation of that significant added feature.

HUMAN NATURE AS A COMPLETE SYSTEM OF EARTHLY VALUES

Human nature is an integrated or wholistic mental-physical-spiritual-artistic human life supporting system controllable by reason. The resulting life-value is fairly evenly balanced between the self- and species-preservation drives. That life-value is so deeply cherished by healthy human beings that it impels us all, by nature, to consider our lives as equal in value to others. That is, our lives are considered just as important to us as anyone else's is to them. My clear perception of the earthly spiritual values stopped there with that equal value of human life.

All of the other moral and earthly spiritual values such as love, charity, honor, etc. seemed to be floating out in space—in the heavens—still coming down to humankind somehow through a mystical process. All the detailed values seemed more or less equal and subject to the arguments for ethical relativism.

Though I do not pretend to be an exemplary Christian, I study all of the major religions and I enjoy good church sermons. Those are the places where one can still find, delivered unequivocally, the strong moral lessons. During a perusal of the Christian Bible, I encountered, again, Christ's statement, "Greater love hath no man than this, that a man lay down his life for his friends." The consideration of such life-sacrifices was in my mind from the effort at writing this book plus from the recent experiences in Vietnam. Despite my long familiarity with the citation, seeing it again in that spiritual (Biblical) context, somehow conveyed more vividly its implied message: this greatest of all spiritual (love) expressions in man-to-man relations (giving one's life for another) is also the strongest possible expression of the scientific species-preserving drive. From that little flash of light, the right question occurred to me: Could it be that all the moral, ethical, and earthly spiritual values are all various expressions of the species-preservation drive?

This was twenty-five years after I had first started the full-time search for the nature of human values. As I thought through each of the familiar moral, ethical, and earthly spiritual values (love, charity, compassion, loyalty, courage, honor, etc.) to see if they fit the species-preservation criterion, it was breathtaking to me as I perceived that each, in turn, did, indeed, comply. Each is a different expression of the human tendency to risk or give of one's self for another where the only payoff (when sincere and especially if secret) for the loss of wealth or status is *psychological satisfaction.*

The theory of human nature and the universal values was complete. I saw at least a total outline of the basic Natural Law that governs humankind. (Doubtlessly, there are mistakes in my interpretation of ramifications, but the outline seems fairly solid.) And this small factor of the exact relationship of the various earthly spiritual values to human nature is of considerable importance just now in history with our inordinate concern for human rights with seldom a word or thought about human duties. That balance, too, along with a couple of other significant but smaller details about human nature as a system of values can now be spelled out. I'll include the explanation of (1) our natural rights and duties and how they work, (2) the issue of whether giving for the spiritual satisfaction is properly called altruism or selfishness, and (3) some detailed explanations of how expressions of the earthly spiritual values cause a risk to the self-half of the life value.

NATURAL RIGHTS AND DUTIES

Rights. On the self-side of human nature, when the self-preserving drive expresses itself, it causes us to feel as if we possess certain natural rights that protect and support our individual mental, physical, and material well-being—our self. Our society has become so attentive to these claims that everyone has become a little jumpy about being sued over anything by anybody. But on the other side of human nature, there is an inadequate societal concern for our natural duties.

Duties. When our species-preserving drive expresses itself in various ways, it creates feelings of natural duties. They cause us as individuals to risk or sacrifice some or all of our self—our social, physical, or material well-being—on behalf of others. The only inspiration for these drives, when genuinely expressed, are feelings of moral, ethical, and spiritual well-being, that is, feelings of maturity, wisdom, and especially, serenity. In the absence of proper attention to this half of our nature, our natural duties, the resulting guilt, resulting stress, resulting tensions, and resulting emptiness are not only filling our individual lives with unhappiness, but even the productivity of the entire nation is suffering.

It is not only better to give than to receive, it is necessary to maintain concern for others in order to maximize one's own health and happiness. (There is a problem here in the modern world of big government and organized charities. To derive the socially healthy satisfaction from giving, a donor probably needs a face-to-face relationship with the recipient. However, this person-to-person relationship would be difficult to achieve in a huge urbanized society.)

One of my top students observed that perhaps the greatest evil of big government, especially of communism, is the fact that it institutionalizes giving. That not only deprives us of the personal joy of giving, it makes us resentful of being forced to give indirectly, through taxes. (In passing, is there a way out of this dilemma? Something along these lines might be worthy of consideration: Charity could be decentralized for personalized giving through neighborhood churches, or Moral Study Centers for the non-believers—all run by persons who have accepted a vow of poverty, to reduce graft.)

THE SATISFACTION OF NATURAL RIGHTS AND DUTIES

Expressions of the self-preservation drive range from the demand for food to the desire for freedom. When satisfied, these self-sustaining values give life pleasure and afford security. When felt and expressed excessively, as selfishness, that is, to the hurt of others, both the selfish one and society suffer.

The species-preserving inclinations or values, range from love and charity through loyalty and honor to truth and courage. In all societies where I have studied, it is always said—by those whom others identify as *highly moral and spiritual persons*—that these values, even though they often cause material sacrifice, are what make life worth living. But when expressed excessively, out of weakness by a person, he or she often becomes a resentful victim of circumstances.

THE ISSUE OF "SELFISH ALTRUISM"

Of course there are those who give, in public, for selfish reasons—to obtain some material or social gain. This cannot be called altruism; at best it is a tricky trade off; at worst, hypocrisy. You may also be familiar with the modern contention that giving is not correctly called altruism if one derives spiritual satisfaction from the act. The spiritual satisfaction, the argument goes, makes the act selfish. Since that view violates the understanding of altruism that we have found is held by most people in the world, we'll not accept it here. It becomes too much of a matter of the modern double-speak that makes communication impossible. I'll mention two examples in the rebuttal:

Do you know the story of Elizabeth Pilenkok, better known to the world as Mother Maria, a Russian Orthodox nun? She worked in a Nazi prison camp comforting the Jewish victims as they were being led into the gas chambers. One day a little girl started crying in fear and was about to be beaten by the guards so she would not panic the other prisoners. Mother Maria took her hand telling her not to cry, "I am going to go with you," she said, *and went.*

On February 4, 1912, by a freak of nature on the frozen river below Niagara Falls, Eldridge Stanton and his wife, Clara, were adrift on an ice flow headed toward death in Whirlpool Rapids. Eldridge could have escaped by jumping from ice block to ice block and to land. But Clara was too weak even to try. Hundreds of people watched while Eldridge decided to comfort his wife in his arms during the trip to death in the rapids rather than to leave her to face those few terrible moments alone.

I'm sure Mother Maria and Eldridge Stanton felt warm spiritual satisfaction during their last minutes of life. Still, despite that possible spiritual satisfaction, would we not now appear disgusting beyond discussion to besmirch either one of those personifications of love by calling them selfish?

SPECIFIC EXPRESSIONS OF THE DETAILED SPIRITUAL VALUES

Truth, ethical truth, is of the following nature. It involves risking the individual self. It says: *I did it; don't blame others.*

Love has said: *I'll gladly die for her or for him.*

Loyalty and courage, in the strongest vernacular of the streets, often say: *You'll hurt them only over my dead body.*

In other words, the great moral, ethical, and earthly spiritual values are nuances of the self-risking others-serving drive. All of them are. *Workaholism* is at times a *misfire* or exaggerated expression of this spiritual inclination to give to the family or to humankind. So is the undisciplined love that spoils children.

FINAL RAMIFICATION

With this final piece to the great riddle of human nature in place, I knew that eventually ethics—the study of right and wrong, good and bad—could be upgraded from its nebulous status into humankind's most important science for our better guidance toward peace and tranquility. We can accomplish that upgrading if we are not already too far distorted or out of natural balance from the conditioning of our selfishly oriented society and from our narrow and excessively competitive educational system. Men do commit suicide; so do groups; so do nations.

TRANSITION

A summary of how the chief characteristics of human nature guided us to successful solutions of the crisis in education will be presented in *Attachment B*. Just now, we shall turn to the pressing problem of solving major cross-cultural and cross-group conflicts. We now have the intellectual tools for that worldwide task. The best preparation for the readers to help pacify the warring globe by this methodology is to review some of the major cross-cultural conflicts that we were able to solve on our projects in various countries. The most challenging and interesting examples follow. As you read them, see if you might have solved them with your current understanding of humankind's equality/sameness, plus the cross-cultural detective approach that together make solutions possible.

Understand that power-brokered treaties or race-relations laws without supporting attitude changes, are reliable only so long as the power holds.

PART II

CROSS-CULTURAL DETECTIVE WORK
FOR ETHNIC CONFLICT REDUCTION

As world history changes from the age of national hegemony to ethnic self-determination, the approach to peace must change to research-guided grass-roots attitude change.

INTRODUCTION

Fortunately, the human brain adjusts quickly to adverse circumstances. Otherwise, even more persons would be neurotic and psychotic than there are now. That sanity-saving psychological flexibility, however, has it drawbacks. For example, men in combat grow accustomed to death and get careless. Similarly, we have grown accustomed to violence in modern society and now we risk taking violence for granted. (Read the morning paper; any morning, any paper.)

A permanent solution to the astounding level of violence awaits values education in our schools. But our schools, worldwide, as we almost all know, are outmoded. Catastrophic modern developments in the world have left the schools back in the somewhat inhumane age of industrializing mass production. That includes the Japanese schools as far as humane respect for the individual child is concerned. Many students in the Japanese schools are driven to high stress tensions, even suicide. Hence, their schools, too, are failed institutions by any truly civilized standards.

Academically, the depth of the trouble is generally admitted outside of academia. The situation is so desperate that the current, ongoing, panicky plan for U.S. school reform is propelling our nation even further into weakness, sociologically. The forward-going plan is dividing our educational system up further into poor schools and rich schools through specialized magnets, business-supported satellites, and other semi-private adjustments, leaving the majority of public schools still poor, failing, and resegregating. It is a disastrous, narrow-minded, short-term solution. It is not only dividing our society further, but is weakening our nation unnecessarily at the roots—all across our work force. We shall at least outline a better, healthier solution in *Attachment B.*

Meanwhile, we need a shortcut to violence-reduction on a national and global scale. We need a shortcut that will substantially eliminate the social animosities that continue to cause cross-ethnic warfare, the horrifying fanatical terrorism, and the insane street violence that makes our city streets dangerous places to walk, even in our neighborhoods.

There is a shortcut to violence-reduction on a massive international scale, faster than by changing the schools. It is through the means described in the previous chapters. The first step, *teaching the theory,* is the most important feature of that methodology and it takes little time. The next step, however, *the social detective work,* takes time. Happily, it is intellectually challenging as well as highly enjoyable. It is similar to working any puzzle, or solving any mystery.

A decisive intellectual footnote to those two steps above may involve the most emotionally difficult feature to accept of the entire process. It is to learn and teach a higher appreciation of natural-resources geography. Poor people in this world, generally speaking, come from difficult environments, and wealthy people, from comparatively supportive environments. This seemed to be a surprisingly difficult bit of knowledge for almost any American to accept until the oil problem almost closed down entire cities in the proud state of Texas. Now, those Texans understand the problem a little better, but most Americans in the wealthier economic classes still do not. They prefer to take personal credit for having been born into the "better classes." They attribute their status to their own hard work and superior intelligence.

Actually, hard work and freedom together, alone, *will not produce anything.* The cooperation of Mother Nature someplace along the line is or was also needed. In fact, the single area of factual knowledge that is most important to peace, second only to the understanding of human nature, itself, is a knowledge of natural resources geography. Yet this understanding decreases as rural society disappears in favor of industrialized agriculture. The resulting urbanized populations more and more believe that milk comes out of bottles and *basic* wealth out of computers.

The inability to appreciate our relationship with Nature is the single biggest cause of bigotry (the deeply felt judgment that other, poor groups of people are stupid or less than equal). Many of my most brilliant students, intellectually speaking, have suffered from this lack of understanding and became unhappy haters in foreign cultures.

If you do not understand what I am saying here, or if you tend to disagree, please consult *Attachment C.* America needs your enlightenment on this matter. The attachment presents a comparison of the U.S., from the natural resources standpoint, with the country of Bolivia. After learning the technique, you may want to test it by applying it to the few countries that are usually cited to disprove the theme:

1. Switzerland; check its comparative location and comparative amount of arable land—more than any country in South America,

2. Israel; check the size of *imported* capital and human resources, and

3. Japan, compared to Korea; check comparative climate, fishing waters, and free access to coal and iron in Manchuria during the period of world industrialization.

4. Also check the comparative wealth of Illinois with my current home state of Tennessee and then dare to submit to these Volunteers that the Illinois people—on that flat land of black soil loaded with minerals—produce more wealth simply because they have more basic intelligence and work harder than those of us from a little farther south (in these rocky lands).

Adequate research will reveal that all of those admirable, comparatively wealthy peoples are admirable indeed, but not exceptions that disprove the basic rule.

5. Also for the same type understanding, check the comparative *disadvantages* of unnavigable waters, poor

soil, and zoological human enemies in most of Africa; this, despite the continent's famous but comparatively unimportant mining industry.

Now let us take up the challenge of the culture-shock, or poverty-shock, cases to test and build your cross-cultural detective abilities.

To solve the major cross-cultural attitudinal roots of violence, learn the technique from these actual cases. The approach will work in Ireland, the Middle East, in former Communist countries with ethnic troubles, in Central America, or in our urban centers suffering from deep cross-group or teen-gang animosities, including, for example, the severely racially divided cities of Chicago or Milwaukee.

CHAPTER 13

THE CASE OF THE SLOW DINNER SERVICE

The island of La Maddalena off the coast of Sardinia is one of those marvelous little spots on earth where visitors might wish to retire and live-out their lives under the friendly Mediterranean sun. This fact was not lost on the U.S. Navy a few years back, when selecting spots where American families might be happy in *homeports* overseas. Prior to the transfer of Americans onto the tiny isle, one large U.S. Navy ship had already been stationed there—a short skiff ride away from a small town that catered to international tourists. Since the ship was busy with some kind of service to other naval ships in the area, only a few of the crew members at any one time were able to visit the little island town. Nonetheless, the old familiar Ugly American problem soon arose.

One day while working on USMC race relations in California, I received a rush request from some U.S. Navy command in England to visit both La Maddalena and Athens, Greece, for the same mission: To try to solve the sudden problems being voiced in the terms: *Ugly Americans* and *Yankees Go Home.*

The difficulty in La Maddalena, as the responsible Navy commander explained it to me, was unclear: "So far," he emphasized, "there is only one little problem. But it bodes ill for the future when the American families arrive. I am not going to describe it to you, but rather take you to it so you can experience the treatment. It is causing some fights."

The town was so small that I figured the entire population of the greater community was not more than a few thousand. The commercial area along the coast seemed to be two main streets forming a Y with the longest commercial street not more than three or four blocks long. I knew that if we Americans could not make friends in that friendly tourist village, I was going to give up work completely in this field.

The commander took me to a waterfront restaurant as soon as it opened for dinner. We seated ourselves at one of the six or eight sidewalk tables and I picked up the menu. From my memory, it looked something like this:

Menu

Salad	2.00
Italian Bread	1.00
Seafood Snack	3.00
Spaghetti	3.00
Beef Steak	10.00
Pork Chops	10.00
Lobster	15.00
Fried Chicken	8.00
Ice Cream	2.00
Chocolate Cake	1.00
Apple Pie	1.50
Tea	.50
Beer	1.00
Wine (Glass)	1.50
Wine (Bottle)	4.00

The commander graciously offered to pick up the tab and recommended the lobster. But we had eaten aboard ship, which served dinner early, so I decided on the surefire Italian spaghetti, salad, bread, and a glass of wine. The commander ordered the same and after the waiter left, he said: "Okay, now it starts. Check your watch for time. See how long it takes to get served. Also notice these customers arriving and ordering subsequently to us and see who gets served first. And observe that we are the only Americans, with our short haircuts, at any of the tables. If others arrive, notice how long it takes them, too, to get served."

I watched. It was easy. We were flat-out last to be served; even though all the other tables had filled-up after we arrived. No other Americans showed up.

After being served, finally, and eating, I ordered a bottle of wine; we sat sipping until closing time. (Sometimes you have to give your all on these detective assignments.) When a waiter finally told us politely that they were closing, I asked to see the owner. Unlike the food, he appeared at once. I introduced myself and the commander, explained my peace-seeking mission, and mentioned the late table-service problem.

He was silent and thoughtful. Then with an action of decision, he graciously ordered another bottle of wine and took a chair at our table. After the wine came and he poured, he sat back and pointed to his eyeglasses. In excellent English, he asked, "Do you see the broken eyepiece in my glasses?"

I allowed that I did. He spoke.

"It was broken last night in a fight with some of your sailors over this very same issue. May I explain?"

He waited for my response. I nodded eagerly. He turned to the commander for additional approval. "Yes, yes," insisted the commander, obviously surprised that there could be any legitimate excuse for the ill-treatment of Americans.

"You see," he said, leaning forward on both elbows obviously emotionally involved but very much in control of himself. "We have tourists from all over Europe and now you new Americans. At first, I was delighted with your arrival because I am very much opposed to communism. But soon a big problem arose with you as customers. May I tell you what it is?"

"Yes, that's what we came to learn," I asserted again, thinking maybe he did not understand English as well as he spoke it. "Why would you hesitate?" I asked, now a little bewildered if not annoyed.

"Because, I know it will offend you; because both of you also suffer from the same problem. And in my culture, at least, it is very insulting."

"Try us," I offered. And trying to keep the conversation friendly, I added: "I'll bet you that last glass of wine that we will not be insulted."

"Well," he said, "it is because you Americans are so stingy."

That comment, of all possible comments, offended me. I felt my face flush. It surprised me so much that after a momentary flash of anger, it made me laugh, because I did feel insulted and knew that I dared not speak. I looked at the commander. His knuckles were turning white as he held his glass of wine. I could see that his tightening grip was going to break off the stem.

Gaining my composure and stifling my disgust at this obviously contrived allegation and therefore intentional insult, I picked up the wine bottle, shook my head in disbelief, and emptied the last drink into the restaurant owner's glass saying, "Alright, you win the bet."

Hoping to find a soft spot in the man's apparent anti-Americanism, I probed with these comments: "You know," I advised, "I have worked all over this world on our so-called Ugly American problem. I am admitting to you that we seem to have trouble everywhere. But the one thing I have never heard us called before is stingy. In fact, on the contrary, of all the complaints, the opposite of stingy is one of the most familiar. It is said that we are wasteful spendthrifts, careless buyers who don't know how to bargain, and consequently thoughtless persons who inflate prices for local people everywhere. For God's sakes, can you please explain why anyone would ever call us stingy?"

"Yes," he said, "you see our tourist season is only a few months long. But we have to earn enough to feed our families all year. Yet you Americans are all the same. You come in here every evening before any of the Europeans arrive, take our few tables, and order only spaghetti and wine. All of the European tourists order the entire meal. That's how we make our money: from those who order a full dinner. But since you Americans arrived, we have lost money instead of being able to save for the dead season. It is as simple as that."

I was delighted and laughed. I knew I saw the answer at once. Do you see it? The main clue is on the menu.

I was so pleased that I had to hold back from blurting out the answer else it seem superficial. It was the only time in twenty years of work that an important answer had come easily. I promised and guaranteed to solve the problem absolutely within a week if he had time for one more bottle of wine. Eagerly he ordered it and pulled his chair over closer to me as people do in the traditional cultures. He advised: "If you can actually solve this, you will change everything for the future of your Americans here. The owners of all the restaurants have been having meetings. We were going to do something because delaying the service was not working. It was just causing fights."

Requesting a menu from a waiter, I laid it in front of the owner.

"I don't really know much about menus in the best restaurants," I advised. "But I know about young enlisted military men. I used to be one. I come from the same American working class that most Navy persons do. And to me, this is what we would call an á la carte menu from which you are expected to pick and choose freely. There is no indication on it at all that one is expected to order a full dinner. To us, this sidewalk atmosphere is very casual, like a sidewalk coffee shop. These sailors are not tight. I'm sure if you would ask some, you would find that they tend to think of themselves as big spenders. But like me, who ordered only spaghetti tonight, they eat an early meal aboard ship, then they come here actually wanting to be friendly. They all love spaghetti; it's one of our favorite dishes in America. But it is considered a main course dish. Just change all of your English menus. Put in only one price at the bottom of everything, allowing certain substitutions... et cetera."

He saw the point but showed skepticism. He clearly wanted to believe me but finally rejected my explanation:

"They know," he insisted. "They know they are supposed to order the entire meal. How could they not know when the tourists from every country in Europe all know?"

"Because," I countered, "the international tourist set is definitely a different breed of cat from us working Americans. I don't know why the European tourists understand, despite that menu; it probably comes from their own culture or class. Or maybe it is just that they are hungry. But our guys definitely do not know better. I didn't, and I came here to try to solve the fighting problem. So you must realize that, except out of ignorance, I would not have committed the exact mistake that was causing the fights."

I could see him starting to believe me. He looked at the commander who nodded an affirmative. The owner began to study the menu.

"Okay," he said and made some kind of an Italian hand sign of pleasure that I did not understand.

"Tell all the other restaurant owners," I added. "Change all the menus and I guarantee you I'll stay on this island until the problem is solved or we drink up all the wine." He laughed and agreed. I was positive the problem was already solved.

We went back to the ship and had a good laugh explaining the matter to the ship's captain. We also made certain the misunderstanding was corrected from the American side, just in case the restaurant owners failed to act.

Now, most important for understanding the real key to finding a solution was the conviction that an answer could be found. Humans all over the world are all alike; we possess the same reasoning ability. The commander communicated to me the same idea by admitting that he had not solved the simple little problem for only one reason: He had assumed there was no answer except either to avoid the restaurants or else win the fights.

A couple of the few outstanding scholars in this neglected field worked with me during those fascinating few days on lovely La Maddalena, the professors Donahue from USIU in San Diego. On that island, we did it right. Before the main body of Americans arrived, we conducted a quick attitude study of the key dislikes on both sides. The Donahues stayed a while longer and helped the Navy team get specific answers to the negatives, rather than typically, just talk about the positives (which need no comments), and plan a good, total, mutual-respect program.

A year or so later, I heard that the *Little America* on La Maddalena was considered by the Navy to be one of the most successful binational communities in the world. The chief credit must go to the dedicated persons themselves who lived there and worked it out. Still, that crucial little bit of detective work that we did there, I suspect, gave it a hopeful rather than an almost hopeless beginning. The restaurant owner advised me, "It's good you came. The menu was such a little thing. *Yet Communist agitation was starting, and in our anger, we were starting to listen. They are spreading rumors about that ship out there and what it is probably carrying. It was getting very bad.*"

That was an easy case; let us try a hard one.

CHAPTER 14

THE GENERAL NATURE OF THE PROBLEM FOR A GROUP OF AMERICANS ABROAD AND A SCIENTIFIC SOLUTION

INTRODUCTION

I have prepared groups of Americans and a few Canadians to go into the Mediterranean area many times over the past three decades. Few changes have been necessary in the materials. Why? Because the peoples of southern Europe have solid *cultures* or established *traditions*. In America, the old-country cultures don't fit; they are set aside, or they just dissipate. Rather than a traditional culture, in America we have an *economy*, a *fast-changing economy*. About the only significant ideas that could be called tradition are the highly vocalized belief in political *freedom* and a deep, even if not articulated, *sense of human equality*. When change-oriented Americans go into tradition-oriented societies, of course, conflicts result.

The following case about a foreign culture was written by an American suffering from deep culture shock. He spoke for most other Americans in the large, civilian, overseas *Little American community.* He was in complete emotional control and a brilliant man. His ancestors came from this *old country* that he is discussing. That was one of the reasons he had gone there. But what he found shocked him doubly: Besides the direct shock, it embarrassed him to be identified as one of the area's blood descendants.

Hold these facts in mind as you consider the case: The group had received more traditional language and cultural training than most groups prior to their move abroad. Still, they had submitted their resignations from their new overseas jobs and were demanding transfers back to the States. We solved the problem in a few weeks.

The Americans withdrew their resignations; they stayed and finished the job admirably, and accepted another overseas contract in a more difficult area of the world. I reiterate: the problem was not the Americans, it was their previous faulty education for the modern shrinking world. How was the solution accomplished? Especially, how was it accomplished so quickly?

It was mainly a matter of attitude change through an effective appeal to the universal human values plus some crucial cross-cultural education. As you read, think; think what you might do to find corrective answers to the negative, self-defeating, American attitudes. Ponder how you might transmit the corrective information to a hostile audience. You must persuade them to change some of their attitudes and some of their behavior.

Understand that there are limits to anyone's ability to change others' attitudes from words alone. It is not *all simply a matter of communication.* There are deep *values* conflicts that communication alone will not solve. As we shall see, changes of situations and behavior patterns are at times also required.

ORGANIZE A MULTICULTURAL TEAM

For solving such "unsolvable" hostilities (roots of war) such as the Arab-Israeli, North-South Irish, Greek-Turk, or the black-white polarization in America, the first step up out of these archaic tribal hostilities is to develop a good *mixed* orientation team. The team members have to be persuaded by you to identify the alleged shortcomings of their *own* cultures and then discover and explain the unseen pragmatic reasons for those patterns or else (more difficult) persuade their own people to start making the necessary cross-cultural adjustments. Here are three categories of examples that call for the most difficult accomplishment: behavior changes, rather than mere attitude changes, in one's own culture. The following examples are situations in which one's cultural patterns threaten another group with one of these three type problems:

1. *Life-threatening situations*—deadly sanitation problems, head hunting, carrying guns at social functions where there is also drinking, etc.

2. *Loose sexual patterns* that are prohibited in the other culture (usually considered a threat to the family).

3. *Actual financial exploitation.*

Two cultures divided by those problems, I find, cannot be mixed happily and effectively until the members of the threatening culture are willing to alter their behavior patterns or the members of the frightened culture are willing to accept the allegedly threatening or looser practices, which is unusual.

Of course you start with comprehensive attitude studies to make certain you have a true attitudinal analysis of the problem, and not some leader's naive or self-serving interpretation.

Section A
The Case

Case Title:

WHY WE ARE ALL QUITTING AND GOING HOME: THEY ARE PINCHING OUR WOMEN, KICKING OUR LITTLE DOGS AROUND, AND RINGING OUR DOORBELLS ALL DAY LONG.

From: Mr. X, The Committee Director

To: Professor Humphrey

Topic: The summarized answers to your questions.

The Problem

All except a few of the 300 paid employees are submitting their resignations. They want to go home and take their families.

The Reasons

Now that almost a year has passed since our company (of 300 employees, 200 with families) arrived, the tourist-oriented literature of a year ago has been forgotten by most of our 1,000 Americans. It has been replaced by a swarm of impressions that are beginning to fit into a pattern of understanding. At best it is an incomplete understanding, limited by short exposure time, language barriers, and the restraints placed upon those who work each day.

Our mission is American in origin, as is our organization and its technical supervision. Our support facilities are of American origin. Our community is American, with corresponding social habits. What are the considerations, then, in the minds of these Americans to life here? What is the reaction of the typical wife and mother who has to make daily contact with the locals? Let's list a few of the impressions under certain categories.

Impressions of the Single Male

Local females don't believe in shaving armpits or legs and there aren't many single U.S. types around. Casual dating of local girls isn't customary. Here, it is understood that dancing with a girl is the equivalent of a marriage contract.

Impressions of Married Male Employees

Among the most aggravating elements of this country are its roads and highways. Even local residents recognize that they are crazy drivers and incautious pedestrians. They drive at high speeds, pass in no-passing zones, use horns instead of brakes, and argue violently with police when caught breaking the law. Unconcerned pedestrians wander in the street talking. Between the automobile operators and the pedestrians and the bicycles, motor scooters, motorcycles, horse carts, pushcarts, and funeral processions, in order to avoid an accident, a driver may dodge off the road into a tree, concrete post, rock wall, or ditch.

If you are a customer in the bank, it takes 10 or 15 minutes and two or three clerks to cash a check and convert dollars into local currency. When the bank is crowded, it is hopeless!

On the work site, the speed limit of 25 miles per hour is obeyed infrequently by the locals. If one of their small delivery cars will do 50, that is the speed it always travels.

After assuring us that dynamiting was finished at a position, and after we moved our own explosives into the area, a local contractor proceeded to dynamite some post holes.

The American employee learns the actual meaning of tomorrow. It is an attitude, a local way of life, perfected to a high degree. It is a polite way of ignoring tasks....

Legal advice demonstrates a peculiar courtesy of the local national. Since the client is paying, he will be given whatever advice he wishes to hear, whether it is true or not.

Most company people... remember and laugh grimly about the series of diagnoses by the local doctor when presented with our first case of hepatitis. The order of diagnoses: influenza, too much smoking, a cold, homesickness (suppositories for treatment), appendicitis, and finally, hepatitis. The patient was a nonsmoker.

Local guards entrusted with the security of the area have been so energetic in this mission that they have completely covered every accessible inch of the guardhouse structure with pornographic drawings.

IMPRESSIONS OF A WIFE AND MOTHER

The elegance of having a maid has shown a few drawbacks. Disregarding minor thefts, rather constant demands for wage increases, and the tendency to shout instead of talk, the major problem is: *Who is boss—employer or maid?* Asking a maid to do it the American way leads to arguments. Arguments lead to new maids. Raising children, when left to a maid, is accomplished with great love but no discipline. Parents lose control.

Starting at about 8 A.M., the door bell rings all day. Small boys or men offer rugs, newspapers, fruit, vegetables, bread, wine, olive oil, and other items; children and nuns bearing tin cups collect for innumerable charities; bill collectors for gas, water, and electric utilities read meters and collect sums ranging from small to stupendous.

Three little girls asked their mother why the local boys played soccer with a puppy before they drowned it. [Word of this spread through the American community, and caused great anger.]

Walking in town during shopping requires great skill in dodging erratic walking patterns, the flailing arms of talkers, dashing children, and purse-snatchers. The nationals cut in front of lines, shove, and push to get there first, but address you courteously as they do so.

Surely nowhere else are the men so constantly scratching themselves. Along the waterfront a few teenage boys stand naked flipping their private parts at passing drivers.

After a few months, Americans feel that they shouldn't be items of curiosity. The continuous stare is still used, especially by the men who must fancy themselves as great lovers. Sometimes, in a crowd, they manage to pat and pinch as well. [This has caused some fights between local men and American husbands. Many American women are enraged.]

The use of enclosed toilets is not mandatory. One can't drive through the city or country without seeing someone relieve himself against walls or bushes or over the wall into the bay.

It is tiring constantly to boil all drinking water and soak and wash all vegetables day after day....

AND WE ADD THE IMPRESSIONS TOGETHER

The majority of Americans avoid contact with local residents as much as possible. There are exceptions, of course, in a few of the more-educated local families, who are friends of many Americans. But the majority of the local people are not well-educated or prosperous. We are distressed by the complete lack of moral, religious, and business ethics demonstrated. They appear to Americans as inconsistent, illogical, obscene, undisciplined, and of animal intelligence; *a semi-animal group of miserable creatures constantly seeking food. Too much is enough.* We are going home.

SOLUTIONS THAT DO NOT WORK

Before we proceed to the solution of this case, let me refer again to a few, familiar, superficial reactions to such cases. These are vital warnings that I'll repeat occasionally for emphasis:

Since this was southern Europe, a sizable minority of the Americans spoke a little of the local language. Did this help? Yes and no.

Some Americans had learned to deny that they spoke the language because it had brought them invitations into local homes where they encountered more culture shock. So they stopped admitting their ability to speak the local language and they stopped speaking it.

A few had *gone native.* As soon as work was over, they changed clothes into something more like the local people wore; they took up residence in a local suburb, secretly, away from the other Americans. They loved their experience there and pitied the other Americans.

Most of the members of those two small groups (the best and the worst adjusted) had something else in common with the local people: the local country was their ancestral home. For all of those Americans, the experience was especially character-testing.

There was another small group of Americans, a few of the college-educated officers of the company, who were unique. This small minority among the officers criticized this *write-up* of the case by their colleague when I showed it to them during my search for answers. When I asked them for assistance with corrective materials, their answers were all the same, and nothing else. It was the answer of the modern college-taught relativist: "Everyone is different, and we Americans must learn to accept those differences."

What is wrong with that answer? Nothing on its face. But in fact, I found it to be *just talk.* The local people who worked in the offices with these *"everything is OK"* advocates advised that in most cases these particular Americans were the most hypocritical. In their personal relations, they were more arrogant and condescending than many Americans who expressed their hostilities openly. At least with the latter, one could start a reconciling conversation, whereas these glib intellectuals refused to face specifics and denied their superiority complexes. Their talk fooled none of the host-nationals. Their aloof, unspoken attitudes were denounced privately as disgusting.

SECTION B
THE SOLUTION

RESEARCH AND ANALYSIS

I started conducting attitude studies, orally, abroad a bus that carried both Americans and local nationals to and from work. The

Americans were so angry (so much in culture shock) that they got loud in their negative responses to my questions. The local nationals heard their denunciations. Arguments started; no fights, but almost. This mixed public research had to be stopped.

Next, I arranged a meeting with a group of about twenty Americans who were working on a remote rural site; wives were invited and many of them were present. The feelings among the Americans were so adverse toward the American company, as well as toward all things local, that I asked the company director to introduce me and then leave. He did. (My mission was to persuade the Americans to sign-over for the job in the next country, not the current one. Of course, incidentally, they had to be persuaded to stay and finish in the current country.)

As soon as the boss left, I opened my package of colored slides to show some pictures of the next country and its problems. But I got stopped by a huge fellow slouched in a chair in the front row. His name was Nick.

"Wait a minute, mister!" he ordered. "I have a question. We heard your name," he announced, looking around to make certain he was enlisting the support of the group. "We know what you are going to say about (the next country). You see, we heard the same lies about this place. But we did not catch who it is you represent. Are you another liar from the company or are you a liar from the State Department this time?"

There were shouts of approval and raucous laughter. (In answer, as a matter of community strategy, one cannot allow *the haters,* the strongly vocal leaders of the culture-shocked group, to mark you as a defender of the host-national culture. Rather, you must establish your correct identity as a constructive leader of your own group, that is, one who will make the group stronger and more successful through a new approach that teaches the group to associate and negotiate more successfully with members of the other culture, for mutual gain.)

Consequently, in the face of this angry personal attack about being a liar, it was important to give no appearance of having been put on the defensive. I was performing a service, not selling. In this particular case, I judged that there was no way to address that hostile group effectively at that moment. So rather than try to respond immediately, I decidedly stopped my preparation toward giving the presentation; replaced the colored slides in their case, and conveyed with my body language, that, obviously, I was leaving— not in anger, but rather as a result of some misunderstanding. Those were my true feelings.

"I am sorry." I acknowledged. "Obviously I have misunderstood something, and have jumped ahead of myself on this mission. My primary assignment was to prepare some of you for your possible work in (the next country). Clearly this group is not ready for that. Whether I am a liar or not, you will have to decide after you know me or hear my comments and then have a chance to check them. As for whom I speak, I am now on your company payroll, but just for a temporary contract. It is not intended to be my life's work. On the other hand, I am motivated strongly toward success. If I help prepare anyone or any company to journey into the country where I have been working, I most definitely want you to be highly successful. You cannot be if you are not happy. And here is the catch: you can never be happy in that tough country unless you, too, are damn tough, mentally tough.

"Now, for some reason, which may be legitimate, your toughness—judging from that cutting welcome that you just laid on me—your mental toughness for life abroad is exhausted, completely gone. This place, compared to most countries further east, is a soft pillow. You can make some financial savings out there, but not happily, unless you are of the pioneering or adventurous spirit. As I say, if this group once boasted a psychological toughness, it is now gone. If you are now homesick and longing for that greatest of all great soft pillows called America, according to my several times around this globe, you will find it there and only there."

I was continuing along these lines; adding a few needles as I talked because they were listening. But I judged I had said enough, had made the point, and had reached the time to quit. (It's a matter of feel, of course. And I learned immediately that I had read that group a little too adversely.)

I picked up my gear from the speaker's table, sidestepped toward the door, expressed my thanks to them for letting me explain myself, and said in closing: "Now, after you think it over, if some of you want to consider the next trip, contact me through the headquarters office, and we can lay this on again for those who are interested. Thanks again."

Before I could take the next step toward the exit, someone from the group objected: "No," he said, "time is flying. I need to make a decision very soon if I am going to change my mind. I came here to listen. So I want to hear your comments now. Why don't we let those who want to leave, leave, and those who want to stay, stay?"

Of course, I agreed (very pleased). Everyone stayed including Nick. It was a breeze. It went so well, in fact, that I broached the topic of their unfortunate unhappiness and asked them to tell me the main problems. They voiced the objections covered in the report above. I took notes and asked if they would be willing to meet with me again to see if my longer experience overseas might provide answers that would help them enjoy their current tour a little more. "It is," I risked, "partly a matter of misunderstanding."

With good-natured skepticism, about half the members of the little group expressed general laughing agreement. The other half left in a still serious, negative mood, but no one attacked me, not even verbally. I left feeling half optimistic.

WIVES AND MOTHERS

Two men dropped-in beside me to talk confidentially as I walked toward my car. One spoke: "We wanted to tell you privately that life here is most difficult for the wives and mothers. If they were happier, the men would be more willing to stay."

"Okay," I answered, "I'll pursue that line of investigation as the first lead." I did.

I arranged to meet with all the wives and mothers in the theater on Friday. I spread the word that I wanted to hear complaints. They came. The complaints again repeated those ideas expressed in the company official's report.

A good many of the women were livid over being patted and pinched by local men and over the local men's use of the lover's stare. Others, a smaller number, were disgusted to the point of emotional heat over the *cruelty to animals* (kicking the little dogs around, killing one).

I requested a week or ten days to research the matters properly and promised to get back to them. The list of issues was long, including fourteen to sixteen items, which caused me some consternation. When you hold a group-complaint session, it lowers the hostility level by letting off some steam. However, that reduction of emotional heat is temporary and you must give fairly prompt feedback or you will likely heighten the feelings of dissatisfaction. (I have not researched that last point adequately, but in several cases I have felt the trouble brewing so strongly that I am almost positive about the warning: Give feedback as soon as possible.) I started my corrective research that Friday evening.

PATTING AND PINCHING WOMEN

That night, at the company's American Club, I situated myself where I could see the dance floor, the tables where drinks were served, and the large swinging double-doors through which the local waiters were busily coming and going. The waiters in that club were not known to pat and pinch, but it had been reported that they sometimes brushed too close or tried to *cop a feel* with an arm or leg. I wanted to be a firsthand witness.

It happened mid-evening right in front of me at the busiest time of the table service. The waiters had to pass between me and a woman. I was leaning against the wall near the front entrance of the club and the woman was half-perched up on the corner of a banquet table with her beautiful naked back facing me through a totally backless dress. The path from the kitchen on my left crossed in front of me and turned left down the central aisles between the tables. There was room for at least three persons to walk abreast between me and the young lady's back.

The waiter who could not resist the temptation to touch that inviting expanse of uncovered femininity could be described as a *dashing rascal.* He was tall, dark, and handsome but obviously filled with mischievous thoughts. Far too bright to spend his life (or evening) just waiting tables, he had come to enjoy the party.

With a tray of empty glasses balanced on his left hand above his shoulder, pretending not to have room to pass between a man's back who had stopped to chat with me and the woman's exposed back, he placed his right hand firmly in the center of that tantalizing expanse of naked skin—ostensibly to protect her from the tray full of empty glasses.

Apparently sensitized by community talk to the risks of being touched, patted, or pinched, she knew at once what had occurred. Screaming over the din of talk and music, she lurched forward to a standing position, half turned and yelled an obscenity at the man. But in that instant that it took her to react, he was long gone. His three or four hurried strides had carried him through the swinging doors into the kitchen (his safety zone). My glance away from the scene at the table saw him duck his head a bit, and laugh as he disappeared into the kitchen chaos.

After work that night, with a financial offer the toucher could not resist, I hired him for the weekend to help me with some *culture-study tourism.*

RESEARCH IN THE STREETS

The next day, Saturday, from 10 A.M. until midnight, we rode every street car, boarded every bus, dug our way through the aisle of every store in the city where I could find large numbers of unaccompanied women whom he might touch, or possibly try to captivate with his *lover's stare.* I wanted a deeper understanding of these questionable customs that were so disturbing to us Americans.

Regarding the *lover's stare,* there was considerable payoff at once. He started it the moment we boarded the first bus. In response to my casual questions, he explained to me what was transpiring. He would catch the eyes of a woman and try to charm her (somewhat like a snake toward a bird, I ascertained). If he got one properly mesmerized, he was then to approach, obtain the address, et cetera. All of the local women, however, during the first hour or so, somehow resisted his hypnotic freeze and turned right away as if they had not seen him. He showed no concern. It reminded me of the patience of a good fisherman.

Eventually, after scores of *turn-aways,* something different happened. I did not notice it but he nudged me with his elbow. A young woman at whom he had beamed his hypnotic glare, had turned away but then turned her face halfway back. I watched her closely. (Caught up in the game, I found my secret disgust toward my rascally friend had subsided. I was actually pulling for him to win this damsel.)

The woman, a girl in her young twenties, never looked all the way back toward us. My guide explained: "She is just letting us study her beauty. Some do that."

By noon, a few women had looked back. My young guide, oozing charm, approached them in a flash, laughing and talking just as if they were old friends. He returned with their names and addresses and some arrangement to meet later. He explained: "There is no easy way to get acquainted here unless your families introduce you. It is not like in your American movies where you have the freedom to casually approach strange women without making certain of that visual invitation. Here it is much harder. It is different."

Still, by noon, there had been no patting or pinching. I was surprised. We had crowded past scores of women in the streets, on the busses and streetcars, and in the bulging aisles of many stores. At noon I suggested we take a bus to the outskirts of town to a restaurant I liked. On boarding that bus and making our way down the crowded aisle, it finally happened.

Among the people busily occupied holding onto the overhead straps and rails to maintain their footing was a woman in a slinky silk dress. Her hips were swaying in the aisle. He laid his hand just as firmly down on her buttocks as he had placed it the night before on the American woman's naked back. Stunned, just behind him, I stopped and watched and pulled back hoping not to be mistaken for the culprit.

He did not look back down at the swaying attraction after he placed his hand, but rather looked toward the back of the bus, very businesslike. He dragged his hand softly across the top of her hips and pushed off with a deft, full-handed squeeze. Still frozen with embarrassment, I could not move, afraid to take up that space just back of the woman.

She had not moved either; there was absolutely no reaction. A step or two down the aisle, safely out of the lady's space, he looked back over his outside shoulder and caught my eyes. With a nod of his head, he clearly invited me to follow his lead and *cop my own feel.* Needless to say, I managed to resist the silky, swaying temptation, but I did burst out laughing. Not just because of the absurdity of his inviting me, a professorial-type with a U.S. government high-level GS status, but rather somewhat the opposite: In the fantasy-land-circumstances, doing my anthropological research, I did not find the invitation completely undignified nor insulting. That made me laugh. (Was I *going native?*)

During the fourteen hours in countless crowds, he touched or brushed two more women. At midnight, I leveled with him and asked for his explanation: What was the touching, patting, and pinching all about? How did it differ from what he had seen in the U.S. movies, or from the American culture which he knew something about from his work in the American Club?

We sat sipping wine the rest of the night as he tried to explain. This is what I thought I got out of it at the time. (Since then, I have learned there is some disagreement in his own culture. But this is all I learned at the time for working this case. And part of that lesson is that you can't wait to complete your Ph.D. on any issue. Time is often of the essence. As soon as you have something honorable that might work, you have to go with it).

"Okay," he said, "there are some sexual attacks here just as there are in the U.S. except that here there are fewer according to the newspapers. I saw one of our men approach an American tourist woman once and just grab her by both breasts. That is different from patting or pinching. We beat the guy.

"I have talked before with American men about this local custom of pinching and patting. To the American men, I was surprised to learn, it is considered a sexual attack. Here, it is more like up in Spain where I have worked. There if you see a strange girl out in public, alone, who is irresistible, you say something loud enough for her to hear about her beauty. The Spanish women, I think, know that it is a compliment, whereas the American tourists think it is an insult of some kind.

"Here, compared to you, we tend to view all attractive women as little girls, just as our women realize that boys will be boys including most men. One of my university professors admitted to me that he had pinched a girl. He said he knew he should not have done it, but he too admitted that it was the little boy in him paying a compliment to an irresistible little girl, sort of like pinching a baby's cheek. What live man can resist every time? He admitted that. But it is not a sexual attack in our minds; what one thinks is what controls what it is."

He struggled for a moment, hit his head with the butt of his hand, and continued: "Let me try to explain it some other ways. And try to catch my feelings while I am trying to explain. You know, the lover's stare that you asked about; that is more of a sexual thing—even though it is not illegal and is more or less respectable. My feelings when I do that, have love motives. The touching doesn't; that is out of the question. It is more like the admiration that I feel when I caress a beautiful race horse out at the track or when I pet carefully the dangerous Doberman pinscher at a mansion where I sometimes work.

"Did you notice that I touched only a couple of women all day long? [He had touched three.] I touched them because they were untouchable for me. They were so unusual as to be out of my world; so I joined that dream world for a moment. I think they know they did me a kindness by letting me. Did you see they did not react? That was all right; they were beyond and above me. My compliments to them were correctly paid."

"How about the American woman in the club last night?" I asked. "She reacted; she screamed at you. I saw you laugh. How do you explain that?"

"Yes, I make more mistakes with the American women. That is why I laughed. Some of those who appear to be the most untouchable, turn out not to be untouchable at all; they look back."

"What?" I asked. "You mean you think that when that girl screamed at you last night, she was looking back at you and inviting you to approach her in some way? Is that what you are saying?"

He shrugged his head and shoulders; lifted his hands in the air in a sign of total confusion and said with a note of uncertainty: "Yes, we don't understand those American women who reject the compliment and want to join you in a fight, of all things; but we know it is some kind of a strange American come-on that can quickly get violent and involve American men. So we just laugh."

Honest, Effective Corrective Materials

That information had one of the two qualities needed for use in this work. It was honorable. After the all-day experience with the young man, a large bottle of wine, and an all-night conversation, I knew I had the honest explanation, from at least one patter/pincher, of the thoughts behind his acts. As long as I presented them only as that, it was honorable.

The other quality needed is effectiveness. That, of course, awaited its actual testing. But since I thought it might ease negative attitudes a bit and start some constructive discussion, I decided to try it as it was, and turn my attention, under the time pressure, to the other deeply hostile issue: Cruelty to animals, the killing of the puppy.

Mistreatment of Puppies

I located the section of town where the killing of the puppy was supposed to have occurred. I knew from previous experiences, elsewhere, that such rumors could upset an overseas American community, yet be entirely false.

THE DANGER OF FALSE RUMORS

In one case, in a Third World country, if you accidentally killed a pedestrian while driving your car, you went to jail for certain for a year; this, despite the fact that by our U.S. standards, the accident and death were entirely the fault of the pedestrian. In the local law, Americans, as well as local nationals, were held responsible and had to serve the sentence. Contributory negligence by the victim was not a defense. If you drove a car that killed someone, you went to jail. That was it.

Those facts alone were terribly upsetting to us Americans. We had at least one American serving his year in a local jail at the time. Suddenly a new development caused near hysteria. Word spread that if an American woman was the driver, she served her year in a house of prostitution for the local national soldiers. The rumor included the assertion that *the local government will deny that this penalty will be used, but it is still absolutely true.*

I checked the rumor through every possible official U.S. and host-government channel. It seemed to be totally unfounded. But it persisted unshakably in the American community. Finally, I stopped all other work and started checking sources of the story. As soon as I heard the story again, I asked the woman to please reveal her source. She did.

I checked with the woman she named and on back to the original source. Within a month I had checked the story back to the same original source through three series of informants: a jolly U.S. Air Force captain.

In the Officer's Club at the bar, the night that I finally tracked him down, he admitted somewhat sheepishly that he had not expected to involve the entire community. Only his wife had been his target, and even with her, it had only been an offhand remark, half joking one day after she had dented the car.

BACK TO THE ANIMAL CRUELTY ISSUE

So back to the rumor of killing dogs: After all of Sunday afternoon, all day Monday, and most of Tuesday, watching the gangs of boys play around the waterfront, I was growing skeptical about the dog-kicking story, when suddenly, almost under my feet, a little mongrel came careening down the street. The poor thing had a tin can tied to its tail and a gang of little boys chasing it and throwing rocks. The dog escaped. When the boys dispersed in that neighborhood, I accepted the story, concluding that this was indeed at least one of the troublesome areas for dogs.

It took the rest of Tuesday and half of Wednesday to line up neighborhood respondents and translators to check out this negative attitude toward dogs. I never use fewer than three translators selected for different attitudes: pro-American, anti-American, and neutral. And without their knowledge, I have them interview some of the same respondents to cross-check responses. It is slow and expensive.

I conducted studies on local attitudes toward ten kinds of animals. The first glimmer of perspective came from the question that asked the respondents to place the ten animals into *most favored and least favored* categories. Dogs, surprisingly, even among the adults, fell into the bottom category with rats and snakes. How about that for man's best friend? The follow-up question was obvious: *Why are the dogs hated so much?*

Maybe it would be something that the Americans could understand, thereby reducing, to a degree, their disgust toward the host-nationals for kicking dogs. I reasoned that most Americans would not be filled with disgust and hatred toward persons who kicked rats and snakes.

In the next go-around, we asked the respondents to list the obvious reasons why most persons would place each of the ten animals in the categories where they were placed. And there it was for dogs: *Rabies!*

Follow-up questions to that response revealed that rabies was an alleged child killer in the area. Stories followed about whose children had died and whose were in the hospital currently; descriptions of the length of the rabies needle that they stick in the poor children's stomachs, and just how dangerous it was to touch any street dog.

PRESENTATION OF THE FINDINGS

When I met with the women that next Friday, I advised that I had researched only the two *jugular vein* issues: the patting and pinching, and the mistreatment of dogs in the area. But I thought the beginning answers that I had turned-up were interesting enough that they were worth submitting at once. We would proceed from there depending on how it went.

I told of my journey through the town with one of their own club *touchers*, and left them to try to guess which one. Fortunately, I was able to make the account as amusing as it really was: especially the part about where I had tried the lover's stare tactics on the local women and had found it so discouraging that I had to quit or become totally deflated. After the patting/pinching explanation, I had another lucky break. I finished the account with the concluding advice that my adviser had given me confidentially for my own wife. I summarized his words:

If she has been here for a considerable time, and has never been patted or pinched even once, tell her she must be walking without any style at all. (I tried to mock his demonstration of how some women walk like slouches while others tingle when they walk right.) It is not a matter of beauty; it is a matter of true ladylike class. Don't forget, now: don't have a dirty mind. It is not a sexual attack; not here. Remember, with me, yesterday, it was only two, maybe three, out of all those hundreds we saw, who could merit my supreme compliment. They were not the ones I visualized as lovers. They were the untouchables who had to be honored with a touch. They were the real ladies with exquisite class. They didn't look back.

Most of the women in the audience were laughing. Some were clapping lightly with enjoyment, and a few were still sour-faced and rejecting. I wondered if they were the ones who had been patted or the ones who had not. The lucky break was the comments from a beautiful wife of a company *big shot.* She walked out to the middle of the floor in front of the stage. The crowd quieted down.

"I knew it! I knew it all along!" she said. "I knew I was being complemented rather than attacked," she declared. "He is absolutely right; what he has told us rings true to me. I knew I should not have let it make me mad."

That took care of the issue. Within a week men were telling me: "My wife came home boasting that she got pinched. I think we are going to be able to stay."

KICKING MORE DOGS AROUND

After the pinching explanation, a stand-up break turned into an uproarious laughing discussion. I reconvened the meeting:

"Okay, let me tell you about the dog issue quickly. Then I want to hand out a questionnaire for a little more input on the minor issues."

Quickly I told them about the rabies. But before I could complete the distribution of the questionnaires, a disturbance occurred in the audience. I was losing control. In this work, you don't fight for control when that happens. On some logical excuse, you call a quick break. I did.

They started pouring out of both huge doors at the back of the auditorium. Concerned, I went over to the lovely woman who had offered the support on the patting/pinching, quickly thanked her and asked: "What happened; half of them seem to be leaving. Have they had some bad experiences with questionnaires?"

"No," she said, "the rabies information caught us all by complete surprise. The ones leaving have children. They are headed home, no doubt, to kick a few dogs around themselves. Your findings could not possibly have been more effective."

I don't recall the exact timing; but within a matter of weeks that group of people had turned around completely. Soon, they became attractive, efficient overseas Americans. It was not all my doing by any means. The company had hired a new director. He may even have been the main saving force. Nonetheless, I had been recognized as effective. I was promoted to the office of temporary director of a company branch for movement into the next country. I began to work through opinion leaders on the minor issues on the list, but soon found that I did not have to bother. These *turned-around* constructive overseas people began to solve those minor issues themselves. A small leadership-group was effective in creating a positive word-of-mouth network to disseminate my helpful research findings.

REVIEW

Don't forget, I presented the ideological materials (hunter's story, baboon story) always before I faced the specific cross-cultural hostilities. The cross-cultural materials take much more time, but the ideological materials are more important. They articulate the meaning of the equal life value that controls human relations. An old religious man in Greece once advised me that, "These ideological materials do not teach the deeper human values; they just reinforce them," he said. "Those values that express the joy of giving," he observed, "reside in the *genetic memory* as a part of the divine spark." Something like that would explain why it is so easy to turn attitudes from negative to positive.

TRANSITION

I have heard that our olfactory equipment has a more direct access to the brain than any of our other senses. *Smell problems* certainly cause trouble in cross-cultural relations. Let us look at a couple of those cases.

CHAPTER 15

THE CASE OF THE OLFACTORY DISCONNECT

To review, human life, worldwide and universally, is humankind's most cherished and sacred earthly value. But the life value is not a selfish—me only—value. It is a balanced or dual value in which species-preservation has the slight edge in our natural tendencies over self-preservation. That is, normal (clinically healthy) people will risk themselves for their loved ones and their in-groups. Recall that there is a lot more to it than that. Our global malady is that instead of logically expanding our emotional circles of loved-ones and in-groups to encompass the entire family of man, we have let our natural, emotionally connected, species-supporting, small-group institutions wither and almost die. The family, the neighborhood, the small community where everyone knows everyone, these are the social-centers of close personal involvement where humans, since time began, gave their love and consideration, that part of life which makes it most meaningful.

It is in relationship to the basic Dual Life Value that *all else is relative.* Hence, the overstatement that *all is relative* has a basis in fact. Almost all is relative, all except the hitching post itself, *the Balanced Life Value.*

WHEN LIFE-SUPPORT VALUES THREATEN LIFE OR HEALTH

All of our human values derive from that basic life value. However, a few of the sub-values that are most important to life possess a pain-supported or comfort-supported existence of their own. The pet cat still instinctively needs to scratch—sharpen its claws—on the expensive furniture. This act no longer possesses a survival value; on the contrary, it now gets the cat in trouble. The point is that the scratching inclination does have a propulsion of its own.

Similarly, in humans, the life-protecting sub-value, *pain avoidance,* has a definite instinct-like propulsion of its own in the nerves that give us pain. This instinct-like (unreasoning) pain will interfere with pain's basic life-protecting purpose when the doctor needs to set a dislocated back or pull a tooth.

Similarly, the sex drive, which is of decisive importance to species survival, has what we might call a "life of its own." In opposition to its *natural* function, it may encourage us to life-threatening overpopulation. Obvious things, but the point is that some of our sub-values do have *independent* instinct-like drives of their own that do not work *rationally* in support of their basic purpose: life support.

In other words, there are semi-autonomous values that will express themselves in ways adverse to their natural life-support function if their supporting drives or inclinations, such as the withdrawal from the dentist's forceps or the attraction to the neighborhood vamp, are not overruled by reason.

RATIONALLY CONTROLLED SUB-VALUES

Many of our sub-values do not possess a drive of their own. They depend on perceived relationships to the life value for their existence. Let us take the cherished value of *truth* to make the point because the nature of truth is so controversial. Truth is a value that is considered very close to the top of all sub-values by Americans and other persons of wealth in the world.

Truth, I have found, around the world, tends to be more of a rich man's value than a poor man's. The rich man can afford the truth. Why? Because he does not have to lie or even slant the truth to get food for his children. But to the suffering *have-nots* of the world, when dealing with the indifferent wealthy, truth is sometimes more like the police force that holds them back from the government food stores when their children are starving. Truth can be the tool of an oppressive status quo. To illustrate this point, consider this hypothetical case once submitted by a college student in one of my classes on human values:

> The city mayor, a Nazi, asked the Sunday school class of German youth where the little Jewish girl, Anne, was hiding. Everyone in the group turned to Hans to let him answer because Hans was known to be the most clever joker when he wanted to be. A convincing lie at that moment was, they all knew, as important as life itself—little Anne's life. Anyone from that religious group who would tell the truth just then, and expose Anne, they all knew, totally misunderstood the meaning and purpose of truth as a constructive value.

AND NOW THE MATTER OF SMELL IN CROSS-GROUP RELATIONS

Similar to truth as a servant of human life, smell is also an extremely relative value. The identical smell seems good to some, bad to others. Yet, once conditioned to particular smells, we award them strong status in our hierarchies of good and bad. Consequently, smells that are attractive to some and unattractive to others can play a significant role as divisive culture-shock forces in grass-roots international relations.

Let me draw a parallel in our own domestic relations before discussing cases on the foreign scene. Such parallels are needed to reduce the probability that foreign nationals will take offense over the embarrassing issues involving their cultures. And these parallels help teach ethnocentric Americans that even Americans suffer from such problems. Therefore, *gooks* and *krauts* and *spics* and countless other allegedly semi-humans like that, who suffer from these offensive (say, smell) problems, might actually also be full-fledged, equal human beings. Don't scoff; nice Americans who are simply terribly isolated and culture-bound need this lesson repeatedly. They need it desperately for our own international well-being. In many cases, the higher the *education*, the more Americans may suffer from the culture-shock illness; the more difficult it often is to persuade them to confront their own bigotry or their loss of touch with struggling humanity.

THE SMELLS OF MUD CITY VERSUS THOSE OF BOSTON

Once upon a time, after several years in Massachusetts, near Boston, my wife, my five-year-old son, and I flew back to Kansas City, rented a car, and drove north toward my old, beloved home in Mud City. Soon, on that warm summer day on the country road, a nostalgic fragrance filled the car. It took me way back to my childhood days playing cowboys and Indians in the haymow of the James Miles barn, of lassoing pigs for wild rides when Mr. Miles was away, of making sorghum and licking the giant pan. I shook my head nostalgically and announced, "Wow! Catch that wonderful smell of the farm."

I glanced down at my young son and over at Peggy to see them enjoy with me that new fresh breath of farm air. Rather than look up at his all-knowing Daddy as he usually did, little Robert with a countenance of uncertainty peeked shyly over the other way at his mother. She too was a bit confused and searched the air carefully in her feminine way for some obscure fragrance she apparently was not catching.

"Bob, I don't want to be indelicate," she said, "but all I am noticing is something that smells terribly much like some kind of animal waste." I shrugged in disgust and lit up a cigar which she hates. The swirling, blue-white smoke filled the car.

"Okay," she said, laughing at my chagrin, "that's a little better." A few weeks later on our return to Boston, we were driving down the back roads along the sea coast on the North Shore. Suddenly, as the road ran down and fast, straight east toward the ocean, I was almost sickened by the rancid odor of rotting vegetation in the backwash of the expansive marsh. With that sudden change in the olfactory atmosphere, out of the corner of my eye, I saw my wife throw back her beautiful face and flashing black hair as she filled her lungs and exclaimed, "Oh, Robbie (our son), smell that wonderful, clean salt air."

COUNTRY 4 (IN EAST ASIA)

Country 4, in east Asia, was extremely poor. A smell problem was one of its two jugular vein issues, meaning we had to solve it or entertain no hope of building adequate mutual respect between our numerous American communities and the host nationals. In the inimitable GI vernacular, "The whole country smells like crap."

When the ideologically naive and innocent American soldier-boys voiced that denunciation, the hate-generating disrespect that they exuded also seemed to fill the air.

Why did this country smell so bad to Americans?

The answer: The local farmers used human waste on their acres and acres of vegetable gardens. These put forth heavy, choking odors into the air.

Consequently, this *human waste issue* presented another of the more challenging and almost unmentionable cultural detective issues.

What can you say?

How would you manage it?

What can you do?

Now, please, again, if your thought is that intellectual foolishness that says, *We just have to accept others' differences,* please close the book and send it back to me. I'll refund your money. The book has already, in your hands, been a failure. That repulsive *human-waste-fertilizer* issue is still out there in many countries of the world. You may run into it in a few new Asian communities around San Francisco and elsewhere. So I ask you again, as a tough-minded cultural detective: What can you do in addition to hoping that some beloved comedian does not appear and use the issue in his local humor? (That happened to me just when I almost had the vocal attitude under control. It is OK to handle these touchy issues with humor—but only *after* they are understood and under control.)

ONE SOLUTION

It is time to focus your attention precisely on the cultural detective's most sophisticated task. You have to recognize the corrective answers if you happen to run across them. In fact, unless obscured in history, the answers, too, (as well as the problem) are often right under our noses.

Now, regarding the *smelly fertilizer* issue, recollections from my boyhood days in the family greenhouse, called back the fact that Dad always piled the animal manure in *compost piles* to let it dry out some in order to reduce the smell. I checked that recollection in the limited available local library resources (in English) and found some confirmation.

The farms that were causing the main problem for us were those along the one main highway that Americans traveled plus the few farms right around the Little Americas near the large cities in Country 4.

Mr. Jan Oh, my driver, chief interpreter, introductory oral-researcher, and unofficial bodyguard started out with me, to find out if those relatively few farmers involved might agree to compost their human waste fertilizer more thoroughly if we Americans paid the costs.

The first farmer was willing, but the social amenities, necessarily included in the arrangements for such a sensitive interview, took us almost all day. The project looked like an endless task.

On the second day, Mr. Oh stopped the car by the side of the road to go in and arrange with a second farmer to meet and talk with me. I opened the novel I was then reading knowing I could get through half the book before Mr. Oh returned. Before I had finished two pages, Mr. Oh opened the car door laughing and shaking his head.

"What's the matter?" I asked.

"Well," said Mr. Oh, "he insisted that I bring you a message. But first, I might mention that you will want to remember this experience to use the next time an American makes the familiar mistake of telling you that all Asians only tell you what you want to hear."

"Sounds like he might have said no," I observed.

Still smiling, Mr. Oh explained: "I had just finished the introductory comments about the importance of good relations and the mutual struggle against communism, and turned carefully to a mention of the smell—the fertilizer. He stopped me from speaking further by holding up both hands the way some Americans do."

"All right, all right," he said, "now I understand; now I know what you want. It is not new to me. I saw you drive up. I thought that was a "big nose" [American] with you in the car. I see them driving by here all the time with those long noses in the air or making a great show out of holding them. Well, please, I want you to go back out there to your American friend and tell him these exact words for me. Tell him and all of your American bosses that I have five children to feed. Tell them that I can't afford any other kind of fertilizer, and I don't want to take chances with any other kind. Tell them that if my crop fails, these children will starve. One year their bellies swelled up with hunger. Tell them that after that terrible winter, every time I come out of this house in the morning and I smell that stuff, it just smells great! I suck it down into my lungs and say to myself: OH! THAT JUST SMELLS GREAT! In fact, you know, when I don't smell that wonderful smell, it makes me sick. Now go! Tell him; tell them. We cannot talk further."

Mr. Oh waited for my reaction. (What would you have said?) I was not sure. This rejection was unexpected to say the least. Finally, I scouted around through my camping materials in the car and found a nice gift and asked Mr. Oh to deliver it with some words of thanks to the man for being so truthful.

I went home and related the story to my wife. "Good for that farmer," Peggy said. "I think he is right." I told the story to my two oldest sons. Their responses were similar. I tried an American Army sergeant, a chaplain, a psychologist, and an Army major. Every one of them laughed at me and sided with the farmer. I strongly suspected that the search was over. We had an effective answer. Why? Because it was based on the powerful, behavior-controlling life-value; *it was reasonable.*

It was successful, always. We used it with at least 100,000 troops over a period of two years. It never failed to persuade a group in general that it was time for us to *toughen up* about the smell issue.

In our presentations, we added these few bits of information, from our massive research, to reinforce the rationality of using the human waste rather than risk starvation for the local children: Our American ancestors used tons of human waste on our own crops right up until 1914 when the Germans invented chemical fertilizer. We mentioned that there was a group of Americans right at that time experimenting with processing their own waste materials through a chemical process for food, if needed, for their own survival, and asked the troops to guess who it was.

Someone, in a large audience, always guessed or knew that it was the astronauts. Of course, we concluded those sessions with the affirmation that when it is a matter of life or death some of our brightest, toughest, most heroic Americans agree with the old farmer: If necessary for life, fill your lungs (or stomach).

How effective were these materials? After the story became well-known in the American community, it was not unusual for me, when visiting some outdoor military function, to observe a few GIs playfully ridiculing *the smell,* and then to be delightfully pleased to see one of the young men boldly, in a humorous but effective putdown of the others, step out front, hold up his arms, fill his lungs, pound his mighty chest, and declare: "TO ME, IT SMELLS GREAT!"

I think this task of general conflict resolution is too subtle to be performed effectively through written lesson materials. One must conduct the educational programs orally, with enough crowd participation to keep it lively and thoughtful. To recover our respected status abroad and healthy strength at home, it needs to be taught in all of our schools. It provides a civilized counter-attack against the rising horror of cross-group hate crimes.

How effective would it be in general, for America, on the overseas front? In answer, I would judge that all industrial nations, on a scale of 1 to 10, would rate about a minus 7 to minus 10 regarding good overseasmanship just now. Our competitors, Germany and Japan, respectively, would earn around minus 10s or worse. As the first to be educated in the universal values, the results for America in world trade, alone, could be quite significant. Most important, we would offer the first sound, universal, secular, moral leadership.

Let us try another *smell case* that involves Americans in a surprisingly interesting way.

CHAPTER 16

THE CASE OF A STRANGE AMERICAN FRAGRANCE

While solving these cross-group conflicts, one encounters incidental difficulties that may seem small but can be decisive. One example is the need to obtain a fairly balanced number of complaints from both sides. For instance, you may be working on conflict resolution between Greeks and Turks or black and white Americans. You will need an attitude study showing the things that both sides do not like about the other. The list needs to be about equal in number of dislikes. Surprisingly, it is not enough that this balance be qualitative; also it must be quantitative. I'll explain through an entirely hypothetical example that is almost identical to an actual case: Say you are working with two groups in conflict whom we'll call *the spitters* and *the shooters*. On your attitude studies of the things the two groups dislike most about each other, 90% of *the spitters* have said this about *the shooters:*

They are shooting at us with guns from hiding.

Only 10% of the respondents even mention a second dislike. I presume the reason is obvious. The qualitative weight of being shot at outweighs everything else so much, why bother to mention anything else!

The shooters mention, about an equal number of times, three objectionable actions of the spitters: *They try to spit on us, they frown at us, and they call us names.*

I show the hypothetical studies to the two hypothetical groups (separately as I always do at first). The reaction of the group accused of shooting amazes me. They complain that my studies are obviously faulty and unfair. You could not guess in a hundred guesses why they say that (unless you are becoming an amazing detective already.)

They complain: "You cannot convince us that those lowdown rascally spitters only had one complaint about us shooters when we have three complaints about them (spitting, frowning, and cussing). It has got to be false, because they are far bigger crybabies than we are."

What do you do? Well, you go back and add two minor, but actual complaints made by *the spitters* to balance it off quantitatively. It makes no difference that shooting carries more danger than spitting, frowning, and cussing combined.

THE NUMBERS GAME

This numerical balancing act is a problem because the main complaint that the rest of the world has about Americans, especially but not exclusively white Americans, *is the worst violence-causing characteristic in human affairs.* It is a devastating criticism: *being bigoted or disrespectful of others.* If true, it tags us as the epitome of human stupidity, violating as it does our own founding value, human equality, and our enabling document, the Declaration of Independence.

We Americans tend to list the relatively insignificant, unattractive accompaniments of poverty as the things we dislike most about others: unsanitary standards, noisy societies, smelly workers, etc. Since those comparatively minor *shortcomings* are often unavoidable in a group of poor people living on stingy land, perhaps they might understand that to have those complaints registered against them, justly or unjustly, is not nearly as bad as what they are alleging about Americans. But human nature does not work that way. Both sides seem to want to see the same number of complaints. So name them for quantity as well as quality if possible.

I took the space to make that rather long methodological point in order to encourage you to identify, articulate, and correct all alleged shortcomings of the more powerful, and more offensive, side of a problem. Otherwise unemotional logic might direct you to devote your time exclusively to the overriding issue of all issues: our bigotry or superiority complex.

OKAY, NOW OUR AMERICAN FRAGRANCE

Regarding the issue above of smelly human waste on their crops, I encountered it also in the harsh land of our great Asian allies, the Koreans. This was a dozen years ago before their miracle of major economic development. But I doubt if even those hardworking people could dispense so rapidly with the use of humankind's most reliable fertilizer.

There was another annoying smell issue in Korea for Americans.

(The Koreans are one of the few people on earth, whom I know, who are so tough that I would risk writing openly about them and not fear false offense. I hope the recent economic development has not filled them with false pride and modernized softness.)

The food staple in Korea was fermented raw cabbage, called *kimchi*. It smells every bit as powerful on your breath as our garlic, except in Korea, unlike us with the garlic, everyone ate the kimchi; *everybody*. When I came home in the evening while I was working in Seoul and picked-up my one-year-old baby son after our Korean maid had made him into a kimchi-lover, I could hardly stand to hold him. His normally sweet little baby breath was worse than King Kong's to me.

Our military men were attended by female Korean barbers. The barbers could not eat their kimchi before work or else they had to wear cloth masks over their mouths to find compatibility with their American clientele. It was a problem if only an amusing one. Nonetheless, we had two strong anti-Korean *smell-issues* to deal with: the kimchi and the fertilizer.

Against that background, I was visited one day by a young member of the U.S. Peace Corps. He wanted me to try to find out why his Korean house-hosts did not want him to stay in their home any longer.

My chief interpreter in Korea was a relatively uneducated but brilliant young man by the name of Mr. Hong. His forte was personality. He could get the self-implicating truth out of a pathological liar.

I presented him with our problem and asked him to try to arrange a meeting with the head of the household involved in the Peace Corps case.

"All right," Mr. Hong agreed, "but first," he said, "I would like to show you something that might lead you more quickly to your answer."

Mr. Hong took me to an orphanage near a U.S. military base. We arrived at a prearranged hour and the orphanage director sent us, immediately, over to a couple of elderly Koreans who were working with a large pile of donated U.S. Army clothing.

"Figure out what they are doing," Mr. Hong said, laughing to himself.

I watched; it was strange. They were taking each article of clothing, holding it up to their faces for a second and then folding most pieces and laying them neatly in a pile, or else, for a few pieces, throwing them into a trash can. The strange thing was that some of the few pieces they were discarding looked better, much better, than some of the worn or torn items that they were keeping. Mr. Hong was by this time very much into the culture-detective game with me, and I knew that I was not going to get any more clues until I figured this one out or admitted failure.

I approached the two busy workers and studied their actions. They laughed, as Koreans do easily when amused. (And as they do also when disappointed or even devastated. In that historically unfortunate land, long savaged by foreigners and the capricious Manchurian winds, they smile over tragedy, as Mr. Hong once told me, to keep from crying. Another elderly Korean once told me, "Ours may be the only land where we tried all the religions, and they all failed us." Korea's history is indeed grim. Mr. Hong's four-year-old son studied by candlelight in their small hovel until late every night. The Koreans are tough. If you watched the 1988 Olympics, you know that what they hate most is losing a fight.)

It was clear: The two elders were smelling the articles of clothing. Yes, they were giving them some kind of a smell test. At once I speculated that the clothes were for the orphans but the children did not like all of the after-shave lotion smell and all the other cosmetic odors that our Americans used. But then, on second thought, why throw them away? Those were expensive, valuable, woolen articles for warmth in a freezing land. The Koreans, of all people, would never be so soft or wasteful. Cosmetic smells could be totally cleaned out. It had to be something else.

I picked up a folded shirt and smelled it. Nice. In fact it smelled of some familiar after-shave. I turned to the trash can; took a shirt out and smelled it. WOW! Terrible! I blew out through my nostrils and pulled back a little trying not to be noticed. They did notice, and laughed. Everyone in the compound laughed. (Our visit had been prepared for and it had attracted a crowd.)

I looked at Mr. Hong and asked, "Are you saying that some of our clothes smell too strong for Koreans to use?"

Mr. Hong just laughed, which was his way of saying, "You got it, Humphrey."

"Okay, let me expand the question: Are you saying that some of our American clothes smell too strong for Korean orphans to use *but some Korean clothes don't?*"

He laughed again and said: "Bow a bit to everyone and thank the director. They just let you in on this secret after I persuaded them you could be trusted. Let's go."

In the car, I asked Mr. Hong how he explained it all. He didn't. He just said that it was an old long-standing problem and added that it was so bad that many Koreans did not like to serve with American outfits in Vietnam because the smell of a U.S. unit could be so strong that the enemy Viet Cong, the Koreans feared, could smell a unit of Americans hiding in the bush.

Despite having witnessed and personally experienced the validity of the orphanage *smell-test* exercise, it was still similar to the restaurant owner, near Sardinia, trying to tell me that they considered Americans stingy. The part that I could not fathom was not the idea that we Americans smell; obviously everyone does. It was the assertion that the kimchi-eating Koreans did not smell worse; that was the absurdity. I pressed Mr. Hong on that point.

"Korean breath, yes," he allowed, "but with Americans, somehow, it is in the whole body, even when the breath is fresh and after a bath. There is whispering about the Peace Corps people. They have a definite problem because the talk is strong."

"What exactly is said?" I asked.

"Well," said Mr. Hong, "The tactful Koreans whisper that the Americans cannot live in our tiny little houses with us because the Americans smell like rancid butter."

I hesitated to ask the next obvious question, but did: "What do the Koreans who are not tactful say?"

Looking straight ahead as he drove, Mr. Hong said as softly as he could: "The zoo."

I left it there for a couple of days. What would you have done?

You Are What You Eat

Was Mr. Hong playing a practical joke on me? It was possible. I spent a couple of days in the American military library; Mr. Hong in a Korean library researching the American smell issue. Nothing.

We started searching out the other Americans who lived in traditional Korean homes, especially other Peace Corps members. These few were serious, subdued, impressive young persons who did not seem to be aware of the smell problem. But neither were they very happy or filled with a feeling of success; so I suspected they had the problem and also did not understand it.

Within a week we ran into a young American Peace Corpsman who was one of the more outgoing and attractive persons I have ever met. He was dressed in a white cotton suit of some kind rather than the popular darker clothes that prevailed in Korea. He was so confident that I broached the smell issue at once. Laughing, I asked him, right after introducing myself: "Did you ever have any kind of a body odor problem here in Korea?"

Jackpot!

"Sure," he said, matter-of-factly, "it is from our heavy meat diet. My adopted Korean grandfather told me that the meat makes me smell like a meat-eating animal. So I took-up a rice diet. It required about six weeks to get rid of my strong smell. I had to throw away my suit. That, in fact, is why I have this nice fresh new one; I couldn't get the body odor out of the other one."

I was almost convinced but still offered one last halfhearted rebuttal. "The Koreans that I know, eat meat. Is your adopted Korean family a Buddhist family?"

"No," he answered, "like all the other Koreans, they grind-up and eat what little bit of meat they can afford in their rice. But they can't afford much."

"What happens," I asked, "when your other Peace Corps friends visit you at your Korean house? Can you, personally, smell them now that you no longer have a strong odor?"

"It's no problem;" he said, "after they leave, we just air out the house. What is amusing," he laughed, "is to visit a Korean diplomat's house after they have had a party with many Americans present. It may be midwinter, freezing cold, and there it is: All the doors and windows open, airing out the house, and making excuses to me— not wanting to tell me why. It is a secret little problem all right."

I was ready. The account was now very honorable, with a strong probability of being absolutely sound. It would probably be acceptable to the GIs. If so, it was a honey of a balancer at least for the human waste smell issue. I tried it soon on a group of GIs. There were no rebuttals. Maybe it was because I was lucky again. When you first present this account to unsuspecting Americans, it contains enough embarrassment that, for a moment or so, it shocks a crowd into silence. In that first group I talked to, there was a lad present who identified himself as a farm boy and was the first to speak.

"It makes sense," he said. "If you put your face against the neck of a horse or cow, their smell is pleasant, sort'a like the feed they eat; or cows, like fresh milk. Of course they eat no meat at all. But meat-eating animals like dogs and cats; man! they can smell strong as hell. Somebody once said it right: you are what you eat."

In my subsequent speeches on this topic, I always included that GI farmer boy's comments. Believe me, that human waste smell issue was one difficult barrier against promoting respect for Koreans among

Americans. But we found that along with the true account of the starving children and the meat-eater's body odor, we could knock it cold.

CHAPTER 17

A Challenging Case Involving Women, Sex, and Military Matters

My first contract of international significance was to help salvage the foundering missile installation project in southern Italy. Grassroots Italian/American relations were volatile. The patting and pinching of American women by local men was one of the more heated issues. We soon solved it with the same approach employed in the extensive case described in Chapter 14. But something really strange was encountered in this Italian case. Perhaps it will help convey the almost overwhelming difficulty of this complicated general issue of *disrespect for women*. It is a worldwide issue that, according to my studies, is little understood by Americans. Yet it has brought disastrous consequences to America in many countries. Its detrimental effects, possibly, are second only to those from the more general issue of Ugly Americanism.

EXPLORATORY RESEARCH

You may have noticed in the several previous cases, that if possible, I sought a sample group of any major clientele, or a key informant, for some exploratory studies. On this Italian missile installation assignment, I journeyed out to a so-called *missile site,* one of the rural areas where a few people were posturing one of the actual missiles (*birds,* they called them). Those sites presented an opportune situation for interviewing Americans without causing more conflict with the Italians. There were few Italians present in these high-security areas. On one site, I saw only one Italian worker. He was the night watchman for a missile.

I began to chat with him during that evening period when Americans were leaving and he was waiting to start his vigil. His English was good. He had once driven a *hack*, as he called it, in New York. My questions to him concentrated on the differences between American and Italian customs. But of course I also asked him about his job. He explained the few details, which I have now forgotten except for one item he mentioned that chilled me. He said almost these exact words: "Also I am supposed to look up inside the bird to make sure there are no sparks up in there which might cause an explosion."

I shuddered at the thought of that building-sized bullet, towering beside me, exploding, but I passed it off because of the way he stated it: "I am supposed to look," indicating to me that it was an inconsequential duty with no real fear of sparks ever being present. As my concentration was on human relations, I turned back to that central topic.

I got to know the young man quite well. Eventually, he confidentially described some of the foolish behavior of both the Americans and the local Italians. (I knew he was leveling with me because my covert Italian interviewer was getting the same views from him at his home.)

One evening, during an interview coffee-break (which is one of the best times to elicit guarded views on the most sensitive matters) my mind returned to my nagging recollection of his comments about the possibility of a spark up in the missile. I asked him: "Incidentally, regarding your comment about watching for sparks up in the bird— did you ever see a spark?"

He looked at me with one of those expressions that indicated, as I anticipated, that the question was absurd. Embarrassed at looking foolish, I quickly apologized saying, "Okay, of course not, but you can see why someone might ask. You did mention it as one of your tasks."

"Are you kidding!" he responded with a sneer, "Sometimes it looks like the American Fourth of July up in there."

His comments caused an involuntary reaction in my nervous system. I swallowed hard and choked-up. Knowing that he had seen my negative reaction, I decided not to play it coy, as good, professional interviewers do. "Good God, man," I finally asked, still managing a sincere tone of confidentiality rather than criticism, "don't you tell your boss?"

With an expression of blushing anger, he declared: "I would not tell those sons-a-bitches anything even if it meant blowing-up the whole country, not the way they talk about our women."

I was shocked. I just sat down on something there beside the missile (which I mused might explode momentarily). He observed my consternation and hunkered down in front of me to deal with my alarm. He surely knew his job was on the line if he was telling the truth about the sparks. In a way, so was my research project. If researchers reveal their sources of negative information, word of this betrayed confidentiality will spread and their research effectiveness is over. So what was I to say, and do?

Finally, carefully, I explained to him those two implications regarding his job and mine. He nodded; he had guessed as much. Then, because of that reasoning about my own work, I explained to him that my next question might seem off the topic, but from my perspective, it was more important than all those other little details about blowing-up Italy, killing Americans, etc. I went to the topic of pinching American women.

PATTING AND PINCHING WOMEN VERSUS VERBAL INSULTS

I explained to the missile guard: "My main interest right now on this job is the pinching of American women by Italian men. To most Americans that is an issue of insulting disrespect for the American women. Yet, here ironically, you have just suggested that you might risk self-destruction to spite us Americans because we don't respect your women." (I tried, at that point, to make one of his Italian hand-and-face signs of total confusion.)

"Oh, no!" he protested with a shout (also obviously relieved to change the subject) "that is all wrong! It is not the same. Only a minority of Italian men do the pinching. They pinch our own women as well as Americans. And although it is wrong, and illegal, here, I think it is more of a compliment than an insult." (There was that thought again).

He continued, "The Italian men who do it have to be careful that the brothers or husbands of the women don't catch them. Still, it is in the way of a compliment. But with the Americans it is different; they yell insults about our women in front of all the other Americans and those others just laugh. That is why I would be willing to blow up this place, it would damn-sure get these insulting Americans."

Now, to the point, I'll relate a similar case, where this sex issue created an even more serious life-threatening situation.

AMERICAN INSULTS OF ASIAN WOMEN

Years later, some ten thousand miles away, I was called in on a case where a host-national soldier, in a united American/Asian command, tried to shoot some American soldiers.

The official story was that an American sergeant had tried to make the Asian soldier collect firewood for his little cottage, where the U.S. sergeant lived with a local prostitute called a *hired wife.*

When I finally got to the Asian soldier, he advised that the official account was false.

"I went berserk," he said, "over anger at all the Americans, even though I did have to carry the wood to the sergeant's whore. But the final straw was the new captain. He yelled out across the compound, 'I can fuck any woman in this country for three dollars.'

"I decided it was time to teach the Americans that they cannot continue to fuck-over all of us in both words and actions. That lying, smart-ass, no-good, son-of-a-bitching captain was talking about my mother and sisters."

What would you do to solve this issue?

Before you contemplate what you might try, to compare with my efforts, you need a wealth of *fill-in* regarding my assumptions as part of the working context. I'll discuss those inputs for you in the happenstance order that they forced themselves on me in the field. Hopefully, for your useful vicarious experience, these flank intrusions into your train of thought will prove confusing, then helpful—as they were for me in the field.

Understand that at times you will encounter one of these confusing, multifaceted cases. I call them *quicksand cases.* They just keep sucking you in deeper and deeper, making for more complicated involvement. To solve them, you simply have to keep turning to meet all new disruptive issues as they arise. You cannot say, as we often do (inflexibly) in the classroom, *leave that until later so as not to lose your train of thought.* It is more like a battle: You have to turn to meet every attack that threatens.

INFORMAL MILITARY ATTITUDES TOWARD WOMEN

U.S. military boot-camp training does not include the veneer of civilization overlaid thinly on us in polite society. Rather, many tough, young drill instructors, notoriously, have searched their brains for ways to shock the teenage recruits out of their *civilian softness.* Sometimes, these methods include the most common misguided and phony symbols of toughness: swaggering, sacrilegious profanity, pornographic vulgarity, disrespect for marital fidelity, tirades against women, et cetera.

I would not mention this verbal iconoclasm if it did not promote harmful disrespect for women in general, or if it did in fact create *true toughness.* It does not. I have trained young men in self-defensive boxing for over forty years. A few men are not afraid to box in public; most are. The toughness involved in the willingness to box is totally unrelated to one's attitude toward women.

Meanwhile, the misguided, phony-tough initiation in disrespect for women in the U.S. military never totally dissipates. Most of the men may rise above it privately, but too many participate in it, semi-publicly, through sort of a good-old-boy, party attitude. Many conclude that in order to get along, you have to go along with the loud-mouths. The members of this compliant majority prove their apparent loyalty to the crowd mainly by showing that when the social situations (the loud mouths) demand, they can join in the irresponsible, immature sex and alcohol games, and use as many "f" words as anybody.

Irresponsible sex is one of the biggest displays of phony toughness. (Even some chaplains have been guilty.)

THE ANTI-FEMALE CONTEXT FOR OVERSEAS CASES

This is the context of disrespectful vulgarity and casual disregard for women that men, in groups, abroad often create. It cannot be corrected through a few more rules against discrimination. It requires drastic changes in basic training toward true toughness so the phony stuff, including the putdown of women, is not felt to be necessary.

I ask again: What would you do in the shooting case described earlier that might be effective?

INSTITUTIONAL CHANGE: GETTING YOUR DUCKS IN ORDER

I went to the general officer in charge of the entire division—thousands of men. On *this case,* I knew that I had to reach all of the men in an entire geographic area in order to alter the thinking and behavior of the few men in that one troubled unit where the shooting had occurred. Trying to change the *generally* strong vocalized ideas in one small unit faces defeat through contamination from neighboring units if they, too, are not changed. (Not so if the negative attitudes are only whispered denunciations.) The general officer listened. He agreed to let me address his troops, about 1,000 at a time, if and when I was ready to try.

First, I held discussions with approximately 50 religious leaders, U.S. Army chaplains in the country, to make certain they were with me if I criticized the sexual practices of our men. The easy sex and disrespect for women was the underlying two-faceted issue in this shooting case; chaplains are invaluable support personnel in guiding the behavior of military men.

AMERICANS AND PROSTITUTION IN ASIA

Attitude studies on anonymous questionnaires from five widely scattered, economically poor, Asian countries held that we Americans were *buying (their) women into prostitution* on a mass scale. In the deepest jungle areas of Lower East Asia, while ostensibly hunting deer, but also checking attitudes, I picked up Communist leaflets showing long lines of beautiful Oriental women chained together at the neck and ruled over by whore-masters who were American soldiers.

Do you think that either the village people who did not know us well, or the city folk who did, believed that vicious propaganda?

Both groups did.

One of the two groups was more convinced than the other. Which one? The village people with little exposure to us, or the city folk who saw us daily?

The city people.

The samplings of city population alleged, admitted, or accepted the proposition as a matter of fact. The villagers accepted it but with less certainty. The belief caused some ambivalent disdain and hatred toward Americans everywhere. Thus, I learned that *exposure to Americans reinforced this negative portrayal.*

AMBIGUOUS PRO-AMERICANISM

In discussing this or other disturbing anti-American problems with a group of Americans, usually at this point, one meets this question: If the foreign people are so disgusted or angry at us, why do so many want to come to the States? The answer is harsh but easy: It is not *to be with us Americans,* whom despite everything, the local nationals may even prefer to other foreigners. The reason is that North America is viewed as a wealthy land where one can be comparatively free from government oppression and where one can get rich. That's it. Similarly, our own ancestors came to find better lives here, not to be with the Indians.

Okay, now, how does one deal with the allegations that we overseas Americans are *buying poor Oriental women into prostitution,* and what would be wrong with it even if true?

Understanding the Sexual Nature of Humankind

Much of the background that was used in this case is based on inadequate (unavailable) research sources. When conflicts exist and must be solved to stop violence, often you are compelled to act fast, with insufficient study and proceed on the basis of your best judgment regarding the nature of things. In these cases, I relied on my judgments as experimental operating facts for my corrective efforts. In this new field of culture-detective work, *general knowledge* is the name of the game—the only pathway to success. But of course it is seldom complete.

In trying to solve a difficult cross-cultural case such as this, one should form committees of researchers and consultants. In committee meetings, many side issues, or blocking issues, arise which must be dealt with before you can proceed with the main issue. We encountered several blocking issues in this case. The most troublesome one was whether or not there are *Natural Law* grounds for opposing so-called sexual promiscuity.

The Question of Pair-Bonding Fidelity in Nature

Some species of animals pair-bond: one male, one female, for life (with cases of cheating). Wolves, eagles, and geese are examples. As in those three examples, these pair-bonding animals usually seem to be hunters of some kind. Conversely, the *harem animals* (with multiple mates) that I have observed around the globe tend to be *the hunted,* herd animals; they are not big meat eaters, they are meals for others. Gibbons, jungle or forest primates, are pair bonders. The other great apes, I have read, use more communal sex.

One of the prevailing tip-offs in nature about the pair-bonders is that about the same number of males and females are born into the species, as is true of humans, whereas among the harem animals, several times more females than males are born and live in the species.

The Human Pair-Bond

According to what I have observed, all over the world, humans are pair-bonders; numerically strong pair-bonders, but psychologically weak ones. Many cheat; but still, we humans, compared to other species, are basically pair-bonders.

After our traditional or natural human habitat, the small group, breaks down, many of us behave like men gone out of town to a convention. Many of us practice infidelity to the pair bond (one husband, one wife). This is done with much more open and common frequency than was true only a few decades ago in Mud City, Missouri, where I was reared. Nonetheless, even in all of those societies that are notoriously harem cultures, almost all of the thousands of men and women that I ever met were pair-bonders. Unquestionably, according to my eyewitness evidence in Christian, Moslem, Hindu, Buddhist, Shinto, Confucian, Voodoo, agnostic, and atheistic societies, I estimate that 90% of all adults marry or live with only one mate (at a time).

To that overwhelming behavioral evidence that humans are pair-bonders, one must add the evidence from nature that approximately the same number of males and females are born into the human species, and we do not possess the herbivores' teeth of the common herd/harem animals. Even as food gatherers in nature, the anthropological evidence is that we were also determined hunters, just as it is still among all of the primitive peoples that I have visited.

The Weakening of the Human Pair-Bond Marriage

Now that the small-group (the historic human habitat) is disappearing, the reliable obedience to most of our species-preserving inclinations has been to a degree, undercut. Why? Because, in nature, instinct-like inclinations, usually develop only to the extent needed.

In the traditional, ultra-conservative human atmosphere, adultery was an extremely serious, if not killing affair. A weak instinct-like inclination toward pair-bonding was all that was needed. Human rationality and social conditioning took care of the rest.

The instinct-like species-preserving inclinations that were further encouraged in the small group through rationality and social conditioning included far more than the pair-bonding tendency. They included the natural inclinations plus social encouragement to love one's identified group members, to protect one's children, not to kill, not to commit suicide, not to steal, not to cheat, not to lie, and similar patterns. (As late as the 1930s in the Missouri small towns, we did not lock our doors at night. The species-protecting values were still strong and effective in the small-group communities.)

PAIR-BONDING STILL STRONG

Despite the weakening of the natural small-group support for species-supporting inclinations, humans remain basically (instinct-like) pair-bonders. According to my observations, persons even in those societies where violation of the natural pair-bond is legal, still generally practice, and prefer, pair-bonding to other forms of marriage.

POLYANDRY: ONE WIFE, SEVERAL HUSBANDS

The only man I ever met who shared a wife, shared with his two brothers. They were from a section of the world that is destitute. He gave that as the reason for one woman marrying more than one man: One man could not feed himself, a wife, and the children of one woman. Later, I read that there are six or seven such polyandrous places on earth—all similarly destitute. This man with whom I spoke stated unequivocally that he and his brothers would all prefer not to share a wife if each could afford one alone.

POLYGAMY: ONE HUSBAND, SEVERAL WIVES

Similarly, in polygamous areas of the world where I talked with women who shared the same husband, they had explanations for that unnatural fact. That is, they did not suggest that it was natural: Rather, they explained that:

1. Too many men had been killed in warfare,

2. Too many men in the very poor areas could not support a wife, whereas there was a small number of super-wealthy men who could support more than one wife and often needed their labor for large farms, or

3. A great leader, in an earlier time, had more than one wife, so modern leaders wanted to copy him.

Those women (relatively few) with whom I talked—and more often their daughters—surprisingly to me, talked of women's desires to outlaw polygamy. The one exception I encountered was a young girl in an old man's harem. She preferred the harem, "...as long as women have to marry older men and work, work, work." She only smiled when I asked her if it was customary for her and her wife-sisters to have young boyfriends.

OTHER EXCEPTIONS TO THE NATURAL PAIR-BONDING TENDENCY

I have seen on television a few men and women in strong religious societies defending their polygamy or, in other groups, defend communal sex. But according to my six times around the globe, it is culturally freakish, similar in the physical world to persons with six fingers or toes. (I've seen a few of those, too.) My conclusion: humans are natural pair-bonders, and therefore can find greater happiness in that custom, versus alternatives including adultery or promiscuity. This conclusion from worldwide observation is confirmed by my own experience in a marriage of forty years.

Consequently (and this is the key point which we'll get to soon), one is on sound ground in the natural scheme of things to discourage the support of prostitution by Americans in all impoverished areas of the world. These areas are especially vulnerable to promiscuity, but that does not make the people tolerant of it.

A SUPERSENSITIVE POINT ON WOMEN AND NATURAL RACISM

Regarding marriage, or the human pair-bond, both men and women can be dangerously jealous. According to my experience, jealously is the reliable, danger-fraught norm everywhere; this is true despite what you may have read occasionally. In some places one can look at another person's spouse, but not touch; some places, touch but not look; some places, use someone else's wife sexually, but not seek her affections (treat her too respectfully). And everywhere, promiscuity is, I warn again, a dangerous business. You had better find out, specifically and precisely, what you can do safely and what you cannot.

And, finally, regarding jealously, men are jealous regarding women in their own identifiable in-groups, not just in families, but also in racial and cultural groups. Even some men and women who are strong intellectual advocates of respect for human equality have trouble, emotionally, about racially mixed marriages. In our shrinking world, it is a growing phenomenon that we have to deal with.

SPECIALIZATION VERSUS GENERAL KNOWLEDGE

In this complicated "quicksand topic" of respect for women, we are deep into the worst feature of cultural-detective work. It suggests one reason why modern educational institutions go into their notorious Ivory Towers of compartmentalized over-specialization. When working in the social sciences, on a scene where problem-solving is the only acceptable goal, you simply have to take the time to pursue all of the possibly relevant knowledge (leads) across all academic fields of study. I must devote at least one day a week to bookstore browsing. And Mrs. Humphrey, the company's full-time researcher, spends at least two full days a week in the libraries scouting out new findings.

Why is this *general* pursuit of knowledge necessary? Because we find that the very finest scholarly specialization leads to mistaken analysis in the social sciences. That is one reason that our modern societies are in such great trouble.

I must repeat, if you have made a point that leads you a step closer to necessary understanding or attitude change, but that point raises another side question, usually you dare not say, as we often do in artificial academia, *we'll get back to that.* Remember, that will cause you to lose your persuasiveness as you have allegedly *ducked the issue or objection.*

The Natural and the Good

The objection that these materials on pair-bonding raises occasionally is that sometimes I seem to be saying that if something is natural or instinct-like, it is good—the natural truth. (For example, I said that humans seem to be naturally possessive about the women or men in our own racial groups.) Yet, on the next line, I might submit that this allegedly natural inclination is a problem (not good) as I just suggested above on that exact point—the natural, possessive racism *is a problem we must deal with,* meaning it is natural but not good.

The elimination of that confusion lies in a review of human nature plus the guiding Life Value it contains.

The Controlling Life Value Reviewed

The natural function or purpose of our instinct-like inclinations is to protect that Balanced Life Value: species- and self-preservation in the ideal balance. This demands the greatest protection possible for the individual, second only to the necessary life-protection of the group. The natural purpose of human reason—also a part of human nature—is also to protect the Balanced Life Value. For example, countless fathers view all of their daughters' suitors with a critical eye and judge them unworthy; that is irrational from a species-sustaining position. Those men have to let their reason overcome their more narrow, instinct-like, inclinations.

That life-sustaining superiority of human reason over the instinctive tendencies, in fact, is what caused reasoning ability to be selected-in to human nature as the dominating feature. It can overcome the mistakes of dumb instinct-like inclinations when they no longer serve their life-protecting function. In this rapidly shrinking, racially mixing world, we have to overcome any natural racism that protects our women from the love and affection of outsiders or else, irrationally, continue to contribute to the threatening global violence and warfare. Very sensitive. What do you think?

EDGING BACK TOWARD THE PROSTITUTION ISSUE IN ASIA

Remember our purpose here: In the field, we were compelled to digress to examine fully the proposition, voiced vehemently by some, that sexual fidelity is *only cultural* rather than a natural universal. We could not proceed in the field effectively until at least our own committee members were supportive of the latter proposition.

MALE-FEMALE DATING CUSTOMS

Recall, again, the extensive case reported in Chapter 14 of the country in southern Europe, where the American complained that dancing with a local girl was tantamount to a marriage commitment. Americans visiting southern Europe found out about those strong marital customs from fathers with shotguns or from a girlfriend's brothers (just as I learned to my shock as a teenager while hitchhiking through some Mexican border towns in the late 1930s). Those foreign ideas about girls, boys, and marriage constitute another phenomenon that can provide one of the more character-building experiences for lonely young Americans far away from home. They can also prove fatal.

In the few Asian-Pacific regions where I spent some time, male-female customs are imposed on their own members. In fact, outside of the U.S. until very recently, I have never been anyplace in the world including the Pacific islands, where teenagers can get married whenever they would like without kin folk involvement.

ECONOMICALLY-DETERMINED COURTING CUSTOMS

In much of Europe, compared to most of Asia, historically speaking, there has been enough economic well-being that young persons could risk the dating (if chaperoned) that leads to early marriages and procreation, but not in most of more destitute Asia. The only way, short of infanticide, that many Asian societies had for any hope of controlling their societies against early, economically disastrous marriages and population explosions was to keep young males and females substantially separated from one another until the time was right for economically feasible marriages. Even then, an economically stable child-rearing couple had to be carefully arranged. Economic considerations had to be considered above all else. Because economics was of decisive importance for survival.

AMERICAN'S CULTURE-VIOLATIONS IN NON-DATING ASIAN CULTURES

When wealthy Americans went into the Asian cultures and violated the local male-female customs, the precluding assumptions against early, love-based marriages because of dire poverty obviously did not apply to the wealthy Americans. They had the money to marry whenever they wanted. It was clear that they could support a new wife, and in addition (a happy thought) her entire family. So when the Americans first made the dating moves toward Asian women, which carried with them assumptions about marriage in the local cultures, the local people did not know that the Americans did not share those *honorable intentions.* And the naive Americans were not aware of any such "stupid assumptions."

Strongly ethnocentric Americans who know, or respect, only American views, assume that reasonable human beings marry only when it is voluntary on both sides and then only through a love marriage. We tend to believe that *primitive people,* with other archaic ideas, have no rational choice other than to change their old ideas and practices and become *modern.* Overseas Americans constantly express this view: A foreign woman is lucky to have the opportunity to date an American. We ignore the fact that cultural *strings* are attached.

American men declare that dating Americans helps the foreigners modernize—an infallible blessing according to American views. The fact that it reduces tens of thousands of Asian women—Okinawans, Thai, Vietnamese, Koreans, etc.—to a dishonorable status in their own cultures is dismissed as ridiculous. It is also likely to invoke anger from the Americans if one questions the morality of it all. The Americans customarily assert that "many of these women and their families would suffer from starvation without our money from prostitution."

A couple of final questions must be answered to fill out the minimum background regarding the shooting incident caused by American disrespect for Asian women.

ASIAN MORALS

What about the morals of the Asian girls who accept local disgrace by associating with American men for money? The *overriding* reason for such sexual liaison is economic. Despite the thousands of such cases in U.S.-occupied Japan immediately after World War II, such associations declined over the years to a small number when the Japanese achieved economic recovery. The answer of the American men just above, that such relationships are *better than starving* is basically accurate. That is the correct explanation. Worldwide, I find that to keep their children from starving, if necessary, good men will steal and women will prostitute themselves if there is no other way: Facts of life and further proof of the species-preservation value.

Comparative Western Morals

The last two questions in the backdrop of pertinent facts that we had to answer were these: Would our own Caucasian women prostitute themselves to keep their children from starving? And two, is female virtue actually a universal value? Angry arguments against both views were voiced in our committees.

If you doubt that Caucasian women would in large numbers prostitute themselves if necessary to save their loved ones, consult some of the older Americans who served in England and France, and, especially Germany during the semi-starving days of World War II and after. Also consult some of the American men who were young and had a little money during our Great Depression.

Many women, everywhere, will prostitute themselves, if necessary to feed their families. But conversely and equally clear, from my travels, women and all societies value female virtue. Even in the South Seas, where, because of low fertility and the need for population, sexual relations were valued openly and smiled on, still, female virtue was also valued. Merchant mariners from the South Sea islands, where Margaret Mead wrote about free sex, were the first persons who told me about girls having to show blood to prove their virginity at marriage. Why did they do that if it did not hold a value? It does. (It still does in America despite the seeming absence of a culture and despite the highly touted sexual revolution.)

Implementing Institutional Change

Those were the primary considerations that gradually forced themselves into our analysis as we struggled with the preparation of materials to try to solve the case of a host-national soldier shooting at some Americans over our alleged disrespect for their women. The goal of our work was to reduce the hatred toward us, or, more accurately, head-off more shooting at us, by first reducing the cause of the shooting: our sexual misuse of, and accompanying disrespect for, their impoverished women.

Deciding If and When to Make
the Educational Effort

The most difficult institutional change step for an issue this touchy had been accomplished: That is, the commanding general in the military area had agreed to let me try to *do something constructive.* I also felt some security from the fact that fifty chaplains had voiced their support. The one big criterion for my corrective effort (in addition to it being honorable) that concerned me more than usual in this case was to find something that was almost certainly effective.

Why? Because if I tried and failed, there was a danger of causing massive anger—by daring to call into question the general and growing American free-sex morality. Anger over that issue might stop the rest of my work. At a lower level of concern, I feared that attempting to address this issue might mark me as *like the chaplains,* someone who meant well but was unrealistic.

I knew I did not yet have a satisfactory answer in all these intellectual materials described above even though they were necessary for answers to questions if asked. And although they provided the justification, and won the committee support, for the effort, they were very intellectual and too involved for effectiveness en masse. I had to find something brief and with higher emotional impact. More research was necessary. But where? How?

The Research Facts Are Where You Find Them

As in my other dilemmas, I needed a personalized story that carried emotional impact and the resounding *ring of truth,* like the hunter's story or the evidence from the Korean orphanage. I decided to try to interview the local prostitutes and *hired wives*.

Disruptive opposition started at once. A full colonel in the military support-group inside my own program advised the commanding general that I should be stopped from looking into the Asian sexual scene as an obvious voyeur. When the general, needling me, confidentially informed me of this opposition from an influential critic, I answered: "He's wrong, whoever he is. You can tell him that I am not a voyeur; I am a stay-at-home; never travel at all if I can avoid it." The general laughed and accepted this attempt at evasive humor.

With the help of some bilingual nurses, I arranged to interview about 100 dance-hall girls and *hired wives*. The nurses knew them well through the VD control programs. There were thousands to choose from. The dance-hall girls sold affection to the American men. In addition (with considerable overlap) there were thousands more *hired wives* who lived in tiny shacks near the military bases. The temporary husbands could slip out of their barracks to their private, cozy little shacks at night and on weekends.

The girls derived their income, for themselves and for their families back in the villages, from direct pay by their husbands and from selling black-market materials obtained from the Post Exchange and Commissary. (Incidentally, I found that some of the dance-hall girls were not selling sex nor seeking American husbands.)

THE PROSTITUTES' ATTITUDES TOWARD AMERICAN MEN

My studies on this topic were a bit skimpy without my usual ability to double-check interviews. But the results from the girls' testimony showed four main, strong attitudes toward American men. The first three views were surprises to me and I learned later that they resemble the views of many American prostitutes. The girls advised that:

1. *They hate American men,*

2. They dislike our vulgar talk,

3. They dislike the strange sex practices, and,

4. They hate and are humiliated over the fact that our money had bought them into an outcast status in their own homeland.

There were reasons why those first three views came as a surprise to me and my committees: No one could be much more vulgar-talking than those girls. We all assumed that all Oriental women knew and accepted all the variety of sexual practices known to Americans. And finally, every American military man with whom we talked, was convinced beyond doubt that *his* girl absolutely loved him.

I had doubts whether these findings would be useful. I thought they would if the GIs believed them. But I still needed something better. I decided to try to check out the common assertion that the girls had been *bought* into their disgraced status. Many Americans scoffed at that idea, insisting that the Asian women had no conscience about sexual matters. Nonetheless, Americans are still kindhearted underdog-protectors. If they decided that the girls *were* being victimized, I knew that the negative attitudes of the morally stronger men would change to a degree.

THE PROCUREMENT OF WOMEN

I found that the *girl procurement* or *white slave* system seemed to be developed in a manner similar to our own here in the U.S.: A man who was a *pimp* or *whore master* claimed or owned a string of *girls* that he often managed out of a bar. Typically (I was told), one particular bar owner/whore master often took vacations in *remote* villages. He returned from such vacations with new girls for the trade.

This man, an Asian, was big, slick, and well-dressed at all times. Guess what happened after he spent a while in the village? In the case I followed, he pretended to fall in love with a village girl who was not unattractive. She had no father, just an elderly mother and some younger sisters whom she was trying to support doing menial work. The man either proposed marriage to the girl or else actually married her and took her back to the city with him to work in his bar entertaining the troops.

We did not follow that girl's case further, but seeing how his system worked, we jumped ahead to interview some of his other girls. These interviews had to be conducted very, very carefully, for the girls' safety, and therefore unreliably, while dancing and drinking. But the facts seemed clear: Most of the girls in that bar were from the villages and, apparently, each had been promised a wealthy, respectable life with the bar owner.

Finally, for the decisive, devastating fall into prostitution, each girl had been told a similar sad story: Because of sudden financial trouble, the bar owner told them he needed their help desperately in raising a large sum of money to save his bar and their futures. He used threats and *fatherly* beatings to help persuade some of them. All they had to do was "be extremely nice to a very rich and respectable GI for just one night," and then it would never happen again.

That was it of course; with the help of much alcohol to soften the pain, it kept happening. The system was not invented for Americans. It had been used for years in that country, and elsewhere, to procure. The difference was between a very few women for the local, wealthy customers, and, now, tens of thousands (over the years) for the Americans.

REACTIONS TO THE PRESENTATION

I picked up one more fact that was useful. These prostitutes were contacted regularly by Communist *intelligence agents* for military information passed along by GIs. Some of the intelligence details were shocking (scary) to any military man.

In my presentations I used three items: that last fact, espionage as a cause for concern, the story of the vicious procurement system, and the fact that the girls were reporting to confidential sources that they hated us, because of their defiled status.

After I had perfected the presentation before small groups of men, I tried it on the first large theater full—about a thousand men. I tied it of course, to the American ideological package and gave it a very soft voice—no fire and brimstone. The men listened quietly and at the end there was no applause, just thoughtfulness and quiet discussion. Clearly, it hit them pretty hard.

As the men left the theater, a few sneered at me, many glanced their approval; a few stopped and expressed their enthusiastic agreement. The general, who had been in the front row observed the generally favorable reaction. I could see that he, too, was calmly pleased. He asked me to come over to his office for coffee after I gathered my gear and finished off the informal conversations.

On leaving, I noticed that one little pocket of four or five ranking sergeants gathered around a chaplain outside the theater. He had not been to my larger meeting in the capital with the group of fifty chaplains. I did not know him. He was reported to be very popular and he was a big, strong, military-looking man. Despite a considerable distance between us, in front of the theater outside, I could hear him shouting. Realizing that he had buttonholed a few of the top sergeants and was supporting me with his own fire and brimstone, I meandered over hoping to cool him down and give the sergeants an escape. Little did I know.

The chaplain was *denouncing* my position, not supporting it. He turned to me and exclaimed, "Humphrey, you have got to stop this! I am not just a chaplain but also a psychiatrist. What you are saying will fill these men so full of conflict over their sex drives that they'll be going crazy."

NON-CONFRONTATION

Regarding tactics, unless personal injury is at risk, in this attitude-changing business, I rarely confront anyone. Rather, I take it slow and easy trying to win critics over to my position or else find the basic rationality in their view to see if I should change mine.

"Okay," I said to the chaplain, "I'm sorry if I have undercut you here. I tried to square the effort with all the chaplains in the country. You weren't present. But I have a meeting right now with the general. Why don't you come along. It's his program really, not mine. I assure you that I'll abide by what you and he decide."

Scowling, he came along.

The general had invited me for the visit, so I spoke first, telling the general why I had taken the liberty to invite the chaplain. The general nodded. I asked the general to let the chaplain make his case against mine. He did.

Then, I submitted as objectively as possible that the chaplain had presented a straight Freudian sex-oriented theory of human nature. That was the nub of the disagreement, I observed, and submitted that our Balanced Life Value theory was definitely a different analysis of human nature; that the men would suffer less mental discomfort and damage under our guidance than under a Freudian policy, but concluded with the thought that the general did not have to exercise a final decision.

I suggested (and would have delighted in) a competing scientific experiment using the troubled area where the shooting had occurred and some other areas for control groups. All the general had to do was fund the attitude measurements through some outside group. They would be expensive.

PROSTITUTION AND THE MILITARY MISSION

"Chaplain," said the general, "you wear two hats. As a psychiatrist, you have advised me regarding the mental well-being of the men—that some are liable to go crazy if challenged about their sexual practices. But the hat that you wear for me is to administer to the spiritual well-being of the men. That job, I think, according to your boss, the Church, must compel you to side with Humphrey regarding prostitution or whatever it is called here. However, aside from those considerations I am making my decision on another ground: the military mission.

"At 5 o'clock every morning, I stand out there overlooking the valley at the front gate. I watch half of my command come struggling up that hill after their night in those little shacks, and I know that we have been in jeopardy. If we get hit in the night by Communist forces, we won't be able to muster a satisfactory defense. What the other chaplains and Humphrey are willing to try may help us. I ask you to help them. We can call it an experiment."

The chaplain, who had not wavered from his position, finally, was silent. He never helped; but, to my knowledge, he never tried to obstruct our program.

I was able to give a few more of these speeches on the female-slavery issue in the target area before being called, suddenly, back into Vietnam on a bigger problem. Despite the inevitable feeling of jumpiness about returning to the combat area, I was relieved by the necessary change back in emphasis to general culture shock rather than the complicated and supersensitive prostitution issue. However, it was not long before I returned to it. The crisis issue in Vietnam was solved quickly. When I returned north, I found myself promoted in a needling way to the status of *sex-relations expert.* I accepted and tried a couple of new challenges in that sad field. (We will continue to explore it in the next chapter.)

EFFECTIVENESS AND PROMISE

On September 28, 1987, *Time Magazine* carried the report that a special committee had reported that "abusive behavior toward all women is...accepted....condoned...(and) encouraged in both the Navy and Marine Corps." The Secretary of Defense then announced that "this kind of sexual harassment will not be allowed."

I am sure it will not; not anymore than racial prejudice will be allowed. The more meaningful question, though, for you as a cultural detective, is this: Similar to the racial issue, how do you change attitudes so that the inclination to harass women will not be felt?

That is, how do you improve the underlying male attitude toward women in general? That is the real issue, isn't it? Meanwhile, be strongly conscious of the fact that some of the continuing opposition to the "female equality" movement derives from two fallacies that are fostered by *some* champions of women's rights. One holds that women should not discipline themselves against self-destructive and socially-destructive behavior *because men don't.* MEN SHOULD! The second assumes that equal treatment means *the same* treatment; it does not. It means *fair* treatment for equal human beings. For example, I treat all of my children (boys and girls) equally by giving them, not the same size and make of clothing, but rather clothes that are different in size and make, suited to *fit* their different sizes and different (male or female) means of functioning.

CHAPTER 18

X-Rated Riddles

Being a college prof over sixty years of age, I often encounter younger persons who think that we elders are from the opposite sides of the mountain regarding the sexual revolution. In my classes on values, when we are discussing principles of family life, occasionally I see a young person smile in toleration of my views. I usually leave it there, knowing that some things you cannot teach intellectually; they have to be learned the hard way, through suffering. This is especially true of the great values that are instinct-like. They depend on, or derive from, our emotions more so than from our logic or rationality; they cannot possibly be explained meaningfully in mere words. This especially includes matters of male/female love, sex, and family. How many million songs tell of that unrequited unwanted love that sometimes ruins lives?

How many persons (especially girls) in the sexual revolution seriously hurt their lives because they thought they could deal with sex logically?

SOME SECRETS FROM THE MORE DISCREET, OLDER GENERATIONS

By the time I was nine years old, much of America was traumatized by the Great Depression. It was not just a financial crisis. Dust clouds covered Mud City, Missouri, at times with a mountain of brown that shut out the sun and filled one's mouth with gritty dust. All of life in the U.S. was disoriented. Dad was forced out of our family business, a greenhouse. He rode horseback all over northwest Missouri selling weekly newspapers as well as an antitheft chicken-marking system to farmers. He sometimes sent us a single fifty-cent piece home in the mail. It bought bread and skimmed milk and helped keep us off of welfare. Mother left home in the dark of the morning to walk five miles on a muddy, dusty, or snow-covered country road to teach all the grades in a one-room country school.

And what was there for grade-school boys, such as I, in the wild Missouri towns of the late '20s and early '30s? (Most such towns had only one part-time law man, on foot and easy to outrun.) The toughest of us boys—along with the most angry—from the newly destitute families, formed childhood criminal gangs. Theft, vandalism, and selling whiskey bottles to bootleggers was our business.

But we could read. That takes me, with a sense of amusement, to the point about the so-called *modern* sexual revolution. Our little clubhouse shack, down on the bank of Mud Creek, boasted a collection of *dirty comic books* that would make modern sexy magazines look sedate. We also enjoyed traveling carnivals, small circuses, and side shows in those grimy days. Many were manned partly by lecherous old men, and young ones, who had not only, as they boasted, *seen the elephant* (knew the worldly facts of life), they had ridden on its swinging trunk. From the exciting sex tales of the *carnies*, and the older boys, by the time I was twelve, I knew more about sex than Dr. Ruth. And in those childhood gangs of the depression and prohibition, it was not all talk. Occasionally, one or another of the toughest street-wise girls was made an honorary member of the club for some *gang-banging* back in the times when it had a less harmful meaning. Of course, she received an honorarium: Indian head pennies, the most beautiful marbles, the cleanest cigarette butts, and maybe some treasured colored chalk.

The sexual revolution (this most recent one of many others in history) did at least four things: two good; two bad. It unmasked and dumped much hypocrisy. It freed many oppressed and depressed grown women. Good. But it lost sight of the line between things public and things private. That's bad. Most damaging to human happiness and social well-being, it dissolved the glue of sexual fidelity that helps hold together humankind's natural institution:

the family (pair-bond). That has been disastrous for too many children.

OFFICIAL PIMPS, VD, AND SUICIDE

My sudden trip out of Country X (previous chapter) back down into Vietnam at the height of my new involvement in that shooting-and-prostitution issue was indeed welcome. It gave me a much-needed moment for some contemplation. I could not grasp, completely, the social dynamics of the sex scene in the Orient for our young teenage men. But I knew I was dealing with something considerably more complicated than the divisible issues: respect for women, prostitution, the sexual revolution, etc. It was some multiple of those factors—a quicksand issue for sure.

How can I describe this social/sexual situation in which our young military men find themselves in some of the poverty-stricken areas of the world, especially during the chaos of war? Ask some of those who have served abroad and now live in your city. Be persistent and have them spell it out. Otherwise few will volunteer the information. Try to picture it: Prostitution everywhere; countless numbers of local women with hidden social diseases and ruined lives, yet attractive and selling hard and cheap—that describes the situation pretty accurately. If you doubt it, as I say, ask some of the men who have seen that elephant in Asia during a war.

During this hectic period, a scandalous article appeared in a popular U.S. news magazine reporting enough cases of VD among our men in Country 4 to include 110%—*one hundred ten percent.* American wives back home began to write their husbands (my friends) asking, "Honey, after squeezing 110% onto 100%, how can that leave you out?"

I conducted samplings on various military compounds to try to get some more accurate estimates. Because of inadequate time to pretest my questionnaires, my research on this topic was the weakest I have ever conducted on any formal study. But as far as I could determine from that shaky research, about 30% of the American men almost never left the military bases and had nothing to do with the local women. The 110% came from men who had caught several doses of VD in a year—some as many as ten times. The hospital statistics were kept without names and were annual. That explained the 110%.

More interesting to me was the fact that about a third of the men were abstaining from the easy, attractive, inexpensive sex. It meant to me that there was a strong nucleus of men who could be called on to help figure out a way to protect the destitute Asian women from being lured into prostitution by our men. These men might be persuaded to pay the girls just to dance with them, or talk with them at the tables. They could possibly establish our taxi-dance institution. (This formula had been used successfully in numerous American cities, and something similar, from the men's viewpoint, had filled our American USO's during World War II.)

On one trip out of Country X, I visited an area of the world I'll call Country 7. It was one of the spots visited by thousands of men on short leave from Vietnam. The first briefing that I sat in on with about a hundred of these young American military men (teenagers remember), could be described accurately as a *pimping session.* The briefing officer spoke:

> Okay men, I'll get right to the point. I know you are all interested in just one thing. (These) are the names of the hotels and bars where you can get it. (Here) is how much it costs. (Here) is where you get your VD wash afterward. Your return plane to Vietnam leaves (on this hour.) Good-bye, have fun, don't miss your plane; don't miss your wash.

I went to the commanding general and asked him about the pimp-type briefing. From his visible consternation, hand signals and body language, I could have been back in Italy. It was clear that he agreed with me at least about questioning the whole thing, but he asked me the hard question. "What do you suggest in its place? Shuffleboard?"

I responded, joking, that his question was dirty pool; the briefings were his briefings, not mine. I had come only to complain. He simply laughed and said, "Figure something out that is better and let me know. I'll listen to anything."

I asked for permission to interview the men in small groups for ten minutes after their pimp-type briefings. He agreed. I interviewed not more than six or seven groups that week, and asked them only one question.

After making certain that nothing was in the offing immediately, and without any appeal to ideology, morality, or anything other than their attitudes, I asked how many would be interested in meeting and associating with some of the "nicer girls" in the country who did not sell sex, nor date unchaperoned? There was one condition: The men could not have both. That is, if they made their trip a cultural study or social visit with respectable women, that was it. (A local high-ranking official had told me: "If you mix the whore-users in with the men visiting our upper-class women, it will never happen again.")

What would you guess was the reaction of our men? Remember, they were on leave from combat to which they had to return and knew that they might be killed.

In the first group I asked, I could see many faces light up in surprise and hands start up spontaneously. Almost as quickly, all eyes darted to both sides and the enthusiasm was killed. Arms were jerked back down. A few hands eased on up, defiantly.

"Good," I said, "if any of you want to stay and talk with me in your limited time, I'll be at (so and so)." I dismissed them. Some came and talked.

In the next groups, instead of asking them to raise their hands, I asked them to just nod their heads to me with a little hand or eye signal. The positive responses always seemed to include about a third to half of the men. On one occasion, a big, timid soldier found my office and pressed me for a *nice girl* contact. He told me that on a previous visit, one of his friends had caught VD and had killed himself. Another boy told me of a friend who made love for the first time in his life—to a prostitute—and had also killed himself.

I didn't have time to try to work anything out along the *nice girl* lines. I suggested a possible program to the general and left it there. I was already overwhelmed with trying to stop the *gook syndrome* in Vietnam and losing. Nonetheless, it was clear to me that something very constructive was possible regarding creating respect for Asian women, that is, if American leadership could ever perceive the need for Americans to win the people of the Third World and act responsibly toward all destitute women.

Understand that what I am denouncing here is the purchase of sex from poor women who have to sell it to survive.

For those many Americans who will tell you that the Asians see *free sex* completely differently from us, test it this way: Find some of the Marines who lived in the Vietnam villages, in the Combined Action Platoons, who were at the mercy of the Vietnamese. The Marines found that they had to leave the girls alone. The two exceptions that I know of were killed in the night *and mutilated.* I was told it was by the Viet Cong, but I doubt it.

On my next return to Country X, I contacted a captain with whom I was working on the shooting case to see how the project was going.

"Fine," he said, "especially for me, which is something I want to tell you. The day you gave that first speech and consulted us about our money pulling the local girls into prostitution, and about the natural validity of the pair-bond, that speech saved me. My two roommates had finally talked me into taking a sex-maid with the argument that so many others were doing it that it was a foolish waste for me not to do so. I had never cheated on the wife and kids before. Thank God for your comments that very week. Whether it is right or wrong or what, I don't know for sure. But the fact that I didn't cheat after deciding to, and coming so close, sure makes me feel good. If it is not a choice between good and bad, it *is* one between fun and something like serenity as you said, and serenity is better. I feel so much stronger and cleaner."

Sex, Race, Self-Doubt, and Better Lovers

Are black men built better for sex than whites? The issue is so unbelievable, and to my older generation, so X-rated as a private issue, that I have vacillated mightily over whether to include it here or not. But since the issue was there, on one overseas base, in no uncertain terms, and was causing fights, I must include it or else bow before the defeating *embarrassment barrier.*

There are some redeeming features to this built-for-love question: It is amusing, and it includes another excellent example of the benefits of *street research* in this tragically neglected area of cultural detective work for both domestic and international peace.

In my graduate-level college classes, I find that about half to two-thirds of the members of an adult audience of middle-management business persons are aware of the old question about black men being built better (bigger) for loving: To the old hard-core racists of pre-World War II, it was the alleged fact that proved that blacks were *like animals.* To the militant black leaders of the 1960s, it was the arrogant boast that proved black men were *better men.* Don't think that the boast did not rankle some *macho* whites. But to most Americans, of the older, more discreet generations it was a whispered rumor of a detail that was beneath one's dignity to discuss outside of the locker-rooms. As a major social issue of any significance in the real world, I would have guessed that it had about the same likelihood of causing trouble as the Loch Ness monster. Yet, suddenly, on one overseas military post, beyond credence, there it was.

The situation involved an isolated unit of fifty or sixty military men on a classified operation. (That is all I was told.) A quarter to a third of the men were black. Some racial troubles had developed in the ramshackle rural nightclub that was about a mile down a dirt road from the compound. Besides that civilian nightclub the only recreation that I noticed on the compound was an outdoor half-court basketball surface with a naked rim. Movies were shown nightly in the mess hall. Pretty austere.

The blacks and whites involved in the new racial hostilities had served together on a previous assignment. The commanding officer insisted that they had been close: *really good friends.* He thought the trouble was over music in the club which had thirty or forty Asian dance-hall girls for *entertainers.* The black men who frequented the club preferred soul music; the whites, country-western.

That was all the information the commanding officer gave me, other than his need to solve this little conflict in his small but important command.

By now, you can guess my first step in seeking a solution: I attended the club. I walked down that dirt road, waited until the bar opened, and was the first customer. The bartender was friendly. My tips were good, and appreciated. As arranged, he signaled me when the men who had been most involved in the fighting entered the bar. One of these, an extroverted white sergeant, could not possibly have been more friendly and talkative. After a few beers, I leveled with him. He laughed about the commanding officer's analysis of the problem as being over music.

"Hell no, it's not the music," he exclaimed pounding the flimsy table with his fist. "That's only the surface; the real cause is that blacks and whites here in this club all have to date the same women! *That ain't fair!*"

At first, I assumed that it was a plain old-fashioned racial prejudice—not wanting to share the same women.

"Why don't the girls specialize as in other parts of Asia?" I asked. (In some Asian clubs that cater to American service men, historically, some of the Asian girls "do" their hair and learn to dance *soul* for the blacks; others make themselves up and dance *white.*)

"I don't know," he answered, "but it ain't fair, the way these black studs are built." He slammed his fist again.

It took a few moments for it to dawn on me what he was talking about.

"Damn!" I exclaimed. "Don't tell me you guys are still falling for that old myth about them being built better than we are?"

"Now look, Dad," he responded, with his anger suddenly turned on me rather than the issue, "don't you start trying to give me that intellectual crap about size not mattering, or that what you call a myth is just a myth. We play a lot of basketball together and shower together. It ain't no myth. Even soft, Dad, they are just built bigger."

For a man so big and so young, his beers had hit fast. He was already loud.

"Okay, okay," I advised, "this issue is a complete surprise to me. But I think I may be able to do something if you'll give me a little time. How 'bout it?"

"What do you mean, 'how 'bout it,' What can I do?" he questioned, obviously seriously interested.

"Stop the fighting," I answered, "until I can check it out." "What you going to do, bring in some round eyes (American girls)?" he questioned, now laughing.

"Nothing as unusual as that; but I do think I can help this situation if you'll give me some time, say a month to check it out." (What I had in mind was to collect overwhelming evidence including testimony from females that size was not as important as finesse— the quality, not quantity, maxim. More than anything else I was counting on the sense of humor of the GIs. It is unfailing and a *God-sent* quality, displayed even in combat. And if I ever saw an issue that was going to cause laughter, once brought out into the light, this was it.)

Humor and a few clarifying facts about the different psychological makeup of men and women, I thought, would serve.

He agreed to give me the time.

Back in the big city, and headquarters, my first stop was the medical section. I explained my amusing mission to a doctor and asked where I could locate some psychologists and psychiatrists.

"You may be on the wrong track," a doctor advised. "I attended a medical conference recently where a related subject came up. In view of the racial troubles these days, plus the importance of that particular operation out there in the boondocks, why don't you follow another lead I can give you. You can always revert. Catch a hop (free military flight) to Korea and talk to this doctor. (As he spoke, he wrote out a name, as if writing a prescription for my ills.) This doctor studies cold-weather injuries. There may be some things that your hypothesis is leaving out."

The man was convincing. I caught a plane to Korea, and found the doctor.

This cold-weather specialist did not laugh at my quest. After I stated the issue, he sat down at a table and thought about it.

"Do you know that black soldiers suffer from much more frostbite than the whites?" he asked.

"Sure, doesn't everyone know that?" I answered. "Don't tell me that military medicine is just finding out about skin melanin? In black skin, developed for hot areas to prevent burning, it shuts out certain sun rays; in cold areas, the pigmentation won't let in enough sun, so black hands freeze sooner than whites'." (My overworked, physically exhausted condition at the time plus my hostility toward overspecialization in education caused me to flare over this apparent wild-goose chase for old knowledge considered new by the medics.)

The young doctor sat watching me for a second without speaking. I thought I had embarrassed him. Then he said, "Yes, they freeze more quickly; their uncovered hands that are exposed to the sun...(pause) and also in their boot-and-sock covered feet."

He smiled as I blinked and tried to process what he had just said. Finally, I overcame my own embarrassment enough to ask in all my wisdom: "Their totally covered feet?"

He laughed openly, at me, and repeated my phrase: "Their totally covered feet."

"Can you explain that in lay terminology for my simple brain?" I queried apologetically.

"Maybe," he responded. He then told me that in addition to the melanin that services our white and black skins slightly differently for hot and cold climates, there is also a small difference in the way the tiny blood-carrying capillaries work near the surface of our bodies and in our extremities. In black-skinned bodies, evolved to stay cool in hot climates, the blood stays out in the capillaries, near the body-surface for cooling purposes. Whereas in white bodies, the blood sucks back in from the surface when the weather cools, so that the body can stay warm and avoid death from the blood freezing. Meanwhile, on the other side white bodies in the hot equatorial sun can burn-up and die easily, whereas black bodies just turn a little blacker and pour out that life-protecting sweat. That was about all he knew.

It was enough. It was another track! Maybe there *was* a considerable myth.

My next series of planned stops was in gymnasiums to talk with weight-lifters and bodybuilders. As it turned out, it required only one stop and I didn't even have to enter a gym. A dozen or so hulking bodies-beautiful, like sea lions on the beach, were sprawled on the steps of a military gym waiting for the building to open. After a few icebreaker questions about the gym, weight-lifting, boxing, and other available facilities, I asked the big question about black muscles being more stable in size (not needing stimulation for expansion).

One white bodybuilder responded nonchalantly: "Sure, it's true," he said. "Pete, over there, has got it made. He can just walk onto a stage, take off his shirt, and show. But me, I got to run back behind stage, fall over chairs in the dark, (light laughter from the group) pump-up like hell, or I don't have a chance."

Pete nodded smiling. No one else said anything.

"'Pump-up?' and 'show?' Are those bodybuilding words or just yours? Can you explain what you just said to me in more detail?" I asked.

He answered, "They are my words, mine and Pete's. But they are real. His muscles stay up all the time. Mine don't. It is a white and black thing. But it *is* unfair," he said laughing.

The young man continued: "Later, after much lifting, I guess, it's not so bad. Ask some of these other older guys."

I looked around. No one else seemed to want to speak. Those were the days of volatile black/white racial troubles. So I did not push anyone verbally—especially not guys twice my size.

I turned back to my informant. "Never mind later," I complained. "How about now? How much smaller are your muscles, when relaxed, than his? And how close can you come to his size after you pump-up?"

"I am fully competitive. We are about the same after pumping-up. But now, before, look at me. I don't have a chance."

I could not see the difference through his clothes.

"You sure?" I asked. "After pumping-up, your muscles will more or less even out?"

"Stick around and see!" He challenged. I did. He was right.

I made one more stop: back to the prostitutes. They confirmed the story. *Things even out.* One woman left absolutely no doubt. Her husband was a white guy; not exactly a high type. He had some financial interest in a local bar. His wife, an Oriental, was a whore madam. She was as rough as a razorback sow. Her husband, she said, had been so concerned about this *size thing* that he had forced her to do some measurements (with a string). "There is definitely a difference, on average, about half an inch when the guys are (relaxed); sometimes more, because when (relaxed) the muscles of some white men almost seem to shrink-up and disappear," she said. "But when the muscles are up, you can't measure any remaining difference with a string."

And that was that.

In less than three weeks after my first confrontation with the fighting sergeant, I was back in that old shack that passed as a bar confidently explaining my findings step-by-step, fact-by-accumulated-fact. The explanation filled him, this time, with table-pounding delight. I did not wait around to see if the fighting stopped but I felt confident.

So did the men in that unit with whom I talked and related the story. Word spread like a flash fire. There was much raucous laughing. No one challenged my facts. I gave the men telephone numbers and names to call if anyone was interested. One black corporal, in good humor, voiced the only negative. He complemented me on stopping "the bad chimes," but said if we ever met again in the States, I was not to "mess around with his myth."

Were my findings valid and reliable? I still don't know. So what is the measure of acceptability for materials when you are trying to stop suffering (fighting, possibly killing) in the field?

The findings were honorable. And they were effective. You keep checking after the crises, and if you find you were wrong, you publicize the fact and apologize.

AMERICAN MALE/FEMALE RELATIONS AND FOREIGN PROSTITUTES

Despite recent token improvements, one of the greatest evils of the military system—according to me—is the continuing official neglect of wives and families. This is not an intentional evil. It is worse; it is so much a traditional fact, accepted as a necessary evil, that it is hardly noticed, like breathing in and out. Short of combat, families should never be broken up for long overseas tours. If at all possible, men in large groups should not be sent into foreign societies without a normal number of women from the same culture because, among other distortions, it corrupts the foreign social balance.

Trying to overcome that evil by letting some (mainly officers) take their families with them to overseas posts, backfires in those areas where the American population (males compared to females) is still terribly unbalanced, and the balance is filled-in by local prostitutes.

The American wives who are in those areas grow inevitably and justifiably angry at the prostitutes because we humans are protective (jealous) pair-bonders. Also because of our racial jealousy in matters of sex, it is not just anger that results. Of all the studies I have conducted in over thirty years, the greatest rage I have ever seen registered on a mass study was from American wives in Asia against those "dirty, yellow" prostitutes. In interviews (before I learned not to interview the wives on this topic), there was often smoldering rage.

Twice, reluctantly, I consented to speak before American Wives Clubs on the topic. Both times I tried to persuade them to be a little more considerate of the local *hired wives* on the grounds of the latter's wrecked lives discussed earlier, those grounds plus the fact that it was *our own men* who were the buyers. Both times, I was nearly expelled from the country and both times on a subterfuge (cleverly alleging that I had insulted the local culture or a third nation) that left me defenseless.

In one Asian country, a prominent American civilian who worked with the military, on arrival in country, moved next door to me. The wife was an Oriental and daughter of a previous embassy official from this same Asian nation. We helped them move into their new home. After his wife's first trip to the Post Exchange, she came home to my wife crying, not wanting her husband to know what had occurred: As she stood in the Post Exchange line at the jewelry counter, a beautiful blond (her words), American wife assumed our friend was a *hired wife* and repeatedly admonished her in a monotone: "You should not be buying this tax-free jewelry for the black market, you dirty whore."

My wife called me home to help with the counseling that our friend needed. I had noticed that one of the chaplains was interviewing wives that day to help in a big Sunday school summer program. Our Oriental friend was a Christian. "Get in with the church," I advised. "Soon, all the Americans will learn of your background, et cetera." She agreed and I dropped her off at the church.

Before the day was over, my wife called me home again. The lady at the church who was interviewing women for the chaplain was that same beautiful blond who had been excoriating our friend in the jewelry line.

When I was exclaiming at the beginning of the book about my successes on these programs, my mind was on the primary jobs for major businesses and military operations. I forgot about those brief experiences with wives' clubs over the prostitution issue. I take some of the exclamations back. On a job like this, you need a team of men and women, both, with representatives from all pertinent racial groups, as well as gays and lesbians.

WOMEN AT WEST POINT

In the late 1970s, after women had been in our military academies for three years, I received an invitation from West Point to address the issue of women in the Academy. After I arrived, I was told that I was the twentieth speaker, as I recall, in three years, and none had been favorably received. In fact, I was warned that the last speaker was the ranking female in the Defense Department, and she had been booed.

Can you anticipate the questions I will now ask you: What would you do on this case (that is, assuming you were foolish enough to accept the assignment of trying to improve male attitudes toward women in a military academy, as I did)? As a cultural detective, what do we do first? Next, how and where do we do the necessary research?

For background research, under severe time pressure (as usual), I scanned everything I could find on women in the military in Israel and Russia. I found nothing really persuasive and inspirational for Americans. Next, I journeyed to West Point about three days early knowing that I had to have some local attitudinal research.

To my surprise, I was quartered in an off-campus hotel rather than in some private VIP residence on campus. Good. I unpacked in a rush and was into the streets buttonholing the few individual cadets—males and females—whom I could find. They were not exactly "hanging out." I spent as much time as possible walking in and around The Academy. Impressive place: Sharp, disciplined, outstanding.

As a Marine, I was jealous. We need a college like that in the USMC.

The female cadets were guarded in their comments, almost evasive. That seemed admirable. Reluctantly, I decided not to press them with questions that might prove embarrassing. But the male cadets were casually vocal about the plight of the females. They described the women as harassed and unhappy, but determined. There was some talk of suicide scares. And much talk of a no-win situation for everyone. If the male cadets were normally hard on the women, there were dangers of being accused of anti-female harassment. If the men were respectful of the female cadets, there was a danger of being accused of seeking sexual attention. No-win! Several men advised that they enjoyed the presence of the women. But all knew there was a problem, a big historic problem.

What I obtained, of substance, in my rushed weekend of interviewing was a general feeling among the men that the women should not be there. Two reasons, mainly, were given:

1. The prized places in The Academy were wasted on the women because they could not go into combat. So for each female present, it meant one less highly trained male officer in the field of combat. Therefore, a less highly trained man might be the one on your flank who would let the enemy through and get you and your men killed.

2. The women's presence, it was insisted, represented unadulterated hypocrisy by the U.S. government and the officials at The Academy who were supporting the women's presence. Why? Because the grounds for their being there was *equality*. The critique was voiced both by cadets who were angry and by cadets who were coldly rational. They said: Everyone keeps harping on the duty to treat the women as equals. Yet, the system and the officials don't. They let the women off through preferential treatment. The women don't have to carry the heavy pack on the marches. They don't have to take their hits in boxing; they get off with judo. And they don't have to do the *pull-ups* for lack of upper-arm strength. You talk of equality! What's all that?

Damn. Nineteen previous speakers and no one with success; the last one booed. I began to feel that old special stage fright of facing a hostile audience and this time with especially flimsy research and untested materials. I made an appeal to my contact officer to let me address the cadets in their classrooms; a few at a time, rather than all at once in the auditorium. I observed that the topic was important enough since it involved, secretly, the issue of possible female suicides. I was testing with that suicide reference. He accepted it without noticing, but responded:

Not a chance. This is one of the most sought-after podiums in America. Men who charge considerable sums of money volunteer to speak here for free, just for the honor. Next, our time here is like lifeblood. We don't do things at thirteen-thirty hours, one-thirty to you; rather, it is thirteen-thirty-one or, to you, one thirty-one; every minute counts. So as far as the class schedule is concerned, to try to change it and work you in for thirty minutes or so, unplanned, into each class... forget it. You came highly recommended from some of the officers who saw you do some things with large groups in Korea and Vietnam. You agreed to face that entire Fourth (Freshman) Class, all (thousand or so) at once. It's tomorrow, bright and early. You are on, unless you cancel completely. That's it.

I asked for and got one concession: "Don't introduce my topic as specifically applicable to women, but rather just to human relations; even that is bad enough." He laughed and agreed, and complied.

When I walk up to a podium, because of my research-backed approach, I always know exactly what I want to say as far as the ideas are concerned. But I never have a prepared, written speech. Only once in thirty years, did I read a fully written speech. That was a race relations appeal in front of some powerful rednecks. Even then, I ad-libbed.

I speak half off-the-cuff because of the overwhelming importance of research. Sizing up the audience is an important step in that research. I do this by mixing into an audience before I start speaking. And I use my first attempted joke in a final research effort. If they are against you, they are reluctant to laugh at the funniest joke. (I use only the proven funniest ones.) If they are "with you," laughter flows without reservation. That reception guides me to the appropriate strength of the message. I deliver the intended message, but the audience will determine whether I whisper that message or shout it.

The large auditorium at West Point that day seemed too dark, and it was fully-packed. After being introduced, I stood silently at the podium for a long time studying the audience, trying to warm up to it, trying to become a part of it, trying to force the silence needed for the deadly serious topic. (The topic of females in the service involves the momentous issues of female suffering, female happiness, justice, alleged unnecessary deaths in combat, and the unanswered question of what is best for the security of the entire nation.) I knew only one thing for certain: I was not going to speak long. As some golfers say on the putting green, *Walk up and miss it quick, or win.* That was my situation there. Just as was customary in the hot spots overseas, here in this unusual situation at West Point, I would either lose 'em or win 'em with very few words. Why say more?

From the high stage in that shadowy auditorium, I could make out the scattering of female cadets down in the front; they would be friendly, I assumed. It looked like all the *heavies* (the officers and civilian teachers) sat up in the back of the auditorium. The presence of civilian teachers at West Point surprised me and would force a slightly different, clumsy choice of words at places in my careful, ongoing message formulation. But I could not make out faces up there in the back. That, too, disturbed me. I take cues from faces during a speech—when to clarify a point, when to re-emphasize one, et cetera.

Okay, I thought, *I'll forget the teachers, and speak only to the cadets.* But that is a high-risk policy. Almost all student movements are started by teachers. (But that is a professorial secret.)

I started, logically, with a war story from Iwo Jima—the one told earlier in which I mildly criticized my younger brother for hiding from sniper fire down deep in his foxhole. Remember? I chided him gently that all his buddies were sitting out on top of the ground laughing at him for being dug-in. Despite its reliable humor for experienced combat men, it is a risky joke with civilians, and I feared the cadets were just young civilians in uniform. Nonetheless, I gambled that the combat officers had taught them some military humor because of its indispensability in combat.

The joke is also risky because it is so macabre or cynical. But it can be hilarious to experienced military men. It delivers a recognized lifesaving message. I suspected that I could rely on the civilian professors to have taught some cynical humor. It was rampant at the time among East Coast intellectuals.

Recall that my brother told me to peek my head up and count how many of his friends were out on top of the ground, exposed to sniper fire, and laughing at him for being dug-in, I peeked, counted, and answered: "Seven." His grim punch line was, "Well, you see, there were eleven of the damn fools out there, yesterday, laughing at me."

Explosive laughter from the cadets. They had let me in. But then I added the real point of the story for the topic being considered. (I did not include it earlier in these lessons.)

My brother, in pleading with me, there on Iwo Jima, to try to stay alive by not taking foolish chances as a platoon leader, had also added: "These Marines who are left are really good fighters. They can shoot like our Missouri boys. But they don't seem to realize that the war goes on in between the hot fire fights. And it is the sniper fire, in between, that is taking us out."

Then I made the parallel (human relations) point that obsessed me in Vietnam, and still does:

"It is America's failures in between the wars—the ideological failures—that is weakening us. That is what is hurting us most in the fight for American respect, worldwide."

As I spoke, the cadets responded with the quiet attention that rewards a serious and sincere message. Coughing, whispering, and foot shuffling stopped. I added these points: "First, militarily, our fighting men won the war in Vietnam, but no one knew that we won (including the press) because we Americans did not join with the Vietnamese people. We excluded them in their own land. We called them 'gooks,' 'f'n gooks,' and 'lazy slopes.' We referred to their women as 'LBFM's' (Little Brown f'n Machines). And their sharpest soldiers, in their white uniforms, we denigrated with the term 'White Mice'."

I concluded this line of reasoning with my conviction about Vietnam: "Totally aside from traditional military considerations, because of these ideological failings, we Americans had to lose that war.

"Second, more specifically, according to me, democracy lost there for two closely related human-relations reasons: One, the 'gook syndrome,' just discussed, and two, 'booby traps!' As high as 70% of the casualties in some outfits were from booby traps (the combat officers had told me).

"Well, here is the combat question: Who was placing many of those treacherous early-morning killers in our compounds?

"In answer, not many male sappers (terrorists) were crawling inside our security. Our U.S. perimeter defense is about the best I have seen in any army. Who was it then? You know, don't you? It was their women! Many a Vietnamese soldier and civilian told me, 'Your American military is naive the way it lets Vietnamese women come into their organizations to wash their clothes, cut their hair, and fraternize with your men on and off duty. Many are spies and Viet Cong soldiers.'

"The Vietnamese, unlike our ineffective American intelligence knew the war was close all along. One Vietnamese officer told me flat out, 'the Viet Cong women with their booby traps, and intelligence-gathering, may be giving their side the winning edge.'" (According to what I was getting from friendly Vietnamese, our military intelligence there was either nonexistent or else totally ignored by command. It was almost as bad in Korea and Turkey.)

In closing, I said, "Incidentally, speaking of women in war, clearly it is a new issue during this changing period of insurgency and counterinsurgency wars, a new phenomenon that our enemy, apparently understands. And one that we don't. Besides my conversations with many Vietnamese about the issue, I talked with our interrogation officers about the captured Viet Cong's attitudes toward their female soldiers, who, as I said, may have given the Viet Cong the winning edge.

"I found that the Viet Cong men did not mind at all if their women were admitted into their top training schools—you know, into their

West Points." (Pause; I thought I saw the bodies tense a bit and thinking start among the cadets in the front rows.)

"And do you know what else? *The Viet Cong men did not complain one iota if their women did not carry the same heavy back packs that were carried by the men.*" (I paused again and looked closely at the cadets up front. I saw some of the women smile and nudge friends in the next seats.)

I added, slowly with extra emphasis, *"None of the Viet Cong men were critical of their women because they did not want to box but studied judo instead."* (Friendly laughter started around through the audience.)

I pressed the needling for one last shot in a much louder voice, also now openly laughing myself.

"The Viet Cong men also knew that their women, who were placing those booby traps, could not do pull-ups, and you know what: THEY DIDN'T GIVE A RAT'S ASS!" There was explosive laughter and applauding.

I looked at my watch. I had spoken only 14 minutes.

Test question: What do you say and do next? Answer: Of course; you think about getting off the stage as soon as possible while you are ahead.

I explained quickly that equality does not mean the same treatment for males and females or even for all males. It means *fair* treatment of equal human beings. For an example from combat, I had my larger Marines in each squad carry the heavy Browning automatic rifles, and I had my 110-pound flyweights do the out-front crawl-scouting.

I thanked the cadets for their time and got the hell off that stage.

The applause exploded again and continued. I walked down the steps onto the front floor. One of the female cadets, incongruously for a military officers' school, walked over with the first little group of cadets and kissed me on the jaw. Harking back to that theater in the Middle East some thirty years earlier, she said simply, *"Tremendous!"*

As my sharp young contact officer told me, "West Point is a busy place." I was hustled out of town so I was not able to do the follow-up research that I always conduct (trusting no one else's). On the plane trip back to California and for weeks later, I kept thinking about the officers and civilian teachers up there in the back of the auditorium and wondering what they had thought. I suspected my words had not appealed to either group. It was not the *need for more bombs* theory that most military officers have fostered ever since the Vietnam loss. And it was not the we *should not have been there* theory of civilian professors.

Whatever the West Point professors thought, no matter, the West Point command invited me back to address the other two troubled classes containing women.

During my second visit, my curiosity was killing me about the West Point internal politics behind that decision to invite me back. The two informal teams of pro and con faculty faces that either smiled or frowned at me respectively in the halls aroused that curiosity further. After the next speech went equally well, I could not resist the temptation to ask a friendly colonel why I had been invited back: "Was it to assist further with the women's problems, or was it to prove that the first successful speech was a fluke?"

He laughed and said, "All I can say is don't ever expect to be one of our permanent civilian professors; you are doing too well on the topic of women in the service." Hmm.

CHAPTER 19

THE CASE OF PETTY THEFT VERSUS THE LIFE VALUE

If you have to deal with a village Moslem who knows the Koran, it is similar to coping with a good Christian in Bible Belt country. You must not say anything unkind about anyone or you might get scolded for your violation of religious principles.

I accepted a job in a Moslem area to try to stop petty theft from an American civilian organization. The company director advised me, "Even though these people are good Moslems, they are stealing from us because so many Americans are so insulting."

"No way," argued his assistant director. "They steal from us just because they are thieves and they are also resentful of our high incomes. They'll rob us blind unless we can find a way to search them as they leave work."

Politically, searching those peasant folk, other than by mere passing observation, was out of the question. We would have found ourselves in jail, expelled from the country, or worse.

I took a supervisor's position over a seven-man crew of locals to see if I could solve the theft problem. They were stealing food and some office supplies, I was told.

I worked overtime to win the confidence of those seven young men, four of whom were married. I *hung out* with them during spare time. They baby-sat my children. We sent gifts to their homes for their mothers, wives, and children.

After only a few weeks, I began to feel and sense the trust and brotherly camaraderie between us. Building such a relationship is comparatively easy in the traditional cultures if you have the time. By the severest Christian standards, these hardworking village

Moslem folk were *good Christians*. If I said something snide about the ugly-acting assistant director who was harassing them, they still winced and made excuses for the man. But the theft continued.

American salaries on the job were approximately ten times those of the host-nationals for the same kind of work. Finally, in desperation, I persuaded the director to double their salaries, up to one fifth the salary of Americans who did the same jobs. Theft continued. The assistant director threatened to report us to the American embassy for inflating the local economy. We had been warned about that.

I persuaded the boss to raise their salaries again up to 30% of the Americans. Theft stopped. But why? I could not figure it out. The boss raised the salaries in his other two small departments with three and six local workers. All theft stopped.

After I moved to another city, I returned about a year later and visited the home of my most trusted employee on that theft case. He had changed jobs and moved up economically.

I explained my actual cross-cultural work and what had transpired on that job with him. After assuring him that I never wanted to learn who had been doing the stealing, I told him I needed desperately to know why it had stopped at 30% of the American's income. He explained:

"It was totally unrelated to the American's salaries," he advised casually. "The men with children, none of the single guys, were doing the stealing. We quit stealing when we could afford two things: three meals a day for our children and pencils for them to take to school. Our government provides everything else except pencils."

Years later in a distant country in east Asia, one of the hysterical charges by culture-shocked Americans against the host-nationals was that *they are all thieves*. And it was not petty theft that disturbed us. If we stayed out too late at night, we would not be surprised to find all our furniture gone with a thank-you note on the door for the fine stereo.

The American joke was that when the children in that country were born, their fathers gave them a pair of pliers to cut through protective wire around our U.S. military bases. "Then when the kids reach six-years-old, they turn in their pliers for tin snips so they can cut through the Quonset huts." (Always good for a laugh no matter how many times it was told.)

UGLY AMERICANS, AGAIN

I consulted a wealthy American businessman about loaning me some of his personnel to help conduct the research needed to combat the attitudes among the Americans about the local theft. He seemed like a nice fellow. But when I asked him for this help, he went into a rage. Here, in brief, is what he said:

Are you crazy, Humphrey? These people are klepto. We had things stolen out of the office until we finally started using an American watchman night and day: radios, cameras, toasters, clocks, everything that was not tied down, especially our personal belongings. Most infuriating of all, when we tore down the front porch to rebuild the office, we found a lot of the stuff under there busted-up where our locals had thrown it when they were about to get caught on the way out. These people are mean thieves. They really busted up that stuff. They decided that if they could not have it, neither could we. So before they threw it away under the porch they broke it up.

Next, the man changed the subject and went into this tirade:

If you really want to help these people, why don't you get the American government to teach them how to grow corn and wheat, and raise farm animals? All they eat, three meals a day, are those stinking turnips. And they think they are delicious. I have to eat with them often. All they eat are those damn turnips. Then I have to ride around with them all over this area in that jeep and all they can talk about are those turnips growing in the fields.

Did you ever notice that these people are so tight that they grow those turnips right up to the edge of the road: the roads don't even have big enough shoulders to park on. And they leave the turnips that grow nearest the road until last to pull; that's because the soil is poor there; so those roadside turnips grow slowest. And the way they brag about the farmers who plant those turnips! Each turnip the same distance from the next with never one missing—what a thing to boast about! Hell, who couldn't measure the same distance between turnips!

SURPRISE TEST FOR THE READER

That write-up of the comments from the angry (culture-shocked) business man is intended as a pop quiz for your cultural-detective work. As he continued to harangue, I realized that he was giving me some answers to the theft issue. Did you notice the clues? (I should remind you, also, that the host-nationals in every country I studied said that we overseas Americans do not respect them. In this country, it was the highest: 90%.)

ANSWERS

That story about the host-nationals breaking up radios and clocks and throwing them under the porch because they were about to get caught does not make sense does it? If a thief were about to get caught, he would not be making noise smashing-up metal toasters and things. So how do you explain those destroyed items under the porch?

Did you suspect vindictive theft?

That's what it was. Through three different host national interviewers, each anonymously consulting one of the workers in that business and paying each for an explanation without names of the thieves, each independently at different times got the same answer. After one or another of the Americans, all of whom were especially *ugly* in that office, had insulted a host worker, the latter destroyed some gear that belonged to the offending American and then threw it under the porch. Obviously there were many insults.

Next, regarding the turnips, if the local nationals were "all thieves" how does one explain those delicious turnips (delicious to the locals) growing right up to the side of the road all over the area and no one stealing them? In many parts of Missouri farm country, if apples or melons or any favorite food grows up close enough to the fence that a long arm can reach, they are soon gone. (And Missourians, of course, are more honest than other Americans.) So compared to Americans, one cannot say that those foreign nationals involved were exceptional thieves.

I used these arguments to upset the attitude among Americans that the local people were all thieves. It was persuasive when attached to the ideological materials. One entire isolated compound of American military men agreed to test the honesty (vindictive theft) theory simply by showing more respect to the people of one local village, mainly by just speaking to them and trying to talk to them. Theft did stop. The Americans even began to neglect the maintenance of their protective fences. Then, suddenly, horror of horrors: three truckloads of coffee were stolen out of the compound. And I don't mean just the coffee; it was trucks and all.

In a desperate effort, I started to organize an internal investigation, thinking that maybe the thieves were *insiders*, Americans. It happens. But before I could get back to the remote compound, a couple of mornings later, bright and early, the trucks were back, still fully loaded, just sitting there outside the gate. *The villagers,* not the local police, had chased them down. No questions were asked.

To avoid further incidents, however, I recommended that the compound quietly fix the fences. As a chaplain friend of mine used to say, "Tempting poor people is a sin." I thanked my lucky Oriental stars that the truck was not filled with "stinking turnips" instead of coffee in that tea-drinking land.

For you *old Asian hands,* please don't think you recognize the nation and business house above in the theft case. I changed many of the non-vital facts. One similar comment: if we Americans learned how to win back the mutual respect and friendship of just one Third World country, we could win them all. Panama and the Philippines make strategic sense for starters. Can the diplomats and business houses do this? Good question. Could the GIs, properly trained? No problem; absolutely no problem! When do those treaties of ours expire? What a Greek tragedy: this endless, needless story of the decline of great nations. A rise into cross-cultural maturity would be so much happier; not easier, mind you, but much, much happier. Meanwhile, of course, and closely related, we still have some domestic cross-group problems to solve.

CHAPTER 20

RACE RELATIONS

Most U.S. race-relations programs have been so unscientific—conducted without attitude studies and without any guiding theory—that they have resulted in deep disappointment among lower economic-class blacks and backlash among working class whites. Some gains were made especially for black elites, but many lower-class blacks say that, on balance, they suffered setbacks. The worst results are these: 1) there is now considerable black/white polarization, and 2) the animosities have gone underground. Equaled only by the related good of reforming our schools, bringing understanding and unity among our racial groups is the most important intermediate goal for developing a happier, stronger, more peaceful America.

THE MOST DECISIVE LESSON FROM
A STRONG BLACK LEADER

While I was working the cross-cultural (gook syndrome) problem in Vietnam, occasionally I was asked to address black/white problems. Since this was during the time of race-riots in America, and since the men in Vietnam carried firearms, those assignments were always very sensitive. For maximum effectiveness, I found it best not to confront the black/white issue directly. Emotions were too high. There had been fights with some shooting. Consequently, I always addressed the more general topic of cross-cultural relations. The problem-solving materials are similar for both conflicts and therefore have crossover effectiveness.

The most volatile of these occasions, that I was called in on, occurred in an area where I was told there had been considerable fighting against Viet Cong forces. There were about one hundred men in the huge dirt-floor Quonset for my address: about forty blacks and sixty whites. All the blacks sat on one side; all the whites on the other. (That was unusual and concerned me.)

The brief address, stressing the human-equality concept, was, as usual, a smashing success. It seemed incongruous for those angry, sweaty, young men, there, in a remote jungle war, divided by racial strife to give a standing ovation to a speech from a passing stranger. But they did.

Outside the Quonset, I asked the top sergeant to send the leader of the black faction over to talk with me as soon as he appeared. I walked about fifty feet over to the edge of the jungle clearing and waited under a palm-leaf roof held up by several palm-tree poles. The man, a low-ranking enlisted Marine, turned out to be a giant—about six-feet, six-inches tall, and probably two-hundred and forty pounds. He was broad-shouldered, hulking, and to me, ugly. (That's important.) Now, understand, all I knew was that there had been some black/white violence. I was seldom given the worst details on these assignments, and I had learned not to probe too aggressively.

The man had huge features on an extra-large head: huge lips, giant nostrils, and overhanging eyebrows. Most impressive: one side of his face had been disfigured—obviously by a knife in some past street-war (in Philadelphia, New York, or Detroit, I presumed). A part of the top lip on his left side was gone; so was a piece out of his left nostril, and there was a hairless slit on the overhanging eyebrow where the facial scar started.

Being an experienced boxer, I always feel a sense of security felt by most hard-hitting boxers that they can whip anyone. Nonetheless, in this situation, alone there in the jungle, away from the others, under that low roof, I was uneasy with this giant black man. I am about five-nine, one-hundred and fifty pounds. Finally, my uneasiness was heightened by the fact that the man was too tall for the low roof. Standing in the middle, at its highest point, he had to hover down over me as my back was pinned to the center pole. Next, the important part of the incident regarding race relations occurred:

"What did you think?" I asked the giant.

"It was marvelous," he said in a warm, soft, deep, voice. Immediately I relaxed.

"What more could be done?" I asked.

"Well, Mister," he answered, in a strangely fatherly tone for a man so young, "you would have to stay and keep telling those stories about equality to the beasts until they really understand." He had taken my shoulder in his huge hand in a reassuring way. I understood why he was the unofficial leader of the blacks. But his epithet, "the beasts," surprised me.

"Good God, man, I uttered, by 'beasts,' you mean the whites?"

"Yes," he said, "not all; but most. It goes back to the slavery, the atomic bombs, and now this situation here: too many blacks dying while our people back home are facing those police dogs and clubs; and even the whites here just getting us killed because of their beastiality to the Vietnamese."

"What do you mean: to the Vietnamese?" I queried.

Thinking for a moment he replied, "Well, you see they don't even know how to give candy to the children. They are afraid to hand it through the barbed wire for fear they'll get their lily-white hands scratched. So they throw it through to the children like they wuz dogs. They just don't seem to understand that in order to win here, we have to show love."

He released my shoulder and held out his huge hand cupped as if it were full of candy. It struck me how white the palm was. He continued: "You see, you have to hold the candy through the wire like this and then as you let them pick out the pieces, you have to keep watching their faces. They will look at you. That's when you have to show them that you love them."

(Now, here is why I explained about his scarred ugliness.) He touched his index finger to his mangled lip and said, "You have to have love in your lips."

He touched that big ugly spit nostril and said. "You have to have love in your nose."

His hand slipped up that scar to the split eyebrow, and he added: "And love in your eyes. The beasts don't understand. You could tell them."

Damn! I ducked out from under the roof so he couldn't see my eyes glazing over with tears. He followed. "Okay," I assured him. "I'll do what I can." He no longer looked ugly, just big and strong.

I began to conduct considerably more research on black/white problems per se; and to write more and more on the black/white issues into the overseas materials. My after-orientation attitude studies, especially in Okinawa, revealed that one could be more effective than I had imagined. Had it not been for that scarred giant there in the Vietnam jungle, I would never have risked taking the Marine Race Relations program. Again, as usual, I didn't get his name. I wish I had, so I could find out if he made it, and let him know that his words were not in vain. (My USMC Race Relations program as I'll mention again was watered down to nothing compared to what it could have been for the benefit of the Corps. But many a black noncommissioned officer has advised me that it did wonders in getting proper respect for the blacks.)

THE NEED FOR BLACK LEADERSHIP

The real lesson of that Vietnam story is that a young black leader asked me, a white, to help. That was his greatest display of wisdom. Following the lead of Gandhi, the leaders of our various ethnic groups fell into the deadly "Gandhi-error" of thinking that each group has to work separately.

Actually, every problem-solving ethnic group needs advisers from other population groups. Cooperation is infinitely better than confrontation. And right now, in America, the division is so great, the unspoken chasm so deep, that constructive whites are afraid to speak. Only black leaders can pull it back. Working through the churches, I would guess, is the best bet. Many have observed that the black church may be one of the few healthy institutions remaining in America. White leaders should be invited in for visits.

I have sent hundreds of college students on such visits in the past fifteen years.

According to their testimony, one visit did more to improve their racial attitudes than all their other education of a lifetime.

The following section details the results of my key findings about race relations. Use them carefully, and double-check them in your area. They are sensitive. Black/white relations are in a class by themselves, much stronger than any other racial conflicts that I have encountered. Across extreme racial physical/visual differences—if there are also cultural, and especially economic, barriers—integration will make relations worse rather than better with only one exception. That exception is when that integration is preceded and accompanied by a good scientific cross-cultural program such as the one suggested in these materials.

The confrontation approach, that was used in the '70s, worked for the elite (that is, where there were no real cultural and economic barriers), but it made attitudes worse in certain ways among the masses. The so-called reverse discrimination promised and caused so much stifled hatred among working-class whites, it is almost as if it was an intentional booby trap planted in the civil rights movement. Henceforth, to overcome that force of self-defeat, as you fight to correct past wrongs, do not let naive elite law-makers set it up so that lower-class whites have to get hurt in order to give the lower economic-class blacks their human rights. Don't allow wealthy whites to conveniently manipulate poor whites into suffering to compensate blacks for past wrongs. Enlist the support of the lower (economic) class whites. Why? Economic class, because of its relationship to survival, easily becomes one of humankind's strongest social bonds.

That is, the growing political force of the black community needs to help get blacks into med schools, onto police forces, fire departments, etc. But if the only entry test is written, for example, and one in which a white earns the top score, make society let that white guy "in" also.

The guiding principle should be: Don't let the elite (blacks or whites) set those of us in the lower economic classes against one another. The problem is a social problem, so society *in general* should pick up the cost—not some hardworking white fireman who might never, himself, have discriminated against anyone.

The Fear-Monster Again

Remember, the decisive methodology is to include white advisers on black-led conflict-resolution teams, and similarly encourage black advisers to work on white-led teams. A close second to that is to realize that the key specter is not bigotry; it is fear. Black-led cross-cultural detective teams must find out what it is the whites are afraid of regarding blacks and then work to eliminate the reason for that fear. White-led teams must accomplish the same type reform in white society.

According to the best research I have studied (especially that by Ralph Stogdill) leadership has a few clearly identifiable characteristics.

- Organize your people

- Organize your tasks

- Press for achievement

- Maintain a sense of kindhearted humor

- Be considerate, make personal sacrifices (within reason) for your followers

- Resolve conflicts

That last item, resolving conflicts, recall, is the big leagues of leadership. And bringing the black and white populations of this nation together into harmony, that is not just the Superbowl, it is also the all-time World Series of all conflict resolution. Are we smart enough and good enough to accomplish that great unifying goal?

Probably so; but not without the elimination of the overriding cross-racial fears. Start there.

I designed the Race/Human Relations program for the Marine Corps under Commandant Chapman. Of course it was based on the self-confidence building, unarmed self-defense STRIKE foundation, a field-tested formula that has never failed. A subsequent Commandant eliminated that foundation, reducing the program to what the enlisted Marines called with disgust, *a pussy program.*

It was not bad; in fact, did considerable good, but it was still, in the eyes of the young men, a soft program. So it was far from the revolutionary unifying program needed. I stuck with it for as long as necessary to keep the Corps from having to revert to the Defense Department's absurd *touch-feel* program.

The upshot is that I have conducted about as many attitude studies in race relations as any person. From those studies, here is a reminder of the fact that assures success if the scientific approach is used: No matter how bad things sound from gossip, you can rely on the goodness of approximately 80% of both black and white Americans. They want humankind's basic equality respected. They want justice for all. That is a good, solid 80% on both sides. You can rely on it.

THE CROSS-CULTURAL DETECTIVE'S CHECKLIST

For closing this section on cross-cultural detective work, here is a checklist I use to analyze a case totally. First I try to see and deal with the jugular vein issues. Then, to make certain I or my associates have not missed something, I use the word, RECTIFY, as a mnemonic device to check every issue in conflict: each letter stands for the key word in each analytical concept on the following page:

R—REASON. Find the reason for the troublesome difference.

E—EXAGGERATION. Stop the exaggerations.

C—COMPARE. Compare the alleged difference to your own culture for forgotten similarities.

T—TOUGHEN UP. Don't let the alleged difference make you into an unhappy camper. You are the one who will suffer most.

I—IN. Join "in" with the local people until you can acquire some understanding of the reason for the difference.

F—FACTS. Get the facts; don't believe everything you hear *or read.*

Y—YOU. You may be the problem, especially so if others you know are enjoying themselves in the cross-cultural adventure; so go back to the "T," TOUGHEN UP AND HELP AMERICA.

CHAPTER 21

LOOSE ENDS, SUMMARY, AND CONCLUSION

INTRODUCTION

I taught overviews of this body of knowledge many times to college graduate classes both American and foreign. The core materials that I always teach are included in those first twenty chapters plus, for special audiences, the materials in *Attachments A* and *B* as well as in the first item in *Attachment C,* "The Reason for Underdevelopment." There are many items of related knowledge that crop up in many classes but are not absolutely necessary; that is, they are not necessary for an understanding of the basic theory or they did not figure strongly into the successful application of the theory in the crucial programs. However, they are important to many students; I'll place them in *Attachment C,* Part II, *Loose Ends.* These are the topics:

- Foreigners' Interests in U.S. Race Relations

- Program Origin and Its Necessary Leadership

- The Upshot—Your Leadership Toward Wisdom

- Good Philosophical Guidelines to Teach Your Children

- The Nature of the Brain

- The Nature of Rationality

- The Green-Eyed Monster: Greed

- The Upshot Regarding Strength, Happiness, and Leadership

- The Mania for Money and the American Monkey's Paw
- A Peaceful Political Revolution
- Communism, Capitalism, and the Life Value
- Russian Leaders
- The Russian People
- Collectivism versus Economic Individualism
- The Cooperative Nature of Americans
- Our Individualistic Nature
- How Much Freedom in Life's Balance?
- Liberals versus Conservatives
- Rational Control
- Justice or VIOLENCE
- Further Remarks about the Natural Law
- The Balanced Life Value and the Human Brain
- Humankind's Philosophical Freedom

SUMMARY

The Balanced Life Value is humankind's only *absolute* earthly value; all else is relative.

The life value along with the sub-values that support the life value provide the best description of human nature for social problem-solving purposes.

Figure 3, page 278, illustrates human nature in its most irreducible minimum description as a life-sustaining system of:

1. self-sustaining, or individualistic, tendencies on one side,

2. species-sustaining, or social, tendencies on the other, with

3. reason, serving as the (possible) balancing, or controlling, factor in the system. (Explain why we must say *possible* balancing factor rather than simply balancing factor.)

In answer, such sub-values as food, order, freedom, beauty, equality, physical contact, and physical exercise support the individual life. But if reason fails, that is, if we fail to use our reason to keep those sub-values or natural drives in proper life-supporting control, they can misfire and become life-destructive. The desire (need) for food can become gluttony; the need for order can develop into authoritarianism; freedom, into license; equality, into a superiority complex, etc.

On the social—species-sustaining—side of human nature, among the sub-values are love, charity, truth, honor, courage, pair-bonding loyalty, etc. These, too, can misfire. The species-preserving drive, itself, when felt strongly as in-group defensiveness can misfire in the form of aggressive war. Love for children can become dottiness that spoils children; honor can be exaggerated into false pride; courage, into recklessness, etc. See Figure 4, page 279.

The ideal government at any level of society, in order to maximize human well-being, must, in its laws, duplicate human nature. See Figure 5, page 280. All the control or cooperation or collectivism must be maintained that is necessary to sustain the group including its helpless members such as the children and the sick. After that, all the freedom possible must be maintained in order to maximize individual efforts, because (as the Communists have finally learned) there are strong individualistic as well as social inclinations in human nature.

As Figure 5 also indicates, the best possible way to maintain the proper (human nature duplicating) balance is through *individual rationality, democratically expressed.* When it is stifled, under a dictatorship, the felt right-to-life defense will threaten violence. We call this feeling, the right to self-defense, or the right of revolution. It is irrepressible. It expresses human nature—the Natural Law.

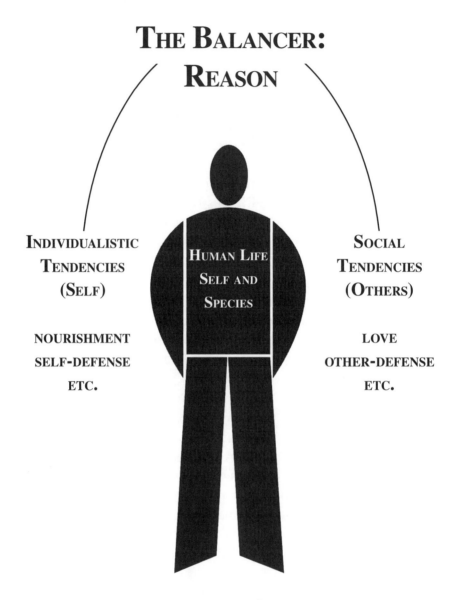

FIGURE 3
HUMAN NATURE SUMMARIZED

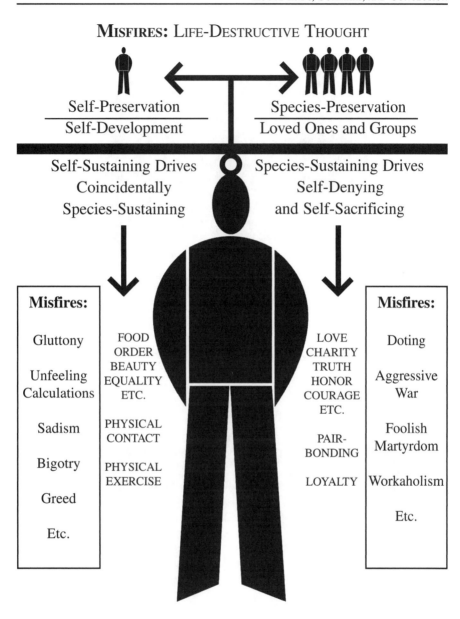

MISFIRES: LIFE-DESTRUCTIVE THOUGHT

Self-Preservation
Self-Development

Species-Preservation
Loved Ones and Groups

Self-Sustaining Drives
Coincidentally
Species-Sustaining

Species-Sustaining Drives
Self-Denying
and Self-Sacrificing

Misfires:

Gluttony

Unfeeling
Calculations

Sadism

Bigotry

Greed

Etc.

FOOD
ORDER
BEAUTY
EQUALITY
ETC.

PHYSICAL
CONTACT

PHYSICAL
EXERCISE

LOVE
CHARITY
TRUTH
HONOR
COURAGE
ETC.

PAIR-
BONDING

LOYALTY

Misfires:

Doting

Aggressive
War

Foolish
Martyrdom

Workaholism

Etc.

FIGURE 4
THE INDIVIDUAL
BALANCED LIFE VALUE
HUMAN NATURE IN DETAIL

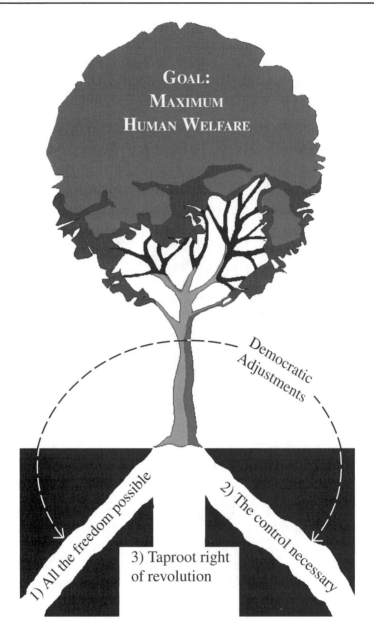

FIGURE 5
THE IDEAL POLITICAL-ECONOMIC SYSTEM:
A HUMAN-LIFE SUPPORTING SYSTEM

CONCLUSION

How does one conclude what is most basically a thought-piece on humankind's most important knowledge: the nature of human nature? I cannot bring myself to conclude with a review of theory. Even the most important theory is important only as a guideline and inspiration for action.

Through the recent years, I have persuaded scores, in fact hundreds, of college graduate students to put the theory of humankind's goodness into action, meaningfully, in their own daily lives. Goodness in a human life, you know, second only to total sacrifice for another, is expressed most meaningfully, constantly in little details.

I assign four exercises for my students to practice in order to establish a life-style of goodness for the dual benefit of their own increased happiness and for the benefit of humankind. I'll not spell out the details, but rather, give you the four ideas; you must experiment with them in your own neighborhood in order to encourage them or assign them most effectively to your own loved ones and students.

Give-Away Happiness and Encouragement. Within reason, to the extent possible, henceforth, give away greetings to everyone you meet in your home neighborhood or around your workplace. Simply nod non-verbally and look away casually, pleasantly, without waiting for the payback of a greeting in return.

Strengthen the Family. Find out what one thing you could do or stop doing to make your own family (or closest friends, if no family) happiest. Within reason, try it for a month.

Strengthen the Nation. Persuade associates from other social groups to allow you to visit their places of worship with them. Do this whether you are religious or not. Advise that you are seeking universal moral lessons and that you are interested in promoting cross-racial, cross-cultural, and cross-ethnic understanding in the nation and world. Of course, be certain, tactfully, to enjoy the visits.

Reduce Tensions. Henceforth, endeavor to allow nothing that happens on the crowded highways to upset you—even if you have to take legal action against some malfeasance. This may be the ultimate test of your growing maturity.

Remember, these exercises in maturity will not just improve society, the idea is to improve you're own well-being.

BOOK TWO

THE

ATTACHMENTS

INTRODUCTION

HUMAN NATURE'S GUIDELINES FOR LOW-INTENSITY WARFARE AND PUBLIC EDUCATION

As Amitai Etzioni and other leading thinkers have stated or clearly implied, the proper analysis of human nature will allow humans to solve our greatest social problems. These attachments—Book II— prove the accuracy of that judgment. Human nature, as described and applied in Parts I and II, allows us to unify humankind cross-culturally by emphasizing our deepest common bonds and by seeing through the divisive veil of our incorrectly perceived, or only apparent, differences.

Attachment A uses the guidelines of human nature to explain how our American military personnel can develop a reliable defense force along with the respect, friendship, and trust of the world's people.

Attachment B employs the guidelines to explain in some detail how all human beings can be educated well and happily through public school reform. Its immediate purpose is national more than it is global: It is to avoid further public school, and national, decline.

Attachment C clarifies uncertainties occasionally raised by skeptics studying the theory. It helps one understand not only what life style is most effective—making for happiness—but also why it is right in that it conforms to the life-protecting laws of human nature.

In general, these attachments exemplify the fact that a proper understanding of human nature will let us solve any of our great human relations problems. Conversely, without these attachments, the impression most likely would be that the theory applies only to the resolution of cross-cultural conflicts.

ATTACHMENT A

WORLD STRATEGY FOR AN ERA OF LOW-INTENSITY WARFARE

INTRODUCTION

In this section I will submit the more serious and sophisticated low-intensity warfare considerations, plus some of the hard-to-get details on institutional-change problems from an actual case. Through most of Book I, I omitted the institutional-change struggles encountered in the field. But unquestionably, they took up more than half of my time, and will be operative against anyone who tries to introduce *anything new* into the social sciences.

PART I

BACKGROUND

Usually, you cannot relate institutional-change case-details publicly without sounding petty or setting yourself up for litigation and grief. The lessons, however, constitute "must-know" items for change agents. The problems are inherent in any major modernizing or upgrading effort in any field. They become almost hopeless barriers in monopolistic fields, such as the military and public education, where there is no accountability in profit-and-loss statements. I'll weave the two bodies of knowledge (military facts and change techniques) together as much as possible, as they are always interwoven in fact.

These detailed military considerations are so important to our modern defense strategy that they merit this special treatment in conjunction with some repetition of materials presented earlier. They include the extensive discussion of STRIKE (unarmed fight training) as the modern foundation-training for all fighting men and women both for high- and low-intensity combat. The effort to introduce this training into the Marine Corps is used as a case study on the difficulties of institutional change.

THE MODERN PROBLEM:
A NEW ERA OF LOW-INTENSITY CONFLICT

Since Vietnam, our U.S. military wisely has struggled for a strategy to use in counterinsurgency warfare, the new name used currently (to avoid reminders of Vietnam) is Low-intensity Conflict (LIC). Meanwhile, out of the frustrating inability to find that strategy, many military officers have argued self-deceptively that Vietnam was only another conventional war. Actually, it was not only something new but also an ominous portent of the future nature of political violence. If we cannot indeed find a new pacifying strategy for unifying our own ethnic, racial, and economic groups as well as for winning back the restless people of the pivotal Third World, a new age of terrorism, little wars, and street-violence is, most likely, just beginning; this is true, especially in view of the high-level corrupting influence of the multibillion dollar illegal drug traffic. Consequently, this attachment focuses on that need for a new, morally oriented military strategy in terms of the rejected or lost lessons from Vietnam and Iraq. No matter how moral our excuses sound, we cannot win the respect and trust of the Third World's captive people if we are willing to bomb and kill them because of their criminal leaders.

In a nutshell, what the new strategy demands is the conversion of our military forces into a true *peace-force* worthy of both halves of the name. To be a winner, the strategy can never again contain a simple Machiavellian America-first policy. It must be a strategy recognizable to the world as based on our high moral principles of

1776, which are beneficial to all humankind, *and are absolutely in our own best interest in the long run, to support democracy.*

Who does not admit that there is somewhat of a moral breakdown, or at least a moral problem, in our new overly urbanized America? It has been abundantly evident across *every* level of society in the past two decades—even in the White House and in Congress. It is past time for someone to set a higher level of moral behavior—a better moral atmosphere—for the entire nation. But who?

It may have to be the U.S. military; most logically, the Marine Corps, or else the Special Forces.

As you shall see, under the enlightened encouragement of two Marine commandants, this values-approach has come close to getting the new strategy started twice in our allegedly ultraconservative Marine Corps. The difficulty that stopped us the first time and possibly the second is ironic: To educate our military personnel to become, virtually *warrior knights,* adequately trustworthy and respected, requires as a starter, their retraining to considerably higher levels of individual self-confidence, higher than was ever before enjoyed by any prior military force on earth. That, in turn, requires a program of sophisticated training in the modern, scientific, *individual, unarmed* fighting skills. As mentioned, the project was approved twice at the top Marine Corps level, but before we could institutionalize either program effectively, each was watered down or distorted into something different and inadequate if not downright negative for combat training.

THE INSTITUTIONAL-CHANGE PROBLEM IN A BUREAUCRACY

Why did those reversals in the USMC occur after having won top-level (Commandant) endorsement both times? Because, for a truly revolutionary reform in a major bureaucracy, it is usually not enough to win only the top-level support. You must also win a network of support inside and perhaps also around the bureaucracy. Otherwise the tradition-bound forces therein will likely defy and defeat the official change. In my Marine Corps program, both times, the reform called for introduction, Corps-wide, of the new, safe form of boxer-punching training (STRIKE). It instills the necessary self-confidence foundation for the properly self-controlled use of force in men who carry weapons legally and have a license to kill. An ethical life, in peace or in war, includes standing against wrongdoers, especially bullies. Consequently, it had better be established on a foundation of physical prowess, or it will likely include many painful failures.

What was the reason for stopping the establishment of this physical foundation in the new USMC values programs both times? Excellent attitude studies are usually required to find the answer to that type of question. I conducted such studies the first time and found a surprising answer.

THE INDIVIDUAL DEVELOPMENT PROBLEM

According to my brief but highly reliable (in-depth interview) studies, the officers, in general, were afraid they could not cope with (learn or teach) the rough boxing skills. (Most admitted that they wanted the skill and started once in their lives to learn it, but were hurt or embarrassed and gave it up.) Since we have developed a method to teach the boxer's punching skills safely—without embarrassment and the customary dangers of deadly brain-injuries—and since key, compatible martial arts add-ons can be taught rapidly, the necessary skills training is finally possible.

Even if we have achieved this decisive breakthrough to developing the individual self-confidence needed to field a worldwide low-intensity warfare strategy, a prior question must be faced. Do we possess the knowledge needed to teach the moral requirements for a successful strategy? That question must be addressed against the background of the nortorious Ugly American problem that alienated us from much of the world and that helped defeat us in Vietnam.

THE BEGINNING OF OUR MODERN GLOBAL PROBLEM

The great Cold War was waged by the U.S. to stop the aggressive expansion of communism during the post-World War II period. That containment was successful. However, as is with all warfare, our American effort was, in ways, heavy-handed. Its worst aspect was the notorious Ugly Americanism that alienated foreign peoples everywhere. It derived from a somewhat innocent but nonetheless offensive superiority complex. Despite the gratitude toward, and love for America, the world's people discerned a root-level ugliness that accompanied our financial generosity, and, unquestionably, this perception resulted in a love/hate attitude toward us worldwide. It continues to express itself in many ways ranging from the budget deficit to acts of terrorism.

The Conclusive Cost of Ugly Americanism: Ugly Americanism rose to its culmination in Vietnam. It was called the *Gook Syndrome.* It was a significant cause of our first loss of a major war. We alienated, helped demoralize, and definitely failed to inspire our own allies, the South Vietnamese people.

To check the probable validity or fallacy of this contention against your own values, how would you react to a group of wealthy foreigners (say Japanese) who came here en masse and constantly referred to all the members of your family as gooks or often something worse: stupid gooks or f'n gooks? (Ask your friends and relatives who served in Vietnam.)

Once the personal trust and confidentiality of the Vietnamese common folk were gained (according to my experiences), we found that many were truly uncertain about which side in that war was worse for them. Our Ugly Americanism kept us from tipping the scales decisively against the Communists. Understand that although we and democracy lost there, it was very close. Had American leadership been adequately enlightened to lead us across the ideological barriers and relate respectfully with those humble peasants, democracy would have prevailed easily.

UNPUBLICIZED ATTRACTIVE AMERICANISM

There was always an attractive American counter-movement to the costly Ugly Americanism overseas during the Cold War. That counter-movement was generally referred to as the win-the-people effort. Many of the foreign elite considered President Eisenhower to be its quiet champion. My specific moral, values-based approach was, unofficially, a part of that general win-the-people strategy. However, for good reasons (such as economic graft and secret assassinations in America's general pacification program in Vietnam) I always kept my projects decisively separate. I introduced no civic action (material assistance) projects in order to avoid the stigma of inevitable economic-graft under the wartime circumstances.

Nevertheless, our program had small chance to succeed in Vietnam. It was a case of too little, too late, not to mention the tremendous blunders on my part. Even though that war for us is now over, the waste of human lives continues; the tragedy of democracy's loss in Vietnam is far from over. Tens of thousands of refugees are still being brutalized in South East Asia.

SIGNIFICANT PROGRAM HISTORICAL DETAILS

Korea: As a result of the 1988 anti-U.S. riots by one of our closest international friends, the South Koreans, I now feel free to mention that a strong love/hate relationship has long persisted between our two populations living and stationed there. Incidentally, many Americans died there in the 1950s protecting democracy. (The 1988 Olympics revealed both the love and hate feelings.)

I was once tasked with improving the attitudes of some 80,000 Americans (mainly military) living there. The specific, assigned goal was to stop the theft of copper wire (essential to the military communication system) along the dangerous Demilitarized Zone. Illogically, in view of the danger to South Korea, Korean guards were allowing Korean paupers to steal the "American wire." The paupers were using the copper to make items for sale in the American Post Exchanges. The South Korean soldiers guarding the wire advised in soul-wrenching terms that they had been insulted incessantly by expression of the gook syndrome. Therefore they had become negative toward protecting things American.

Thanks to the strong, quiet support, and tactical guidance of one U.S. Army General, Bonesteel, breaking the back of the theft came surprisingly easy considering the difficult nature of some of the issues. I was able to reduce and control the negative attitude and related theft problems through a whirlwind speaking tour along the Demilitarized Zone addressing ten thousand troops, one thousand at a time.

It is easy when top command support is present. Top leadership support in any society makes social problem-solving fairly easy rather than virtually impossible. (Just don't forget your supporting network in order to preclude a backsliding when command changes.)

The point is that Ugly Americanism overseas is not the fault of the masses of young, enlisted personnel; they respond favorably to good values education. The problem traces back to inadequate leadership—that is, to poor education and uninformed training.

EVIDENCE OF A SECRET WEAPON

Another research project in Korea provided the most startling and informative group attitude change work that I ever observed. We conducted an experiment to see if a large team of military trainers with only twenty hours of training, and without my personal participation, could inspire fast attitude improvement among one large organization of U.S. troops. (My participation was omitted in response to the critique, proven false, that it was my personal style rather than the scientific approach that was achieving the program successes.) The results of the crash course at first were that attitudes rose for the entire contingent of Americans, but, disappointingly, only up to the line of minor, if any, statistical significance. However, an amazing thing happened: In a follow-up study, we found that in reaction to that small improvement in American attitudes toward the Koreans, the attitudes of the associated Korean soldiers toward Americans *skyrocketed off the charts!* That event revealed the greatest secret weapon any nation ever possessed: Our underdog-oriented young Americans in uniform. If they were trained and tasked with winning back the respect of the world, these young Americans (many only teenagers) would succeed without question, especially in the Third World. I also believe the increasing number of females in uniform will help us with this civilizing mission. Why? Judging from my thirty-five years in the field of promoting human consideration, or deeper respect for life, in all of the cultures I have studied, women are considerably superior to men.

The problem is that this secret weapon, the respect-winning potential of our young enlisted personnel, is still unrecognized, if not doubted, by many American leaders who come from upper middle-income social strata.

Neglect and Denigration of the Secret Weapon: Many military leaders speak of the high-type young enlisted men who stand for the best in America. But, too often, when out of the public eye and in the field, some officers appeal to the lowest human drives when addressing enlisted men in combat outfits. These misguided leaders believe that such leveling with the troops is necessary in order to establish reckless, aggressive attitudes for combat. Drinking, vulgarity, womanizing, and immorality are often winked at, if not endorsed outright; even infidelity. Along with the detriment to our nation, this lowlife encouragement among our modern, already-skeptical teenagers promises problems for the officers in combat, not excluding fragging (murder of the officers themselves).

From Okinawa, the In-Depth Nature of Cross-Cultural Misunderstandings: After America decided to turn Okinawa back to the Japanese in the early 1970s, it caused strife; there were demonstrations at our military gates. I accepted the contract to try to hold the lid on violence during the most crucial period. Since I was already conducting programs in three other countries, preparation of the orientation team for Okinawa was somewhat rushed and superficial. Fortunately, the members of the (military) training team became dynamic teachers. That fact as well as the opportunity to use STRIKE (the unarmed combat training) gave us adequate success at the crucial time.

After we left (stopped the special training), negative attitudes boiled up again. That type of backsliding in this work is inevitable. Under the stress of modern transient and crowding population conditions, values education is not a one-shot deal. It must become a part of our basic education.

A Terminology Question: Warfare or Diplomacy? Perhaps the most striking success of this (research-guided, values-based, behavior-changing) program was the installation of the missile system in NATO, mentioned earlier. After ninety percent of the Americans had grown so dissatisfied that they were quitting and going home, once called in, we were able to reverse the negative attitudes within a few weeks. The recovery was so fast, recall, that despite my lack of an engineering education (and mechanical ability), I was made temporary director of the company's branch subsidiary for its move into the second country.

These cases suggest the possible payoff in the fields of management and leadership from this new body of knowledge in human relations. The term *ideological warfare* is useful in working with military personnel; but with overseas civilian operations, the term *mass diplomacy* is also equally accurate and more descriptive. (It can contribute as much to the reduction of our trade deficit as any purely economic factor.)

THE MORAL-VALUES-GUIDED PROGRAM IN COMBAT: REVIEW

Toward the end of my seventeen years in the overseas work, I was invited into Vietnam. I was asked to introduce the approach into the war specifically to upgrade the Navy and Marine Corps' Personal Response Programs. The Navy was attempting unsuccessfully to integrate its riverboat patrol fleet with Vietnamese sailors. Similarly, the Marines wanted to expand their daring Combined Action Platoon (CAP) program. In the latter, Marines, uniquely, lived and stayed overnight in the Vietnamese villages. Once the Marine Corps ran out of volunteers who were naturals for this frightening, friend-winning duty, they needed a special training program for men to be assigned to that unusual combined task of winning friendship by day and fighting at night. I got both the Navy and Marine Corps assignments (and donated both efforts after my Marine brother, a Gunnery Sergeant, was killed there).

In Vietnam, since the approach expressed a heretical (friend-winning) formula for victory, it was especially necessary to conduct it quietly and unassertively. Also, long before we went into Vietnam, my civilian contract director in the Army Research Office advised (ordered) me, to work unobtrusively, *in the woodwork,* was the term he used. Hence most of my civilian programs as well as the Marine project required confidentiality regarding my role as an ideologist.

After the war, a more troublesome obstacle to describing the program's success and potential soon developed. This barrier was the face-saving explanation for the loss of that war.

THE FACE-SAVING

My military students tell me candidly that when nations lose wars, many military officers make the excuse that the politicians caused the loss. *Vietnam seems to be no exception. The argument, sincere and well-presented, goes this way: Vietnam was never a people's war at all. It was entirely conventional. We lost because the politicians did not let us make it even more frightful—more bombs, more mines in harbors, more hot pursuit, etc.*

My objection to that thesis is not that it might not have merit. Rather, it is their accompanying argument that the winning the people would not have worked better, and with much less loss of life.

INTRODUCING THE WIN-THE-PEOPLE APPROACH IN AMERICA

During the closing years of the Vietnam fiasco, Pepperdine University offered a worldwide Masters degree extension program that was pursued mainly by mid-rank military officers. I was asked as an itinerant professor to teach our new values-based, educational-reform and conflict-resolution method in that degree program.

The officers (students) sent back critiques of the course to the university. The following are typical evaluations that were submitted to the University which later forwarded copies to me:

- From a Marine officer at Parris Island: *Taking this course was one of the most significant events of my life.*

- A Naval officer, Norfolk: Super!! *Best leadership course (personal and professional) I ever attended.*

- An Air Force officer, Homestead: *The best course I have had in 18 years.*

- An Army officer, Fort Jackson: *Excellent. Action!*

- A Marine officer, Iwakuni, Japan: *Changed many of my attitudes toward making changes in my job and my home.*

How does one explain these enthusiastic responses from experienced combat officers to a mere college course during the especially cynical (post-Vietnam) period of military history? The answer is contained in another evaluation from an officer/student in Hawaii. He wrote: *Finally, a college course that offers some hope.*

THE NATURE AND SOURCE OF THE NEW VALUES-BASED STRATEGY

Why is it that this new values-based problem-solving approach is effective for previously baffling human-relations problems both at home and abroad?

As spelled-out previously, the new approach is based on a more complete, research-obtained description of human nature. That description provides the guidelines for a total, properly balanced (mind-body-values) education. Further, it clarifies the hierarchies of moral values that make conflict resolution possible on reliable, lasting grounds. The goal of this values-based, attitude-changing strategy is nothing less than the cessation of war plus the decisive reduction of all domestic violence.

COLD WAR FIELD PROBLEMS

My initial Cold War assignments, first, as a State Department (USIA) grantee, and later, as a military contractor, recall, were to overcome the culture shock and the resulting Ugly Americanism in and around the overseas communities called *Little Americas*. Those bustling communities sprang up all over the world like wealthy outposts in the post-World War II American era of history. (Those overseas communities were, incidentally, ideal field laboratories for study of our current and growing domestic urban, ethnic problems.)

The total solution, we finally determined, had four, and in the most difficult cases five, steps:

1. Overcome culture shock suffered by Americans,

2. Reduce the *resulting* Ugly Americanism among Americans toward their host-nationals,

3. Eliminate the active anti-Americanism among the host-nationals (that had arisen almost entirely in *reaction* to the insulting Ugly Americanism) and then,

4. On that improved attitudinal foundation, improve the allied effort ranging from better multicultural office work to greater combined-action effectiveness in combat.

5. In those situations where general physical fear of the foreign men was involved, it needed to be removed by teaching the Americans some unarmed combat confidence. (This is a new historical phenomenon for Americans. When America was basically a rural—very physical—society, until shortly after World War I and into the World War II period, boxing and hunting were two of the few common-folk participant sports. No more; self-confidence suffers. Similarly, in cross-cultural relations, if there are important intellectual insecurities, such as the

inability to read, they, too, cause trouble and need to be relieved.)

After the old method of preparing diplomats for foreign cultures, through language and culture study, was found to be ineffective for changing negative attitudes (and often made them worse), we started from absolute scratch to try to find a successful approach. Through persistent, research-guided, experimental efforts, gradually, ever so gradually, we succeeded. However, success definitely required the development of an entirely new human values (moral) understanding of human nature, and a new educational method for conflict resolution based on the resulting new, advanced understanding of human values or human nature.

SHIFT OF ATTENTION FROM MY WORK TO YOURS

Recall from the book that my ultimate goal is to encourage and inspire others (you) to use and improve this values-based method for violence-reduction. Here, before the next few pages, please make a strong change in mind-set from my work to yours of the future. Read each warning, no matter how casually worded, with the attention you would give a police car that stops in front of your house in the night with those multicolored lights a-flashing.

The Almost Insurmountable Opposition to Change. I want to discuss with you, again, the notorious difficulty humans have in accepting anything new in the social sciences. I am sure you have encountered the problem. Whether we call it the *Kill Socrates Syndrome,* or the *Not-Invented-Here Rejection,* or simply, inertia, most of us criticize the closed-mindedness involved. Yet, we all tend to be guilty when we are the ones confronted with new ideas that encroach upon our own familiar ways.

Why are humans like this? We are all so inclined, you know— not just the bad guys.

One answer is this: All change that renders our established knowledge obsolete actually threatens our status, and possibly, our personal material well-being, at least in the short run. It feels a little like a survival threat. As explained in *Attachment C,* there is also probably a certain *fix* in the psyche in favor of one's active values, or against change. (To accomplish a change of attitude—to reinforce and activate the deep, constructive, universal values, that is, to open the closed mind—new knowledge must be presented with emotional impact.)

Despite the reasons, this apparent increased closing of the American mind becomes more dangerous than ever under modern conditions as our frontiers disappear. Communication and transportation improvements facilitate negative forces, such as the giant illegal drug cartels.

Consequently, if we well-meaning members of society do not open our minds to new (different) ideas offering better answers, we can be defeated more easily by the negative interests. Great nations do fall. Remember that all leading nations before us did decline. The odds for us, judging from that history, are not promising. Our domestic problems are simply too serious for us to continue to remain strong and lead without solving those problems: education for all, adequate medicine for all, a system of justice for all, and drug control. The international situation is equally challenging. All, at bottom, are moral issues.

ATTACHMENT A

PART II

VITAL LOW-INTENSITY CONFLICT PREPARATION AND DECISIVE INSTITUTIONAL-CHANGE CONSIDERATIONS

That completes the background for delving into the most serious aspects of a new values-based, low-intensity warfare strategy and the almost insurmountable institutional-change problem. Let us now consider the more sensitive, vital, and decisive details of those two closely related topics.

THE LEADERS WHO DARED AND THE SUCCESSFUL PROGRAMS

Several high-ranking overseas American leaders used this new approach and gave credit. I'll cite a few of the most important overseas achievements with men's names or at least with the official positions of the outstanding persons who made the success possible. I hope that the inclusion of this information will serve to the credit of these men, and will inspire others. Also hoping to stimulate needed debate, I'll cite these past *quiet successes* in the context of the most important topic of this attachment: America's best possible military strategy for this Low-Intensity Conflict Era. Related decisions on that topic will determine America's rise into the trusted moral leadership of the world, or conversely, our degeneration into a selfish, nationalistic predator nation sustaining our standard of living off the sufferings of others around the globe.

Musing just below the surface of clear articulation in our society, especially in military circles, is a great debate regarding military training. Primarily, for what type of warfare strategy should our military be building and training?

1. Nuclear war?

2. Massive and irresistible conventional, big bomb war (Iraq)?

3. Fast-strike commando-like attacks after having delivered overwhelming artillery and air strikes against civilian populated areas, as in Panama. (How bad is this? Think of your city police force acting so irresponsibly in your neighborhood rather than, themselves, risking close-in gunfights with criminals.)

4. Ideological (win-the-people) efforts by our worldwide military personnel during peacetime and also during combat operations where all killing is carefully targeted at the officially identified and condemned top level criminal leaders, rather than captive civilians *and soldiers.*

That four-sided issue, inside the U.S. military, and increasingly sensed by the people, started seriously in Vietnam. Shortly after the easy, and therefore, popular, victory in Iraq (where over 100,000 were killed and 200,000 wounded), the issue has resurfaced.

THE WIN-THE-PEOPLE PROGRAM IN VIETNAM

Inside the USMC's oral history, confidential whispering about the superiority of the Combined Action Platoons persists. The better CAPs were among the most successful *combat outfits;* that is, they were not just people winners. Official records reveal that they also had the best combat records of any type organization. Yet, semiofficial Marine publications, occasionally, vehemently, attack the truth of that knowledge or else identify the Personal Response Program as a mere comparative-religion study, as it was during an early, *intermediate stage,* a period of failure.

When I was asked to introduce the ideological training package into the CAPs, I was told that the religious model had failed completely to inspire average Marines for the tricky CAP duties. As a point of relevant ideological interest, that religiously oriented program (mainly for the study of Buddhism) had emphasized the thought that the Vietnamese are *As Different on the Inside.* That was the name of their key training manual when I accepted the ideological task. Our ideology reversed that message. It teaches, as you know, that all persons, basically, are the same: equal human beings with the same motivating values on the inside.

Program Use in the U.S. Army: Eventually, after being advised that our new materials had been borrowed unofficially from the Navy, by the Army, I attended one of the Army's in-country reorientations for newly arriving advisers in Vietnam. They were using our Navy materials verbatim. Unfortunately this was too late and too little in the overall struggle. But through this values-based approach, according to my experiences, in Vietnam and half a dozen other countries, democracy through more constructive grass-roots efforts eventually could have prevailed where communism, dictatorship, or confusion now obtains. That thought takes us full into the issue of the best possible military strategy where a primary consideration is relations with the many economically poor populations of the world.

AMERICA'S PROBABLE, BUT LOSING, LOW-INTENSITY WARFARE STRATEGY

Since the Cold War's nuclear massive retaliation policy and conventional warfare containment strategy are no longer feasible for use in Third World *insurgency wars,* the question is: *How do we devise a strategy that will fit a low-intensity warfare era?*

The absence of a suitable strategy derives from too many wealth-spoiled and isolated American leaders with a childlike perception of foreigners. The Evil Empire has disappeared. Isolated Americans are still afraid to deal with any foreign peoples who might be poor and angry. They become the new monsters who justify irresponsible violence that risks little to the drivers of the war machine. These perceived monsters, these alleged fanatics, are actually the same desperate paupers of the world that I have been interviewing in Asia and Latin America for many years. Do you know who they are?

They are mainly—and I mean even the peasants who grow and sell illegal drugs—illiterate, angry men whose families are facing starvation while their poor lands are being exploited by outsiders ranging from absentee landlords to drug barons. They seem to be fanatical enemies, but are the same as, just more desperate than, our American workers when they go on strike.

Waging warfare against these men and their families with artillery fire is similar to shooting down West Virginia's striking miners and their families in front of the mine shafts.

This is a semi-fascist formula that promises only to further alienate the entire Third World. About all we can do with the commando approach is to sit off the shores of Third World countries (or inside of isolated, fortified enclaves) with our *killer-outfits* to be unleashed against suffering peasants involved in their anti-feudalistic revolutions. Is that to be America's low role into the 21st Century? Hopefully not.

There is a better alternative for our low-intensity support of world peace, one that promotes, for all the world to see, equal respect, justice, and democracy for all the world's people. Those three goals can no longer be separated in the realpolitik of the increasingly well-informed world.

THE SECRET TO SUCCESS: NICER BUT TOUGHER FIGHTERS

The win-the-people alternative is not only good, but admirably American. We can train our American young persons, especially, our teenage enlisted personnel, to seize the initiative during peacetime by winning respect and friendship among all Third World peoples.

This is not through so-called pacifist *do-goodism;* rather it is through increased individual fighting abilities that provide the confidence needed to approach and build closer friendship with foreign peoples. Then, risking one's life to defend destitute foreign people and democracy, if requested by those grass-roots friends, will make sense. It did not make sense to the ideologically untrained young Americans in Vietnam who were in an American military society that scorned the local people.

During our Cold War programs, as described in this work, we gradually struggled onto three innovations that gave us the training details needed to prevail in the anti-dictatorship struggle in this new era of low-intensity conflict:

1. A way to teach unarmed, confidence-building fighting skills fast, safely, and effectively (as the indispensable physical foundation for a self-risking, *others-protective—* or ethical—behavior pattern),

2. The educational materials needed to re-inspire our 1776 democratic ideology and to reestablish mutual respect with the world's people, and

3. A successful cross-cultural conflict-resolution methodology for use on a mass scale.

The Individual Fighting-Skill Training. First, in response to the decisive need to build greater personal confidence in average military personnel (especially for the most difficult programs), we learned to teach the professional hitting skills of the boxer/puncher without boxing's dangers.

Although this required a sophisticated, high-type coaching staff of not only experienced boxers but unusual coaches (at its core), it was a significant breakthrough that allows the training of masses of men and women. Their newly acquired fighting ability allowed the average man—including the physically weaker ones—to walk unafraid of, and therefore, with a friendly manner toward, strangers even in a foreign land.

This superior confidence derives not from the fancy footwork and jabbing ability of most successful amateur boxers, but something considerably simpler and better. It is the penetrating, close, inside, stand-and-fight, power-punching ability understood and taught only by the world's best boxing coaches. Those few who can teach it, guard the almost-secret skill for "their boys," and few could explain it anyway. They can only gradually coach it into action. But it is a skill that should be conveyed to our military men if we find that they will accept the moral values of *the defenders* versus those values of irresponsible kids away from home, or of cold killers.

As one medium-sized Marine lieutenant observed after the training: "It allowed me to approach and befriend groups of men in the Asian ports who used to put me off. Previously, I crossed streets in the middle of a block to avoid them. Now, I actually find myself walking up to them, smiling at them, asking them questions, and thinking to them in my mind, 'I am not afraid of you any more, so, now, we can be friends.'"

Multiply that attitude by five hundred thousand to a million overseas American military personnel and contemplate the effect. Of course, it also requires the ideological and cross-cultural conflict-resolution training; but success with those lessons comes quickly, *but only,* after the physical confidence of trainees is in place. Why? Because those lessons bring with them the uplifting sensation of the universal constructive values in human affairs and require only self-confidence to activate.

The boxer/puncher's close-in, confidence-building skills can be taught effectively in a short period of time when the new safety features are built into the training. This speedy training solves the frustrating time problem that has discouraged military organizations all over the world who have tried to use the martial arts for this and similar goals. The martial arts either take too long to teach or else force coaches to teach the easy-to-learn, dirty fighting techniques in order to provide anything effective in the short time allotted for this instruction. The dirty-fighting lessons create a frame of mind that undercuts both the protector/defender feeling and the protector/ defender image. Both of the latter are especially needed by Americans considering the persistent Ugly American problem, not to mention the devastating widely publicized My Lai incident.

The Role of the Martial Arts. I am a devoted student of the martial arts and I have encouraged my children and students toward that study. But the main reasons for that interest and encouragement are not to acquire fighting skills. For that, I practice and teach primarily the short, direct hitting skills, that is, to hit close-in, without *telegraphing* actions, and with total body power.

I study and encourage the martial arts because they involve self-discipline and the study of philosophy (if they are authentic); they help develop flexibility and they can provide some good grappling techniques as add-ons when hitting fails or should not be used.

The martial arts fighting techniques were developed two thousand years ago for unarmed men to use against warriors with swinging knives and long spears, or against men in heavy armored-type clothing who could be kicked off-balance and down. As the expert martial artist, Bruce Lee, found, and as I did while judging cross-matches in Asia, the stylized martial arts techniques are not at all effective against even a fair amateur boxer.

It is time, it seems, to develop a complete (practical, effective, safe, ethical, easy) American martial arts style that is realistic as a fighting skill. Such would blend in effective techniques and especially a life-guiding philosophy. Former Marine Jack Hoban's *taijutsu* program in New Jersey and California represents an unusually enlightened effort that may fill this need. As for the comparative ineffectiveness of the martial arts against a good amateur boxer or wrestler, don't confuse the average black belt martial artist with a *lifetime* expert such as Hoban or his teacher, the great Masaaki Hatsumi. I have seen Hatsumi subdue *good* men with only slight movements. He is quite amazing.

If you are going to give your life to the unarmed fighting skills, take a year to learn to box well, and then change to a martial art for the rest of your life's study. Don't consider becoming a pro boxer unless you are very hungry and super-good and willing to get hit hard... brain-damagingly hard.

As a sincere change agent, and probably an intellectual, you must know that without these skills, I have found it to be virtually impossible to activate the moral base and do the cross-cultural detective work on a grass-roots basis. It is too terrifying for most of us. The evidence for this is the fact that when I left the fighting skill training out of the more difficult programs, the programs never got off the ground.

The Moral Base. As the most important breakthrough (for use in all low-intensity warfare programs), we have learned to teach the American free-and-equal ideology in the way that is highly motivational to both Americans and others in every land tested. This is the ideology of our basic American documents, which voice the universals. That straightforward ideology is not to be confused with the specious interpretations of Jefferson's thoughts found in many modern American academic documents that attempt to downgrade his egalitarian principles. I refer instead to the unequivocating ideology of Thomas Jefferson, written forthrightly in our U.S. Declaration of Independence. It is the free-and-equal ideology that was expressed emphatically in the thousands of questionnaire responses from American and foreign common folk in a dozen countries around the globe.

Cross-Cultural Detective Work. Guided by that American and universal common-folk ideology, we have developed a cross-cultural conflict-resolution methodology that is unquestionably & revolutionarily effective. It is truly a conciliatory system based on equal respect rather than combative, human-rights programs oblivious to duties. Do you understand?

All race relations programs that I have seen used in the U.S. or in the world (including the distorted version of my own program misused in the USMC during the 1970s) have been driven by power politics rather than exclusively, as they should be, by scientific studies, for the agreed (persuaded) benefit of all factions.

PROMISED RESULTS IN THE
ANGRY ANTI-AMERICAN COUNTRIES

If the total educational program described in this work were mastered and taught to an entire military division, it could win the people of a hostile country such as Libya, Iran, Iraq, or any Latin American country so strongly to our side, ideologically, and as friends, that no leader in that country would dare speak against the U.S. unjustly.

This, of course, is the ideal ideological foundation for a worldwide low-intensity warfare strategy.

ADDITIONAL EVIDENCE AND RESEARCH POSSIBILITIES

For additional information regarding the bit of history made by this program, but that is being lost, here are key leads that could be pursued along with those mentioned previously.

Military Testimonials and Commendations. Official commendations for this program from the United States Army, Navy, and Marine Corps as well as the Vietnamese Navy are historic documents of record. These include the Civil Actions Medal awarded by the Republic of Vietnam (General Cao Van Vien). The most convincing documentation, perhaps to Americans, derives from the bottom-line figures: the official financing. The records of the Army Research Office will show that the consistent success on each of these projects for a period of over ten years resulted, each time, in a succeeding contract. Meaningful funds (several million dollars in program expense monies) were allocated.

In addition, many interesting attitude studies conducted to guide the development of this program can be found in an official manual prepared for the Army Research Office. The manual is entitled *Fight The Cold War, 1964.*

Also on record are copies of an official message from the American Naval Commander in Vietnam recommending to the U.S. Chief of Naval Operations, in Washington (twenty years ago), that this program be considered for use by our military forces worldwide. That message was never delivered. Why not? It was short-stopped by some daring opposition in the Navy Annex. This answer carries an important institutional-change lesson: The fault was mine for not arranging to hand-carry the world-changing suggestion back from the headquarters in Asia to Washington.

Thanks to a Navy Chief, James Hummel, an outstanding illustrator, a series of three manuals was presented for culture-shock issues in Thailand. That program, too, received a U.S. Army commendation. The cross-cultural program was named, officially, *TARGET*, 1969.

Finally, many of the inspirational ideological guidelines can still be found in Marine Corps leadership manuals written during the troubled 1970s. They can be identified by their emphasis on *the equal human life value* in peace and in combat.

Cabinet-Level Civilian Assessment. There is an interesting footnote to military history that verifies the hope that was seen in these values-based programs in Vietnam at the time when all else there was being tagged as a part of the hopeless failure.

That footnote was the transfer of the values-based program from Vietnam to the U.S. for use in reducing racial hostilities in the USMC, worldwide. Unfortunately, this bit of military history also included the strangest peacetime disturbance that ever convulsed any nation's military forces at any time anywhere. Because of America's failure in Vietnam, plus (more importantly) the race riots which hit the military in 1969, the Defense Department forced all the services to join in one unusual training program indeed. It was intended to be a race-relations program. However, because of the so-called *touch-feel group-therapy* fad that was sweeping the nation at the time, the military, through these race-relations programs, was also forced into the touch-feel movement. This is understandable because it was under the supervision of modern psychologists and chaplains.

Officers and enlisted personnel, together, were forced to remove their insignia of rank and, then, in groups, were facilitated into shouting obscene denunciations at one another. I observed many such sessions—the undercutting of discipline and necessary respect for authority (for combat) lasted for years. (One can verify that unbelievable historical military episode through questions to former military personnel who served during the early 1970s.)

At the request of USMC Commandant Chapman, I asked and received from the Secretary of the Navy, John Chafee, an exception from that touch-feel program for the USMC on the grounds that we would substitute our values-based program. The exception was re-approved by the succeeding Navy Secretary, John Warner. However, prior to implementation, the program was watered-down to minimal usefulness by an incoming Marine Commandant who was afraid to use the physical (STRIKE/boxing) base for a human relations program.

The issue was debated vehemently at the top echelon of USMC leadership. I knew that if I proceeded with the race relations program without the physical-confidence (boxing-like) base, the enlisted Marines would reject it as *do-goodism,* which many did, calling it a wimpy program.

I pressed the argument until I either had to give up the STRIKE/ boxing or else cancel the contract. I relented when the brainy and gentlemanly General Simpson stated it bluntly and poignantly: "The Commandant really fears that the public would not understand the use of boxing to help solve race relations problems."

The rationale behind my concession was this: If I did not concede, give up the physical, STRIKE, base for the values program, and instead, canceled the entire race relations contract, the Marine Corps would have to revert to the touch-feel, group-therapy, Defense Department program. All Marines knew the touch-feel program would absolutely destroy the discipline needed in the Corps. So my Marine friends argued that it was my duty to stay with the watered-down ideological approach even against my better judgment.

Now Here are the Institutional-Change Lessons:

1. I, not the Commandant, got blamed for the soft, all-talk program that was implemented. That hurt my future chances for

another effort at a full program. Rather than accept the undercutting compromise, I should have canceled the worldwide contract despite all pressures from Marine friends.

2. The greater mistake was, initially, in not devoting the time and money required to conduct an educational program on behalf of the innovation. After the program was accepted for the USMC versus the one being forced into all the other services (no small accomplishment), I should have taken the time to arrange an explanation to key congressmen of the connection between the high-physical-confidence and the strong, *active* defend-the-right values needed to really solve racial hostilities (which has still not been accomplished in America). Then, I would have had a network of officials powerful enough, and insightful enough, to deal with the inevitable incoming second-guessers. (My only excuse: my naive belief that as the program failed to measure up to its overseas predecessors, top command would upgrade it as I suggested. As a change agent, don't be naive; build your support network for any new program even after it seems to be in place.)

Research Sources from Combat. Two interesting research sources of information about the use of this approach in combat would be former Navy Commanders Richard McGonigal and Earl Fedge. Both were chaplains who introduced my program in their ongoing Personal Response projects in Vietnam. A researcher could get a broad perspective from those two men and their noncommissioned officer assistants. (The Marines will not know of my personal, *secret* involvement; some Navy personnel will.)

I'll mention one enlisted man from the Marine program because his was the only CAP that I ever visited openly, officially. He was an outstanding black corporal by the name of Brown (from Norfolk, I believe). He can be located easily if still alive because he became a Marine warrant officer, another outstanding and unusual accomplishment. And he ran one terrific CAP.

Commander McGonigal did not take my training himself. He simply rewrote my educational materials into a Marine Unit Leader's manual to give to the young CAP Marine leaders in each village. As a result, the Marine CAPs varied from outstanding to poor. That is, the new ideological lessons were not centralized and orally delivered with proper emphasis for tested and proven effectiveness. Rather, the young individual CAP leaders were relied on to pass the lessons along as best they could to their troops from those books. Those individual former CAP field leaders can be searched out and interviewed for varying attitudes and comparative successes. I found upon interviewing them, that they did not understand the *comparative* importance of the various lessons.

Commander McGonigal especially should be interviewed because he was, personally, indifferent toward, if not opposed to, the secular ideology and was doubtful about the importance of the cultural materials. Still, under Lieutenant General Victor Krulak's direction, he was objective enough to let it all be included in the manuals for its possible effectiveness and validity. His views, insights, and experiences regarding ideology should be obtained especially for their possible critique of my work. We disagreed rather strongly regarding the approach to the sensitive sexual issues in the Third World.

Commander Fedge's experiences with the Navy's ACTOV (the turnover of the riverboats to the Vietnamese) are even more important. Commander Fedge took my full training course and improved on its effectiveness with communication techniques. His program was entirely oral. It was taught centrally, at headquarters, under his own close supervision—the optimum method for high quality control. However, the oral program approach runs the risk of being lost to history. That Navy program has received almost no publicity since the war. Why? I think it is because of the bigger picture: the Navy is not interested in infantry-type (riverboat) fighting. Nonetheless, as a Marine, I suggest begrudgingly that their Riverine educational program in Vietnam was considerably more effective than ours in the better-known Marine CAP project.

McGonigal was a friend to all men. Fedge was much more volatile, aggressive, and at times abrasive, especially to big brass; but with no uncertainty, he turned men around in groups for better relations with the Vietnamese. His efforts definitely stopped some *reconnaissance by fire.* For that reason alone his program should now be researched in depth before Fedge and all the program's young leaders are gone. The basic human-equality ideological position that Fedge accepted and taught is the secret to maximum success in low-intensity warfare in the Third World.

Rationalizing the Cover-Up of the Win-the-People Programs. In fairness to the military officers who are denying or overlooking the successes of the win-the-people efforts, few know the truth. Most military men who participated in the Vietnam conflict were involved in the traditional, losing effort. Most are unquestionably sincere in blaming the politicians. I am strongly sympathetic; the first bombing lull, specifically, is what got my own brother killed. Nonetheless, the truth about the win-the-people successes should be revealed. Knowledge of that high-potential approach could be decisive regarding America's strong rejuvenation or unnecessary decline in this age of low-intensity conflict.

I know many tradition-minded military men who reject the win-the-people approach. I think most of them suffer from the human frailty of protecting their own traditional knowledge in the same closed-minded, self-protecting way that most of us do in our own fields. Most know nothing whatsoever about the successful win-the-people efforts anywhere. Some are familiar with the approach and scorn it for emotional reasons. That is, similar to countless overseas Americans, many suffered from culture shock themselves and a few are flat-out racists. When I inadvertently incite some of them to anger in classroom discussions regarding the best way to fight in the Third World, occasionally one will blurt out the group's true feelings. They advise: *Next time, we'll nuke 'em till they glow.* That monstrous thinking is not predominant, but it is afoot.

THE FULL TRUTH SHOULD COME OUT

On the other side of the argument, the win-the-people side, there are only a comparatively few who really know anything about the win-the-people approach from successful experience. They are the men who participated in the better Marine Combined Action Platoons, the Navy riverboat project, and perhaps a few other similar, unique programs. There were of course that scattering of strongly moral men and women who, from their home or church training, always stood against any immoral or amoral action by the crowd. As examples, I'll mention two former Marine troop commanders who did not even allow expressions of the gook syndrome in their outfits. Even though this was unusual indeed, a message is carried to us by the fact that those two young officers rose to the rank of Brigadier General in today's USMC: Chuck Krulak and Tom Draude.

That is where the situation lies today regarding military strategy. Military training can set the new direction needed in order for freedom with justice to prevail globally, peacefully. The know-how exists as I have attempted to record and present in this work. Using the knowledge for better trained (moral values-trained) military personnel, constitutes our most powerful hope for peace through strength. We should commit such Americans into Ideological Warfare (or Mass Diplomacy) if we wish to see democracy with justice prevail. It would be the wisest national policy for us to maintain and globally deploy a rather large military force at this time of history just to perform this grass-roots violence-preclusion for the future of the world.

And I repeat, the more women we assign to that force, the better. Why? For one reason among several, the presence of American women tends to have a calming influence on those American men who behave irresponsibly when away from home. (However, judging from my experience on Iwo Jima, women and more than half of all American men should not be assigned to rifle platoons. Stress is too unbearable.)

THE NEW IDEOLOGICAL WARFARE URGENCY

A negative fact has long persisted beneath the surface of pretense regarding our troop/community relations, worldwide—in Spain, Portugal, Greece, Turkey, the Philippines, and South Korea, not to mention Latin America and all of the Third World: From the earliest post-World War II days of massive face-to-face relations, a dangerous hate from unrequited love for Americans has smoldered all around this globe. Actually, as unrequited love, it was almost falsely named *anti-Americanism.* Recently, however, some of it has metamorphosed into actual anti-Americanism that is burning out in the open, not just as terrorism, but also as official action, against us. Spain started it with the closing of a U.S. military base; this, before the apparent demise of communism. Many other allied nations are considering similar actions. It is a great historic tragedy for America, because much of the unrequited love is still awaiting fulfillment. In this matter, believe me, our leaders in the past have been unbelievably blind and ignorant.

If we do not now train our overseas Americans, especially our large numbers of service personnel, to toughen-up psychologically so that they can mix-in constructively with all the world's earthy common folk, the consequences are clear. We are going to be less and less welcome in many places, and more and more likely to draw violence. Still, I insist it is not too late. We should not resign ourselves to that isolated fate of the ugly outsider.

Admittedly, turning that corner, taking that new win-the-people direction in military training, will not be an insignificant leadership achievement. But in my extensive experience with enlisted personnel (as one Marine General Smith once observed, as long ago as 1970), the enlisted men "eat it up like sugar candy." Why would that be true?

Because they like the challenge. They sense that something good (unity and democracy for others) is the possible reward for their self-risking contributions. Many are willing to take reasonable risks, when properly led, to associate with and help the humble peasants of the world in their austere conditions.

What are the immediate chances?

They are not bad, and apparently, are gradually getting better if we can judge from the Marine Corps.

New Hopeful Signs

During this writing, a probing, controversial training-reform of revolutionary proportions suddenly was introduced into the allegedly unchangeable Marine Corps. Not surprisingly, it was inspired by a prior enlisted man who became the USMC commandant. Reform-minded to a stunning degree, he sought the solid upgrading of the Corps through development of a new (or old) level of toughness. He announced the need for a new basic *warrior training.* I corresponded with him briefly—through an exchange of three or four letters—in terms of the *high path* suggested above and laid it out as follows:

Make the Marines tougher but also more socially responsible. Teach them the unarmed hitting skills of the boxer/puncher for three reasons:

1. To raise individual self-confidence on a massive scale all across the Corps,

2. To teach the principles of small-arms combat as preparation for the much higher level needed for close-in counter-ambush type combat,

3. To serve as the foundation for the *protector/defender* attitude toward the Third World's humble, struggling peasants—as well as toward civilian Americans.

If this revolutionary development could be institutionalized in the Marines, I knew its inevitable inspirational success would set the pattern for all of our overseas forces. We would soon win back the respect of the entire Third World and others. Meanwhile, if combat became necessary, we would also be more effective fighters.

Coming from a former Marine boxer and combat rifle-platoon leader, my suggestions were entertained and then accepted. I was asked to prepare, and introduce, the first two phases of a new unarmed warrior-training program. For me, understandably, this was not only a great honor, but an inspiring patriotic duty. I agreed to do it for free (that is, for expenses only, plus $1).

First lieutenant Jess Humphrey, a son, had been experimenting with the STRIKE-training/infantry-combat fighting-parallels in the field and was returned early from overseas to help prepare the manuals and movies for the special training. With the help of Lt. Humphrey, and another son, a STRIKE-trained civilian coach, Galen, I introduced the program carefully through rigorous tests to one experimental group of Marine athletic instructors at MCRD, San Diego; to one Noncommissioned Officer Class at San Diego; to one Drill Instructor Class, San Diego; and as a decisive test, through the Drill Instructors, to one typically double-sized boot camp platoon of recruits.

Every facet was a measured success. Almost 100% of the anonymous questionnaire responses along with the supervising officers' critiques showed:

1. Overwhelming popularity among both male and female Marines,

2. An obvious new level of safety in contrast to the dangers of boxing,

3. High effectiveness in building fighting skill and confidence,

4. The necessary time-efficiency.

The new recruits were especially enthusiastic about the new "hitter's" training and a platoon of field Marines was even more impressed with the effective parallels for close-in rifle (armed) combat. They acknowledged that it was of lifesaving importance to them. This platoon also participated in a boxing-match smoker against fighters from the rest of the battalion and won all seven of their matches. Demonstrably, the STRIKE-training, when completed through the third (power/punching) stage, is better than traditional boxing (unless one is matched against the rare boxer/ puncher with much experience and proven *knockout punching skills*).

GOALS

The goal of this training is to prepare our young Americans to meet the challenge of the low-intensity conflict era. This means upgrading the services to the Peace Force posture of the better Marine Combined Action Platoons in Vietnam where the better CAP Marines *really* experienced the true feeling behind being a military man. They may not like to say it publicly, but they always admitted it privately. *They, unlike any other group of Americans in Vietnam, wanted to sign over. Why?*

Because, whether they liked it or not intellectually, they got emotionally involved in protecting those village folk. With that, under the combat circumstances, those Marines rose into the most satisfying status known to humankind: The defenders of innocent human life at the risk of their own. *NO GREATER LOVE HATH ANY MAN...* Willingly risking it, psychologically, is the same as giving it.

If the military role, properly lived—as that of a competent defender—is that satisfying (and it is), why not now develop, at least our Marines, to serve in that proper military role anywhere in the world. Actually, the sooner that attitude is assumed, the less likely anyone will have to die performing it at its highest expression. (Strike has not been fully adopted as yet in the USMC, but it has a chance.)

Please make certain there is understanding of what is being said here. The late Robert Heinlein, the great science-fiction writer, and Naval Academy graduate, in a lecture to the Academy, once described the nature of the military-calling in its most meaningful terms. He told of a nameless stranger, a hobo, in Heinlein's hometown, who happened upon and went to the aid of a woman who had caught her foot in some railroad tracks (at the switch crossing). A train was bearing down on them from around a curve and was certain to kill them if the woman did not break loose so they could jump to safety. But the hobo could not pull her foot free. Still, he stuck with her; kept trying without flinching until the train killed them both. Heinlein concluded his account with these words:

This is how a man dies...
This is how a man...lives.

I would add: This is the way the future American military person will choose to live and risk death anywhere in the world defending the defenseless of any status or any color. For truly, this is the essence of *the military calling.* It will, however, require much better training *and more enlightened (nonmaterialistic) recruiting.* That training must overcome all of the informal, misguided, selfish training that is coming out of all of our institutions including too many of our negative role-model professional athletes, and out of our current culture's neurotic admiration for wealth even if ill-gotten. Fortunately, our young Americans still feel some need for the opposite—the inspiring, self-giving roles in life. Why? Because those virtues reside in their deepest, most satisfying, natural inclinations.

Other Good Signs. Two perceptive military advisers, whose works are encouraging, are Bill Lind and John Boyde. Lind stresses the need for maneuver warfare as the necessary tactical methodology of the low-intensity warfare era. This is almost irrefutably sound. However, the rush of literature that I have read on maneuver warfare contains a fatal flaw. This is almost inevitable because so few living Americans in uniform have experienced patrol duty or small group movement in heavy sustained combat. The essence of such combat is not movement; it is integrity. This requires: a combination of strong patriotism, a knowledge of rectitude, a feeling of self-risking duty to comrades, personal courage that comes from exceptional combat skill—fighting and shooting ability—and great stress control. If there is a prevailing inclination in our modern young persons to think first of self, you can forget maneuver warfare as a winning formula for America no matter how much it is needed. Consequently, success in modern maneuver warfare, where young, low-ranking men must lead small groups, unobserved by anyone in command, depends on the type of military training—now substantially nonexistent—fostered in this document.

Boyde, besides spelling out principles of combat in clear, new terms provides us (America) with the best overall guideline I have ever seen with regard to major strategy. Briefed down somewhat, he says:

"What we need now, for the long haul, is a vision rooted in human nature so noble... that it attracts the uncommitted... undermines the dedication of the adversaries... and magnifies the spirit and strength of its adherents."

Iraq Epilogue: Of course we cannot close on a word about our possible American nobility without facing the worldwide allegations of our "callousness regarding the Kurds."

From a Man-On-The-Street TV Talk Show Guest:

> "It constitutes 19th century barbarism for us to assert that we can—through legalistic pretense—justify, (1) going to war for oil, (2) fostering the peasant revolt as a part of that war, and then, (3) denying responsibility for the inevitable counterrevolutionary extermination of those peasants. After bombing Iraq back into the stone age and then expressing refusal to *interfere in their internal affairs* to protect Kurds constitutes hypocritical legalistic absurdity."

In closing, I am compelled to reveal my view because it is unpopular. From a strictly moral (life values) position, here is my analysis of the Iraq war: The thirty thousand body bags were ordered mainly for the lower class Americans in the front-line infantry. They were not volunteers to give their lives in that war. But as soldiers, they had to go, or go to prison. Of the men in the Congress *who voted* to see them die, *not one* had a loved one at risk. If all had, there would have been no war, just sanctions.

TRANSITION

Of course, for the long run, the rise out of these Late Dark Ages demands more than enlightened training for our military forces or for overseas cross-cultural understanding. Elevating troubled and violent nation-states, worldwide, into the full light of civilization requires abandoning educational methods and policies in our public schools that are harmful to children. We shall not see that warm light of true civilization and the satisfactory reduction of violence until we defer, for human development, to the self-enforcing guidelines of human nature in our schools. Let us now reexamine those natural laws that control the effectiveness and happiness of our lives, and try to reorganize our educational institutions accordingly.

ATTACHMENT B

MEANINGFUL SCHOOL REFORM IN ACTION

> **To High School Teachers and Administrators:**
> *Education's failure in America was not your fault; more so,
> it was ours in the colleges and universities. We establish
> curricula.*
>
> *– Sincerely, Bob Humphrey*

PART I

INTRODUCTION AND OUTSIDE
APPRAISALS OF THIS NEW PROGRAM

The Status of School Reform: In the past ten years, following various respected and alarming declarations that our American schools are failing, there has been a flurry of reform efforts. Do you understand that those efforts have been mainly token? They have not been designed to change the outmoded educational system; rather they have been designed merely to improve the worst features inside the failed system. Our educational system is similar to our old, worn-out Model T Fords. We can shine them up and even speed those old engines up a bit; nevertheless, they are now obsolete. Until the need for a more effective model—educational curriculum—is seen, teachers' groups will blame outside social ills, and politicians will force on us a more elitist, less democratic, system.

Caveat

Our public schools *as they are currently organized* cannot educate our children for modern needs. There are at least nine reasons for this, that come out of human nature, one negative and eight positive: The one negative is that we humans are not natural readers, writers, and mathematicians. Those so-called 3Rs, the basics of academics, are recent inventions in human history. They did not come easily; they came late because they were difficult to develop, and they remain difficult to learn. They are virtually impossible for many children to learn outside of an historically natural learning environment. A natural learning environment for humans must be consistent with at least eight human characteristics. We humans are:

1. *Small-group beings*—so our huge schools need to be reorganized into mini-schools; or even better, deconsolidated into neighborhood schools, again;

2. *Total participators*—so all children must participate somewhat equally in all extracurricular activities of importance;

3. *Very physical*—requiring good diets, considerable exercise, and enjoyable athletics—remember, *for all children*;

4. *Right-brain or whole-brain learners primarily*—requiring much learning through stimulation of the thinking processes and imagery rather than only through rote techniques;

5. *Artistic, and humor lovers*—requiring constant participation in these higher fundamentals of life along with all these other seven basics during the daily difficulties of learning the 3Rs;

6. *Social*—to the point of being self-risking group-protectors therefore needing stimulation—as muscles do—of our

satisfying social inclinations such as love, belonging, loyalty, respect, courage, and life-defense abilities in this still very violent and dangerous world;

7. *Equal human beings*—in our feelings—demanding respect from all so strongly that stereotyping or branding children in any way, such as with the totally false and misleading "C student" or "D student" status (just as with a racial epithet), is inevitably resented and destructive, and,

8. *Role-model followers and aspirants*—needing well-cultured and loving teachers rather than so-called specialists.

Most schools under the current multi-headed control are virtually unchangeable. Every possible positive change of significance will get blocked by one vested interest or another. No state will be able to educate its children to meet our modern challenges without the appointment of an all-powerful commissioner tasked with making the schools successful. This would have been done long ago if the failing schools had been considered as important as any big money-making, professional sport.

The new, school-reform commissioner for each state, according to our experiences, must be charged mainly with decentralizing the system and modernizing the curriculum. Four drastic changes are necessary:

1. **Organize a crash-program to reeducate all interested adults, especially teachers and parents, to make them aware of the suggested need for the updated curriculum that conforms to those characteristics of human nature listed above.**

2. Place all of the power to educate the children in the hands of the local teacher-teams, and hold the teachers responsible—at risk of being dismissed—for the educational *success of all children.*

3. Place the power to hire and fire teachers (logically without regard for certification in a failed field), in the hands of the local parents, logically, just as if they were hiring tutors for their children.

4. Make all other school officials deemed necessary answer to the teachers as their support system for one purpose only—to educate *all the children.*

PROGRAM EFFECTIVENESS WITH THE MENTALLY HANDICAPPED

The following letter, dated April 15, 1981, describes the effectiveness of the values-guided approach with mentally retarded young adults. The counselor/supervisor writing the letter is discussing success with the two most difficult students in the program. Both names, of course, have been changed. The letter does not mention that the student, Joe, when not heavily sedated on drugs, could not be allowed out of a padded room, most of the time. He was too self-destructive.

The Letter:

The clients (students) at the Aristotle Group Home were particularly difficult. They simply were not making any progress. Shortly after hiring Brad Humphrey, things began to change...

One young man we worked with was frighteningly obese. He had been diagnosed as manic-depressive by our psychiatrist and his prognosis was bleak. He was taking large doses of Thorazine (300 milligrams a day) as well as three other kinds of medication. He also had a mild heart condition. He was terribly uncoordinated and socially very withdrawn. He would not even enter a 7-11 store to buy his own cigarettes—he smoked about a pack and a half a day.

On his brief visits home he antagonized his brother and sisters constantly...

Things are different today. In seven months, Joe has lost sixty pounds (from 207 to 147). He no longer smokes. He is completely off medication, in tremendous cardiovascular condition, and more than willing to engage in normal social activities. Our psychiatrist was pleasantly astounded.

Brad and Galen (Humphrey's) success with Joe was not just a lucky shot. Their approach was equally successful with Susan... The remarkable thing is that in some respects Susan was even more severely disturbed than Joe. Susan had been in institutions most of her life. Besides being out of shape, hooked on cigarettes (a pack a day), addicted to coffee (up to ten cups a day), and heavily medicated, she was also extremely self-abusive and antisocial. On several occasions she attacked our personnel. On others, after biting herself and banging her head against the wall, she ripped off her clothes and ran down the street screaming obscenities.

Like Joe, Susan has undergone profound changes. Her self-abuse and hostility toward others is almost completely gone. She no longer smokes, does not drink coffee, is in much better physical condition, and enjoys normal family outings.

> Sincerely,
> Donna Lepine
> Behavioral Counselor
> San Diego County Association for the Retarded

HARD-CORE DROPOUTS

On Sunday, June 20, 1982, the following article appeared in the San Diego Union. It was six columns wide with headlines half an inch high.

STREET CORNER SCHOOL HAS
EDUCATORS KNOCKING AT ITS DOOR

In 13 months, Brad Humphrey has taken 30 pill-popping, glue-huffing, law-breaking, dropout teenagers from the streets... and turned their lives around... Arthur Jokela, a research director at California Polytechnic Institute, one educator who has taken an interest in the program puts his feelings this way: *If it can work for those kids who cannot be educated in the traditional manner, just think what it can do for those who ARE able to learn in the schools.*

At a glance, the Humphreys' methods are far from intricate. If anything, they are startling in their simplicity, and as Humphrey says, *More basic than "back to basics"...* Human beings are naturally unsuited to many of the ways Western-style education forces upon them... The Humphrey's... method suggests... teaching according to basic human nature.

Human beings, the Humphreys say, are small-group animals... are physically active... and right-brained creatures...

The current Street Corner School, located in one of National City's rougher neighborhoods, opened last year after Brad Humphrey, (a teacher) who... wanted to test his father's methods, went into the alleys of National City and recruited his first students. The rest of his class roster was filled with dropouts through help from... a juvenile counselor with the National City Police Department.

I wanted only the kids who others said couldn't be educated, said Humphrey, who thought he could best prove his ideas with this group...

He got that and more. His first classroom full of *unreachables* including alcoholics, a young man who had been charged with being an accessory to murder, a large number of glue huffers and runaways, and probably a dozen who had been involved in knife fights and had the scars to prove it.

Many of them were overweight, most were chain smokers and drug abusers and just about all existed on junk food.

Humphrey's brother, Galen, 27 years old, (and a good amateur boxer) was called in as a second teacher. One can easily see the miracles the Humphreys have performed by comparing *before* pictures of the students with the students as they are today. The pictures show [what were] out-of-shape, sullen, angry, non-communicative youths. The teens now, however, are bright, sparkling pictures of health, who bubble with enthusiasm when asked about their lives and plans for the future...

George Webster, executive vice president of the National City Chamber of Commerce... said: *The Humphreys...have found the key to success in learning.*

If George Webster was right about our approach finding the *key to success in learning,* here is the explanation following the outline, mentioned above, along with a few additional details:

1. **Truly Compulsory Attendance for All Children.** No dropping out allowed. Each morning Brad, Galen, or another brother, Jess, went and rounded up the children who chose to skip school; exciting, dangerous work. After experimenting with corporal punishment, we do not approve of it. But we do use physical restraint to keep the children in school. If this results in a fist or knife attack from a criminally-inclined student, we meet that force (with the minimum force necessary) and win, or else call for help.

2. **Role-Model Teachers.** Brad, Galen, and later, Jess, stopped their own minor vices—mainly eating junk food, and drinking coffee and an occasional beer. They got into good physical condition, went on health diets, and boned-up in all subjects so that they could teach all courses: mental, physical, moral, and artistic.

3. **Small Group Classes.** To respond properly to humankind's small-group nature, they used a one-room school approach—the same teachers stayed with the same students all day (and occasionally took some home with them at night).

4. **Drastic Curriculum Changes.** The curriculum was upgraded to include *for each child:*

   - an exciting, healthy, and fitness-oriented athletic program,

   - an enjoyable artistic-expression and art-appreciation program,

   - a moral-strength building program with activities in helping others plus the training in the unarmed self-defense for personal confidence and for defending others,

   - thought-stimulating, fast-learning methods through whole-brained (or right-brain) imagery along with the traditional education.

One might ask, *Where does one find the time to teach such a complete curriculum effectively?* The answer lies in the last feature listed above. The imagery and thought techniques for learning are so much faster than rote learning that it has the effect of doubling or tripling the length of a school day or school year. The time saved from the learning chores, frees up all the time needed for the complete program. The fast-learning feature, however, has not been considered the most important by parents in the schools we have run. Almost unanimously, parents have been most pleased about the third item, the improvement in the moral strength and behavior of their children.

In order to prove the full worth of the program, it had to be delivered at less cost per student than was being spent in the public schools; it was. However, the long-term goal was and is high-paid teachers as the most important professionals in any society. In evidence that this can be accomplished, Brad and Galen Humphrey, together, were offered one hundred thousand dollars to teach in a Canadian school for nine months.

INSTITUTIONAL BARRIERS

Brad and Galen ran the first experimental school (with the California dropouts) for three years. Then, their younger brother, Jess, kept it going for another year. During that time, in addition to constant press and TV coverage, we had visitors from all over the U.S. and as far away as Australia. One San Diego State University professor allowed course credit to his criminology students for attending our school as observers in order to learn our methods. The brothers, as teachers, received the county's *outstanding* awards from the Greater Industry and Education Council, and also from the Corrections Department for juvenile offenders.

Eventually, we received a call from the Office of California's Superintendent of Schools encouraging us to try to expand the approach into all the high schools in California. That request, of course, surprised me. Why would the State Superintendent's office not ask that they be allowed to promote that improvement rather than ask us to do so? I pursued that question through various sources.

I learned that of all the remedial programs in the state at the time, there were three that were deemed to be outstanding; ours, the best. All three had a common problem: *The educational establishment, especially at the local school board level, was trying to close them all down!*

Of course, I knew from this response that I had my first specific *research handle on the institutional barrier* to school reform. To further investigate that lead, I put a brochure together on our school and sent it to a dozen high schools, school boards, and universities in the area. Only one recipient, a university, even bothered to respond; that was with polite advice that they had no problems in their educational system. I called the president of one local school board as a follow-up. She denounced me for bothering her, suggesting that remedial education is *just so much politics.*

Within three years, it was clear that our experimental efforts in southern California could go no further even though we had already started placing some of the *hopeless dropouts* into the local colleges. Jess, my youngest son, while awaiting his call to Marine officer training, decided to keep the school alive for another year in deference to the pleas of parents. But Brad and Galen knew they had to move on in order to expand the experiment usefully. The more successful we became, the more the official opposition, not support, became.

We favor a strong public school system, we were not interested in *going private.* One of the visitors to our school was a North American Native (Indian) educator who offered the next best thing to public education: trying our approach in a school for Natives in Canada.

On March 2, 1984, (slightly abbreviated) the following editorial in the *San Diego Union* announced the decision of the Canadian Indian representatives regarding the desire for our program.

INDIAN TEACHERS FIND HOPE HERE
BY MICHAEL SCOTT-BLAIR

Martha Many Grey Horses' eyes sparkled yesterday as she watched a group of former National City area school dropouts perform educational tasks that would have made any teacher proud.

"This is what we need," said Many Grey Horses, who was wearing the ceremonial dress of her Canadian Blackfoot tribe. Faced with a staggering 95% school dropout rate, she and other leaders from the major native Indian tribes of Canada had searched the world for some way to help their people. And they believe they have found their answer at the National University's High School, an experimental school for local students who had dropped out of local high schools and taken to the streets.

"We have searched through many native populations from India to Africa to find ways of addressing the unique educational problems of indigenous people, but found none until we came here," said Many Grey Horses, who worked with the World Health Organization in Africa. She is the first person in the history of the Blackfoot Confederacy to earn a university masters degree, and even her high school education is a rarity in her nation.

"I can think of Indian communities of 450 people in which only one person has graduated from high school in the past 15 years. That is indicative of our problem. Our youth suffer terrible problems with alcohol, drugs and dropping out of school. Many of them are getting no education at all," she said.

Before her stood one of the 30 students at the National University school, proud of his achievements.

"I was in and out of trouble for years," he said. He at one time had been arrested on charges of attempted murder after a gang fight. "At 16 years of age, I had never read a book in my life," he said. Now 19, he has read and turned in reports on 14 books, including *The Old Man and the Sea, The Last of the Mohicans, The Count of Monte Cristo, The Call of the Wild, and The Black Stallion....*

As the Canadian educators watched yesterday, it was the students, not the administrators, who showed the success of the program. One of the students, not atypically, can tell you every president of the United States, in order, with the years of office and two major events in every administration. (Workbooks are) six inches thick and filled with indexed completed projects....

Twelve student volunteers stepped forward to memorize a list of 21 disassociated objects called out by the audience and then repeated them without error.

Even without voice training, any student selected by a spectator was willing to step forward and at least try to sing a song.

"Look at the confidence," said Humphrey, director of the school. Bob Humphrey and his two sons, Galen and Brad, a former public school teacher, operate the program...and seek to provide three educational goals: the knowledge to make a living, the body health for long life, and a value system for a good life....

Every student must be able to jump rope 1,600 times in 10 minutes and have mastered multiplication tables from two through 15.

They learn self-defense from Galen Humphrey, himself a former boxer whose philosophy is that the students should be so confident of their ability to fight that they do not need to fight.

As part of their values training, they go to the local public elementary school and teach young children how to read.

Many Grey Horses looked on. "This program teaches respect; it teaches confidence, gentility, enhancing life, and prosperity. It teaches how to live the good life with personal values. It is very good," she said.... "Indians in Canada and the United States have the same problems often based on the abuse of alcohol and rebellious behavior said Many Grey Horses.... and a huge percentage of the prison population is Indian," she said. Asked why, she explained:

"There is so much pain and hurt deep in the Indian heart from what has been suffered over the past 100 years and the pain has not been dealt with. As a result it comes out in deviant behavior.

"Much of the problem comes from the low self-image the Indians hold of themselves. This school program helps overcome that with strength, yet with gentleness.

It is what our young people need," she said.

RESULTS IN THE NATIVE CANADIAN SCHOOLS

A year after we established a *Life Values School* for the Indian children in Canada, the inevitable public and official appraisals started. In collaboration with a parent, child, and family counselor, the president of the local school board wrote a long evaluation for the biggest newspaper in the Province, *The Edmonton Journal.* Here are the most descriptive excerpts:

Following a successful pilot project last year with selected students who were chronic dropouts and educational failures, the system was introduced into the entire high school this year...

Carl Christensen has 18 years experience in education and has been the principal (here) for five years. He says he "has never seen a program work as well as this. Not only does it deal with the academic component, but also with an equally important element – how to live a healthy and a good life."

Since the implementation of the program, Christensen has seen dramatic improvements in the performance of the students. "Truancy has decreased dramatically. Students are healthier, due to a workout program and improved diet and a decline in the use of drugs and alcohol. They show more concern for themselves and others, and more perseverance, responsibility and reliability."

Traditional education does not deal with the chronic social problems faced by many native children. The conventional school assumes children will have help at home. The fact is many native children live with the consequences of extreme poverty, unemployment and lack of education.

Our medical examination of all students was initiated to improve their health care. In the process, we learned just how big the challenge is: more than 90% of our high school students admitted they use drugs and alcohol regularly. Almost all of them smoke.

It is popularly accepted that 85% of native students drop out. Last year, 59% did not complete the year. In stark contrast, in the pilot Life Values project for 25 dropouts, attendance averaged 98%. This fall, attendance was more than 95% in the entire school. We employ a child-centered program that is caring and effective... We emphasize whole brain learning and the use of imagery... (rather than role learning).

Our program succeeds because we redefine the role of the teacher, the role of the peers, the role of the classroom, and the evaluation process. The teacher is a role-model and acts as an educational guardian.

The classroom is self-contained. Students stay together in a small, cohesive group during the day. The teacher is a social worker, parent substitute, truant officer—whatever it takes to help a student. Physical education funds and facilities are equally available for all students including women...

Students are not just names on a roster. The teacher knows who they are, whom they date, how they react to stress, what their expectations are, how their health is, whether they use drugs, where they hang out, who their parents are. Based on this knowledge, teachers intervene to help students.

Nutrition is also important. There are no longer any junk food vending machines on campus.

Some observers consider the physical aspects of the program most important, although we do not agree that any one feature can be singled out. The program is integrated. The focus is on values. Because exercise is essential to health and improves confidence and the ability to learn, it is part of our daily activity.

There are other important values-vehicles. *One is the use of consequences for misbehavior; another is the use of incentives for positive behaviors.* Another is STRIKE, a values-based defense training that includes values stories, the Life Values philosophy and the vocabulary of nonviolence.

We have found it effective to provide a simple, immediate consequence, like a short run or push-ups when a student is late. If a student is caught using drugs, it may mean a 12-kilometer walk with an instructor. The consequences are individualized; students are offered a choice of consequences and always have the option of going to another school if their parents agree. When consequences are used properly, students accept them and feel better about themselves.

STRIKE teaches students to defend themselves and to be responsible and respect the courage and emotional control that make it possible to be nonviolent.

There are only two instructors authorized to teach STRIKE through actual sparring, which is done across a rope separating student and instructor. Other teachers teach the forms and footwork and related values stories. STRIKE has the added advantage of serving as an ideal arena for the development of emotional control while providing an adrenaline-charged experience that teenagers seem to need. *When school is exciting, students don't need to turn to crime, drugs or dangerous activities for thrills.* "The Life Values System" is consistent with our traditional (Native) values. And it works. No one, including critics, has said it is not working. Some people may dislike it or disagree with it, but the results speak for themselves...

Surveys of parents indicate they are strongly behind the program. They like the discipline, and the fact that their children learn to respect others.

Reports from parents mention that children are sharing and are more considerate. They help without being asked, fight less with siblings and act more responsibly. They look forward to attending school. Parents also approve the stand against drugs and alcohol. They want their children to have an education and feel they are getting it."

Signed: The President, Native Education Council.

Critics of the program (drug-hooked students, drug pushers, alcohol salesmen, Native educators from competing, failing schools, and oil interests who wanted to industrialize the reservations) forced outside evaluations of the school. They backfired.

Professor Joseph Couture, from Canada's Athabasca University, adjudged the program: *The educational breakthrough of the decade, at least in Canada.* The Native evaluator from the U.S., John Windy Boy, Jr., with similar praise, advised that the program offered the first hope he had seen of saving the Native culture.

THE INSTITUTIONAL-CHANGE BARRIER

School board politics among the Natives in Canada do not take a back seat to ours in the U.S. schools. To inspire the Indian children upward to the cultural rejuvenation and personal pride desired by constructive citizens, our research showed that it would be necessary to upgrade (salvage) the Indian reservation ecologically. We would have to alter the school curriculum to foster development of more traditional Native agriculture on the reservations (in addition to allowing the industrialization of certain areas). Research revealed that this *more exotic Indian culture* could be made economically viable through realistic outdoor Indian Camps and training for white youth to become blood brothers in those camps. The elders and an overwhelming majority of the Natives were enthusiastic about the project. It was called a sure bet.

The day I announced those research findings, officially, to the most powerful Native on the school board (the one who had written that last laudatory newspaper editorial above), he abruptly cancelled our contract. Later I learned that he was, himself, an industrialist, *pit-mining oil tar sand* on the reservations.

We finally admitted to ourselves that the institutional barriers are simply too high and multi-headed to engineer the necessary educational reforms from inside the public schools.

Upshot. It will be wise for you to dwell on the barriers to educational reform in your children's schools. Find out exactly who is obstructing in your school and try to enlighten them or remove them democratically.

ATTACHMENT B

PART II

A PROMISING EDUCATIONAL REVOLUTION

If a revolution cannot be advanced from the top down, directed perhaps by your state governor, then, short of national decline, that revolt must come, more roughly, up from the common folk.

THE ACE IN THE HOLE REGARDING SCHOOL REFORM

We lower-income and middle-income families have a new ace up our collective sleeves with which to help force the necessary school reforms. It is not well-known yet but is becoming so. That is the new home-schooling movement of growing popularity. A family need not move to it permanently. We can use it safely and constructively for only a year or two if that is all we wish. Others may wish to stay with the home school for a long-range program.

Read this passage slowly from the book *Home School Burnout,* by Raymond Moore, Doctor of Education, and Dorothy Moore, Masters Degree (Wolgemuth & Hyatt, Publishers, Inc., Brentwood, Tn, 1988):

Fifty years ago... Carnegie, the Progressive Education Association and others spent four million dollars to find out which children learned more, those who were taught by teachers or those who were left to develop and learn for themselves. (It was an eight-year study.) Researchers compared fifteen hundred children who were taught in conventional elementary school classrooms with fifteen hundred who learned in very flexible situations or who were not taught at all—where adults were available only to answer questions or help the children find materials. The children were paired by age, sex, social background, aptitude test scores, vocational interests, etc. The results... On every variable, on every parameter, including their grades in high school and college, academic honors, leadership capacity, and even attitude on the job, the children from the flexible classes out performed those in the conventional classrooms. But the children who were not formally taught at all had the highest scores of all in all areas measured.

That is incredible. *Children who have no schooling at all, just strong encouragement and assistance from parents to educate themselves, do better than school children. Do you understand what that has got to mean? It means that there is a general atmosphere in the schools that is handicapping everyone, even the best students. It is that general atmosphere that must be changed. The "I hate school," and "This place is boring" must be changed to "I love school, I am having fun, and I am really learning."*

In our large group of Humphrey families, two have changed to home schooling. One family has three children; one, four. Every single person in both families has shown marked gain in every way from the change. Making the adjustment was hard at first—but as the mothers eased off in their teaching efforts, which is the secret to good home schooling, everything improved. Read, again, the second paragraph of the citation above.

I am advocating the use of home schooling only as an ace in the hole if educators will not help us reform the public schools properly so that they serve all of the children equally and adequately. The end goal is a society where the home in fact does have the primary responsibility for seeing that each child is educated, but the public school is the family's public institutional partner in that task. Some children might spend less time at school, but many might spend more time there—with everything considerably more individualized and definitely more enjoyable for each child.

For national good, we need to upgrade our entire educational system, including our overly specialized colleges and universities. We Americans have deluded ourselves into believing that our colleges are succeeding even though *their institutional children,* the public schools, are failing. The self-deceptive argument has been that our colleges teach thinking better than foreign colleges. That argument is highly questionable. Japanese, German, and others are starting to win the contests for registered inventions at the U.S. patent office.

Obviously our universities and colleges constitute the ultimate source of the problem in our lower schools. All of the high school teachers and administrators are products of those post-graduate schools. The latter have to be at fault.

Our universities and colleges by and large are misguided by faulty theories of human nature: pseudo-Freudianism, irresponsible relativism, and Adam Smith's *invisible hand* or the selfish *economic man.* The last philosophy is probably the most influential in causing the modern failure of our educational institutions in general. Actually, it is not even the true philosophy of Adam Smith: He was an altruist or humanitarian according to the way I read him—a member of the brilliant Scottish Enlightenment.

The Political Usefulness of Home Schooling

Meanwhile, the statistics on home schooling allow us to say this: Even if we, as families, wish only to use the home school for a one-year or two-year sabbatical from the child-destructive rat race in the current highly pressurized schools, it provides an educationally safe method to break the back, economically, of the school forces who refuse to make the school reforms that are consistent with human nature.

That is about all I shall say about our ace in the hole, the home school. Good materials on the topic are available. Order the books on that topic from your book stores. Especially get the Moores' book, *Home School Burnout.* Also consult the families in your community who are already using this method to educate their children (you may be surprised how many there are). Ask them especially about the social and economic advantages in addition to the academic gains.

SCHOOLS, TEACHERS, AND HUMAN NATURE

Humans are hero worshipers. As children, we learn best from, and in many cases only from, our role-models. Also we are small-group beings; we are uncomfortable, if not lost, in the crowd. Consequently, let us force the schools to deconsolidate, or at least go back to the one-room school approach by creating mini-schools inside our large, prison-sized institutions. (Racial integration, incidentally, under these circumstances—involving only small groups—has a much, much better chance to be effective.)

Each group of fifteen children or so (we find) should be under the daylong educational guidance of the same role-model (educational guardian) teacher. Usually, we combine two such groups to fit most school-building classrooms built to hold thirty students. The two role-model teachers team-teach most of the subjects. For special subjects such as advanced algebra, we bring in specialists; teachers move around, not pupils (calculate the time saved with that feature *alone*). One or both of the educational guardians remains present while specialists are teaching. His or her assignment is to make certain that every child gets constructive encouragement just as if he or she were home under the watchful eye of a loving parent.

These role-model teachers must be carefully picked, of course, and specially trained. They must be persons who are willing and able to teach effectively the universal values as well as the academics, physical education, and the arts, including good humor.

The values include only the noncontroversial values that we all teach in our homes: the species-preserving or altruistic values (compassion, consideration, human equality, giving) and the success values (perseverance, determination, reliability, punctuality). The arts include participatory artistic values (singing, drawing, acting) that make daily life more enjoyable.

These role-model teachers do not have to be brilliant scholars, just persons who can stimulate every one of our children's natural love of learning (rather than kill it).

They need not be athletic champions, just persons who stimulate the healthy and enjoyable physical development and athletic skills of every child; this, rather than the sedentary school teacher who kills off an interest in athletics in most children, relegating them to the status of overweight spectators whose hearts and lungs are deteriorating even in childhood. Human beings, especially children, want to participate, want to play, want to do it themselves. The most glorious aspect of our modern high schools, the athletic varsity system (addressed later) may be a more destructive crime-causing influence than any other force in society. When *winning is the only thing,* society loses.

Morally/spiritually our teachers need to be persons whom all the children feel are being fair, and by whom the children will be encouraged, from example, toward human consideration.

Role-model teachers need not be accomplished artists. But they must be persons who will introduce the enjoyment of singing and other arts that help give life meaning. All of the children in our schools learn to sing solo, enjoyably, in front of a crowd. Finally, in academics, the teachers must be willing to reeducate themselves to teach the highly stimulating whole-brain or right-brain learning through imagery and thinking, rather than continue to numb the children's interests in education through only the deeply entrenched, monotonous rote-learning. The latter dominates all of our educational institutions right up through our graduate schools. Rote learning is fine and useful, but learning through imagery-and-thought is far superior and not taught currently, even in our colleges.

Of course we must pay these teachers well. We can save money on buildings. We did. Parents are willing to pay more for good education for their children, but not for the questionable education they know they are getting in the existing schools.

Critics ask two questions: Is such a system realistic and does it not take more adults than are currently involved? In answer, it is simply an upgraded or modernized version of the one-room school that served us well for over one hundred years. It takes *fewer* personnel. Small groups of children are much easier to deal with than large anonymous groups. Students and teachers can do many of the administrative and labor jobs currently assigned to non-teaching adults. They all involve valuable lessons and skills for life.

QUESTIONED DETAILS OF SUCCESSFUL SCHOOL REFORM

While holding in your mind the general outline of the necessary school reform, consider the following details that are always requested in our teacher-training seminars that teach school reform. They include answers to both friendly and unfriendly questions. For realism, I shall use recorded questions and answers from various college classes and educational seminars attended by school teachers.

COMPULSORY EDUCATION

A Familiar Question: Is it not true that some children are just not right for education?

Answer: That is the most misinformed proposition to come out of our failed school system. To test its validity, Brad and Galen took over the group-home, mentioned earlier, for the mentally handicapped. They found that there are very few *dumb brains* inside those heads. The challenge is to find the communication channels into those brains. Even a manic-depressive student, that is, a teenager who had been adjudged officially manic-depressive, turned out to be not manic-depressive at all. Within a year he was out of his padded room; his weight, which was actually 207, went down to 147. He later won the school record for skipping rope after allegedly being hopelessly uncoordinated. He turned out to be able to sing delightfully, and eventually could accomplish menial tasks (little jobs). His proudest moment was when an army recruiter tried to recruit him and spoke favorably to us of his winning personality.

Brad's final conclusion about the mentally handicapped was that to help them—give them happier lives with more laughter—the central key is that they must be held to higher standards than they and society usually establish for them. But make no mistake about this: They absolutely require hands on love, both of encouragement and at times correctional. (Counseling is ineffective, as it is with most students; almost useless.)

Question: You raised the issue of compulsory attendance and truancy duties, can you actually force children into school? Will you not get taken to court? What is more, at least in our school, it is the educators and the school board members, themselves, that are suspending and expelling the children. So how can the parents force them back into school?

Answer: That question always reminds me of a favorite quotation of mine by President Teddy Roosevelt. He once said:

> We have duties to others
> And duties to ourselves;
> And we can shirk neither.

It is the *sine qua non* to success for the nation to reinstate the truancy system everywhere. Brad Humphrey states it this way: Every child is entitled to be forced to get an education so he or she will not later have to go on welfare, into crime, or into prostitution in order to make a living. Forcing education into children is similar to forcing air into the lungs of an attempted suicide from drowning. That principle includes the duty of every adult and every community to get all of our children educated. Hold to that principle. Get rid of school board members and state legislators who disagree. Vote them out. Also use the home-school revolt system. That removes the negative influences of the public schools from your own children at least. Remember, the education that we recommend for your children is *not at all* the "education" that is going on now. I would not force today's education on any child.

PHYSICAL EDUCATION

Question: The responsible educators are actually stopping all physical education in our high school now. Could you comment rather fully on that topic. That is, since the children are not learning to read, is it not wise to use all school time for teaching reading, if necessary. And if the schools won't provide physical education, what can I do at home? But remember, I am busy as a single parent, always in debt.

Answer: In addition to disagreeing with your description of the educators who are stopping all physical education, because they cannot be classified accurately as "responsible," I must start a full answer by going clear back to the topic of diet.

Diet: Do you know the diet that—as far as science now knows—will give your child the happiest, longest life possible?

(Let us keep it very simple, and check my answers with your doctors. If one disagrees, please seek a second opinion.)

I am told by doctors and fellow coaches to cut down primarily on the sweets, salt, and heavy—red and fat—meats. So, as parents, what foods should you keep in your home and eat as the proper example for your children? Fruits, vegetables, whole-wheat breads, hot cereals, fish, fowl, and a little red meat, doctors now insist.

In our Life Value Schools, we have raised the reading scores of some of our children simply by persuading them to change their diets, which were mainly junk foods, and worse.

How do you persuade the children to change their junk food habits?

I guess it goes without saying that you may have to be willing to upgrade your own diet in your home if it has not been good. And why not? It will give you, too, more years with more love.

One method we have used successfully in our own homes is to limit our heavy fats and sweets to the weekends, or to Sundays only. Eventually, one begins to lose one's taste, to a degree, for the fats and sweets. Don't get impatient or angry about early failures. It is not easy or we all would have solved the problem long ago.

Exercise: It helps to start a little exercise program for yourself. No one is so busy that he/she cannot afford the minimum needed, 20 minutes every other day. In fact, if you want to live longer and help avoid some sickness of your own, you cannot afford not to exercise: run, or swim, or skip rope in the garage or bedroom as I do, or just walk part way to work as my wife does. Time is not the problem; just finding the resolve is. This is the easiest part to persuade the children to join with you. Also purchase a scale to weigh yourself every day. Keep a chart. If appropriate, try to lose a pound every ten days; take it easy. That is best.

Personal Involvement: Now the courage factor: Visit your children's school, or at least telephone, and start exerting pressure on the school administration to improve the diets available in the school cafeteria and food-vending machines. You fear the children will go elsewhere to buy junk food? True, for awhile, we find; but they begin to give-in for convenience; they begin to like the improved diet; begin to follow the example of the teachers who change. So put pressures on all the teachers to act as constructive role-models. Enlist other parents in the effort. Use the PTA, even if you have to start one. Understand and stress the fact that the issue is not simply to avoid decline in the future. Overcome the possibility that we are already too far gone into decadence as a culture. Decadence means too soft, too selfish, and too cynical to care.

Make democracy work at the grass-roots: School reform is a grass-roots matter. Don't be a milquetoast. Be a force, a life force. Put more direct time into working for the health and strength of the ones you love. If you do, you'll like your own life better, especially as it gets closer to the end—where it adds up to *success or failure.* I repeat, the life that contributed to the health and strength of the species—to the health and strength of your children and others—is the successful one *in nature.*

Measuring Physical Success: Can your school children tell you what their resting heart rate is? Their exercise target heart rate? Is your child getting any good physical education worthy of the term? Did you? Are you at all knowledgeable about your resting heart rate? It is a crucial concept for health. How much good exercise are your children getting every day, or every other day at their school? How much do they need in order to keep the heart, lungs, and muscles healthy? Can your children tell you? Can you tell them?

Heart disease is the top killer of Americans, a direct manifestation of poor diet and lack of proper exercise. I continue to marvel at the timidity of our educational system when it comes to health matters. It has the ability to stop the number-one killer of Americans; yet, instead it is driving in the coffin nails!

Your Own Child's Learning and Health: You say your own school officials are stopping physical education for your child. Have you personally confronted them? If so, do they deny that the basis for an effective mind is a healthy body? Do they admit that the bodies of our American children today in their schools are getting sick from lack of adequate exercise?

Confront them tactfully: Don't forget, your tax money pays these public educators. They work for you and they have the current and future health of your child in their control. Do not be deceived or intimidated by their naively happy, self-satisfied attitudes, their promises, or their educational degrees—in a failing field.

Accountability: Is that school giving your child a good education? Or is it doing the opposite, hurting your child's confidence in his or her intelligence? When a mechanic fails to fix your car, do you accept his diversionary talk about the fact that someone else broke it? If the school is failing with your child, recommend to the superintendent, the principal, and the teacher that they start producing for you at once or that they get into some other field of work where they can succeed. Accountability to you is the decisive factor.

Courage: Put the pressure on; get your friends to visit the school. This may seem embarrassing. It does require COURAGE; do you have it? Or do you make cop-out excuses and rely on the prominent people in the district? They'll speak up all right; but not for your child; for theirs. The needs are often different. For example, they may have the money to purchase adequate exercise at the local private clubs. Do you? If you do, join the club; if you don't, raise an issue at the school. If the other parents are not with you, start educating them, tactfully, to our national needs; you need their support.

Physical Education, the Fun Part of School: Regarding compulsory attendance, if all children are not included in the fun part of school, all cannot be kept in school. Many will become too disruptive or underconfident. If you still have a physical education program in your school, is your child receiving *equal education* in athletics? Does she/he receive an equal amount of the coaches' time? Or is most of the coaches' time going to those who are already good athletes and therefore need the encouragement least?

Have you been duped into letting the system use your tax money for the other families' children to have all the *varsity system?* Is your child being pushed aside in school-sponsored sports and therefore taught to resent school and secretly doubt himself or herself? Does he or she feel like an outsider in his or her own school that you pay for? Is your money being used for the fun of only those other persons' children who are tall enough to play basketball, big enough for football, or rich enough for golf and tennis?

Have you allowed yourself to be snowed with the line that participation in extracurricular athletics is a privilege for excellence? If so, what has excellence got to do with who is the tallest, biggest, wealthiest, and, recently, the most willing to use steroids? Have you been told that football pays for itself and other school expenses in high school? If so, ask about the cost of building the stadium and all the other fixed costs.

The exhilarating athletics, the fun part of school, may be the most important factor of all education, that is, for development of the self-confidence in your children for their entire lives. According to what I have observed in the still natural villages of the world, *athletic activity may be one of the top second-level human values*—second only to the Life Value, itself. Why else would it be possible for a high school dropout to make ten times more money in one athletic event, a prize fight no less, than the U.S. President makes in a lifetime? Why else would a dropout who can throw a good curve-ball make twice the money of a major corporate director? Why else do great soccer players, who use their heads mainly to butt balls, receive more money and fame than Einstein?

An Organizational Question

Does this mean that we have to kill the varsity athletic system? No, it means we must adapt it to the *total participation or equal athletic education system.* This requires the change, or simple defiance, of some state athletic policies, but so what?

Back to Intramurals

Question: Professor Humphrey, what you said to our small group shocked some of us. Frankly, I was pleased. However, before I ask a sympathetic question for clarification, Coach _____, here, respectfully, would like for you to reveal your athletic background in answer to these questions:

First, did you make a varsity athletic team either in high school or college?

Answer: Yes, with letters in football, basketball, and track in high school, and boxing in college. In addition, all of my sons lettered on varsity teams and my daughter was a cheerleader.

Question: Okay, great; I won that bet. (Audience laughter). Now, would you please hold forth, then, on your suggestion to us that the varsity system may be one of the more destructive elements of high school.

Answer: I'll be brief. The current varsity-cuts system rejects and neglects the majority of our children. Being cut from a varsity team can have a lifelong effect. The corrective approach simply establishes a total-participation system with mini-school and neighborhood teams inside the prison-sized schools. Students earn their honors, mainly, on those neighborhood teams. The neighborhood teams help rebuild the small group that our children need. All-star teams are then selected to play other schools but not so often that it disrupts education and the healthy, confident development of all the children.

Question: Will this reform be popular among all the children?

Answer: It was in virtually all of our schools because we had such outstanding extracurricular systems. However, in one, it was not immediately; a huge cross-section of the student body was already substantially lost in despondency, alcohol, drugs, etc. Many students objected to every feature from the new healthy diets in the cafeteria, to participation in athletic programs, and even to having their rotten teeth fixed. But within a year, strong support developed.

Question: Will this system fit in with the college-varsity program that leads to the professional-athletic, big-money system?

Answer: It will not seem to at first. But don't worry about that. Put proper physical education for all of our children first. Soon the system will adjust, and more young persons, including the late bloomers, will have a better chance in big-time athletics. Either way only an infinitesimal percent ever make the big time you know. The possibility—and the childish vanity involved—is hardly worth the price of the entire nation's physical health.

ACADEMICS: IMAGERY AND THINKING

Question: You mentioned accelerated learning through imagery and thinking versus the rote system. Could you please elaborate?

Answer: All of the scientific studies I have seen, corroborated by my twenty-four years in school, advise that about 80% of a student's learning-time in school is spent memorizing. The method used in modern schools is the so-called rote system. You read things and review them or say things over and over until they are more or less grooved into your brain. Very boring! Is it any wonder that so many children lose interest?

Assume you could place your child in one of our Life Values Schools. Even if he or she were in the bottom third of the class academically, in about a month we would teach him or her how to memorize through imagery and thinking. How much better is this system? We'll teach him or her how to memorize from three to ten (or more) times faster and from three to ten times (or more) as much as he or she can learn now. We would give you a money-back guarantee. The point is that any school could do it if the universities were training school teachers in these superb learning skills developed by the ancient scholars.

For the children who have any interest in math but can't seem to learn by the currently boring rote system, we would teach them their crucial math tables not just through the tens but through the fifteens in a week or so.

Why don't most teachers know about and teach this system? There, the failing of the teacher's colleges, is the root of the failing high schools.

Anyway, put pressure on your administrators to encourage your local teachers to learn the magic-like imagery system. It simply includes, first, creating and forming a mental image of anything you need to learn. Our brains retain pictured images infinitely more easily than mere words or ideas. Second, through one or more thinking processes, one commits that visualized item to the short-term or long-term memory as needed. The simple act of memorizing by this process teaches one to think through practice-thinking: associating, creating, linking, comparing, etc.

Now, obviously, you cannot find one of our few Life Values Schools since there are only two, and those developmental experiments will soon end. And it will take time to reform your local school. Hire a memory expert if one is available to teach your children. Second, order the little *Memory Book,* by Lorayne and Lucas. Believe that you can do what Jerry Lucas (the great basketball player) insists you can do with that system. If you do not want to learn the system yourself, hire any sharp local student to learn the system after you buy him/her the book, and then have him/her teach it to your children. Children in grade school can begin using these systems. As they grow, they learn the more sophisticated techniques. (Older, established educators, however, tend to resist or reject it. I did until my sons forced it on me.)

LETTER GRADES

Question: I have heard that you do not use letter grades in the Life Values Schools. Why not?

Answer: We equate the psychic branding of students with letter grades with physical branding. Our Life Values School teachers serve more as academic coaches. Tests are given more through an outside objective system. We would no more give one of our children the demoralization of an "F" for something he/she is learning than you would if the child tried something at home but did not do too well; you would still be encouraging. If the child, on an objective test, achieves an unsatisfactory 50%, we encourage him/her appropriately and set the target for the next effort, say at 80%. (Our system is known as "mastery learning." Research the term. Some schools already know about the use mastery learning to a degree. The military has used it for years and is far ahead of our schools in that regard.) In all academia, there is no scientific evidence that letter grades serve any useful purpose to the children. And you all know they were often unfair to you when you were in school and at times they were demoralizing. I have never met a teacher who could allocate them justly, and only one at the college level who was foolish enough to insist that he could. In the first few years of a child's education, especially, avoid branding children as "F students," "C students;" use what is called the "ungraded" grammar school.

COOPERATIVE LEARNING

Question: I have heard about cooperative learning. Do you use and recommend it?

Answer: There is much talking in our classes. All students are busy most of the time. Seldom is the class just sitting and listening or half-listening to some lecture. At least, all students are making *mind maps* (drawing pictures) of ideas from the teachers' comments. There is much individual work and much structured cooperative learning. The latter is quite good for more than academic achievement.

Some innovative educators at the University of Minnesota, the Johnson brothers, have conducted research in this field. Seek it out.

Question: I have heard that the Japanese, Germans, and other foreign countries' children who have excelled beyond ours, attend school a month or two longer annually. Do you advocate a longer school year?

Answer: Sure, if the student *wants* it. Conversely, I recommend a shorter school year for those who can handle it or will profit more from productive outside experiences. With the current system, parents resist a longer school year insisting their children need the vacation time. As of now, I agree wholeheartedly.

The total Mind/Body/Arts/Values curriculum solves the problem; school is more enjoyable, much more enjoyable, long vacations, then, are not needed.

THE TRADITIONAL CURRICULUM

Question: Do you use the traditional curriculum in your schools?

Answer: Even with thirty children in a class, and at different levels, each student should feel that he/she is in his/her own magnet school, adapted to his/her special interests. Make certain they are constructive interests of course. As Brad Humphrey is fond of saying, *Each child is the curriculum.* Many teachers say: "If you save one child, you are doing your job." Conversely, Brad teaches his student-teachers, "If you lose one child, you should contemplate leaving the field of teaching." This means the curriculum must be adapted to each child's level. If you use the same curriculum for 30 children, you have at least 29 students in the class working either above or below their own level and therefore wasting time. Each child must have individual attention *if you want to educate each child.* Where does the teacher get the time needed? From not talking so much in front of the entire class, and from using the imagery and thought learning techniques. When the children see that their program is individualized, they are more motivated to succeed; they work harder.

Not losing one child, we learned, means you must be willing to drive five hundred miles; take the boy out of the gutter; fight off his drug-enraged knife attack, and control him all the way back home before he cries and admits that he is grateful for your continuing efforts and love.

THE ARTS

Question: You have rated the arts right up with the other three fields of human development, yet you have not said as much about them. Could you add anything?

Answer: Any time a visitor comes into any one of our Life Values classes, that visitor is likely to think he or she is visiting an *art class*. The children are *drawing* as a part of all their note taking. Some are asked to sing in most classes. Why? Art expression is probably about as close to the bone of human nature (as close to the brain stem) as the need for physical exercise. Art expression helps make life more enjoyable for human beings.

Are your children having trouble with their math? Sit down with them, whether you know math or not, and have them sketch pictures or diagrams of their math word problems. It won't take long. Have them use as much drawing as is possible in both their note taking and in figuring answers to problems.

Is there a good book that teaches the drawing for analysis of the written messages? Yes, right now, in the 1990s, Tony Buzan's books on *mind mapping* are excellent. Ask the librarian or bookstore clerk. Encourage the use of these books or something similar along with one of Lorayne's *memory books,* or something similar, in your school. Insist that your teachers learn these ancient systems. They were used for over a thousand years by scholars to memorize the contents of entire volumes before printing was invented. Now, with the flood of information and the increasing need to change jobs, we need these magnificent systems again.

Make certain there is at least enjoyable singing in every classroom.

REMEDIAL READING

Question: How about teaching the basics? I have a child in the fourth grade who can hardly read and a girl in the ninth having trouble with math, especially with word problems. What can I do?

Answer: Well first, calling reading, writing, and arithmetic *the basics* of education is a misnomer. The true basics for your child's and for all human beings' education consist of the four areas we have been discussing:

Physical Development: One should exercise enough that he/she is aware of his or her muscle tone and muscle development.

Spiritual Development (Earthly): One should have his/her need to assist others properly trained so that he can enjoy the life-inspiring feelings from such actions, including physical defense.

Artistic Development: Music and art appreciation should be made a part of one's life even before one can walk. And it should continue through life.

Mental Development: Of course the students should be taught to think as well as learn by rote. For this, the system of learning through imagery helps. (It is my suspicion that the use of Chinese picture writing in childhood provides an advantage over mere sound symbols, in the development of the brain.)

If those four areas of learning are being satisfied, it will be easier to cope with the more difficult, highly sophisticated, narrow basics of academics: reading, writing, and arithmetic. As I have mentioned, these are actually very recent, highly advanced skills that humans did not develop until about two thousand years ago—comparatively speaking, the last moment in human history. They are difficult concepts for our picture-loving brains.

If your high school children seem to be having trouble with reading or with understanding what they read, *you* sit down with them and have them read aloud, a few lines, or a paragraph, of the troublesome materials. Help them learn how to analyze one written line, a phrase, a sentence, a paragraph at a time. Ask them what each means. If they don't know, find out why. Is it the meaning of a word, a lack of interest, a lack of experience, what?

If you can't find out, then get help. Arrange one session with a remedial educator for an analysis. Or if there are no experts available, hire a tutor, just for a few hours—one of the better students can do it if you supervise. Make sure the slow, careful analysis is going on just as you would analyze any other of life's problems carefully. It won't take long. Consider education your child's job. Help him or her just the same as you would help if the child were having trouble doing some job around the house but needed to learn better.

Watch for a physical problem: inability to see or to hear well. If there is a hint of such a problem, seek professional examinations. Some of these physical maladies are very difficult to pick up (such as visual perception problems), but can be the source of a child's learning difficulties.

If you cannot find anything wrong, especially if the child is older, go to the *high-confidence builders,* the unarmed physical fighting skills and the so-called right brain, imagery-learning skills mentioned above. As a spin-off they have never failed to get impressive improvement in the basic academics among our students.

MORAL/SPIRITUAL TRAINING AND THE FIGHTING SKILLS

Question: Earlier, you mentioned the unarmed fighting skills as a part of the moral training rather than physical. Some in our discussion group, thought it was a slip of the tongue. I could tell that it wasn't. Can you explain more fully?

Answer: There are two lessons here. They are important; I will say the least possible so you have time to discuss them in your groups and can ask further questions if needed.

Lesson A: Teach your child by example to speak-up against discrimination. Don't pretend to be a spiritual person unless you can do this, or start doing it.

Lesson B: If your children do speak-up against discrimination or against other common wrongs of some persons toward others, they will eventually get into trouble unless they know self-defense. And if they get in trouble, without the self-defense tools to defend themselves, they will stop speaking-up after they get bloodied or embarrassed a time or two. They will start walking through life afraid to speak up for what is right. Teach them not to fight: but teach them *how to fight* so they can protect or defend when necessary.

How? Hire a responsible boxer. Your children do not have to do any serious boxing. You may wish to teach them that boxing is bad because it damages the brain; fine, but still have someone teach them how to hit. (Similarly, teach them how to light fires, but not be arsonists.)

Have the boxer teach them how to hit fast and effectively (hard) without stepping back or *telegraphing*. That's all they need. It will take less than a month of lessons. Then make a light, heavy-bag that they can hit with light gloves; no striking-bag gloves are necessary. Get a barracks bag, or sea bag, and stuff it with some old feather pillows. That is the best. Keep it hanging some place always accessible for occasional hitting practice.

Work on the skill to hit shorter and harder with the totally relaxed, short distance, explosive propulsion of the entire body behind your fist or open hand, yet retain your balance.

Tensing your arm muscles will be the most difficult mistake to avoid. To avoid it, relax your fist making sure to keep your wrist straight. As you get to hitting too hard for comfort, begin to wrap your hand and wrist. Ask a boxer to show you how.

Teach hitting to all the members in your family. A quick *jab by women or hard cross* with fingernails extended will stop some rapes; one hit to the eyes, then run. Everyone should stay in running shape. You may want one of the Asian martial arts. They are wonderful if one has the interest, but they take many years to perfect. The boxer's modern, scientific hitting skills are the most practical and efficient, and they can be taught very quickly. Teach them not as a part of athletics but as a part of the spiritual training—*to be more willing to speak for what is right and to be able to defend others.* If one of your sons ever *stands by* in fear while some woman is raped, or while some child is bullied or abused, without at least speaking up, face it, as a parent, you are a failure. You have contributed to the growing weakness in a softening America.

For additional earthly spiritual values training, we use *help-others* assignments, and true stories of sacrifices—also good literature— the classics are full of good, inspirational accounts.

LOVING, PHYSICAL GUIDANCE

Question: At the break I asked you about the use of force on students. You promised to answer in class when you had time. How about now?

Answer: Good, all right. This will require some time so we shall make it the last question and answer. It also presents research results that we did not expect or like. That's one trouble with a scientific approach.

Among the dropouts that we have educated over the past eight years in our high schools, for every violence-abused child, we estimate that we have had at least ten love-abused—meaning spoiled—children who were out of emotional self-control.

I repeat, for the sake of the nation, force an effective truancy system into your area. Get all of our children into restructured mini-schools. Then, make certain the laws and policies allow for historically effective hands-on encouragement and discipline in the schools. That necessitates hands-on love both for encouragement and correction for some. *Of course, work this out with the other parents, the police, the welfare officials, the social workers, the teachers, with everyone.* But do not condone the timid view that allows children to be suspended and expelled because no one has the courage and personal interest to control them physically to keep them in school, or to keep them from committing assaults on other children or from committing other crimes.

When the schools are made interesting with much learning going on, our experiments have revealed that even the most dangerous, criminally active teenagers will tolerate and support the strict truancy and *negative physical consequences,* for antisocial acts, from their role-model educational guardians.

Don't forget, the reasonable competitive athletic program *for each child* is a necessary factor for establishing the constructive school context. We use one-on-one unarmed combat matches for every child in school occasionally paired against students from another school. Even though these are friendly events in which no win-or-lose decisions are made, it is *very* exciting. Every boxing fan knows that judges cannot tell who wins a close fight anyway. Each student feels the butterflies for both self and school. For students who are absolute pacifists and cannot abide hitting anyone, don't fight it; allow a suitably physically demanding substitute.

Accelerated (imagery and thought) learning is a close second for making schools adequately interesting and worthwhile. *Each student maintains a self-development notebook with his or her illustrated record of achievement.* This student-responsibility for learning along with strong discipline and artistic expression, probably tie for third.

Those are our tentative findings. Even though we have worked with tough male teenagers whom everyone said would try to kill us if we touched them, in general, we found the opposite. They accepted physical contact, both positive and negative, as a constructive factor in their learning. They just do not want to be touched completely unjustly or in a discriminatory way. They must know from your previous dealings with them that you mean well, and genuinely care for them.

Teach all of the success values such as punctuality, tenacity, work completion, etc., by using timely positive and negative consequences. Allow for no excuses, if you let them off, you might as well tell them you don't care.

You might ask what is the difference between physical consequences and corporal punishment which we oppose.

In answer, they look similar, but there is a significant difference in the idea. We use physical consequences mainly to force students to do constructive things in place of the negative acts they were trying to do. Of course it may get violent; a student might refuse and then we would assign another duty such as studying. Then, he (usually he) might try to leave school. We would stop him. He has to accept the constructive consequences, or ask for a transfer to another school with parental approval. If the latter is impossible, he is stuck with the increasingly negative consequences. If he finally tries to fight, we increase the power against him until we win the fight. The psychology is definitely different from corporal punishment. The students do not confuse the two.

None of our students would ever go home and tell a parent, *"I got spanked today;"* however, some have gone home and said, "I fought with a teacher today. Now I have to read an extra book over the weekend, run five miles extra in my conditioning program, and do an extra community-work project." Of course the student could talk a parent into a transfer to another school where he or she would just be expelled. It happened once; the child was soon a complete dropout and in terrible trouble.

In another case where a drug-using, criminally active student was beating his mother to the point of splashing the kitchen walls with blood, Brad walked in on the horrible scene, fought with the attacking boy and won the fight with decisiveness. Brad reported the entire incident to the police; they, along with the mother, were pleased with his action. However, had Brad administered that kind of treatment to the boy as a punishment, he would still be in jail. As far as we can determine, these five years later, it appears, Brad saved that tough, recalcitrant teenager. His mother was considering institutionalizing him for life when we took him into our school. The main idea is to keep the child in school rather than *throw him away,* that is, rather than suspend or expel him. We humans are physical creatures; that fact cannot be ignored. Sometimes only physical experiences can teach us.

When one of the new boys in our schools continues to use drugs, we know why. It is to get that marvelous *high.* We catch him as soon as possible and try to teach him that for every such high there is a worse low coming. Beside the so-called sobering-up showers, there will be long hours of catch-up study and athletic workouts (always in conjunction with good medical exams). When we catch a boy with a needle, in the act, we take it away with as much force as is necessary. That is not punishment, the force is administered with the same feelings needed in a last-chance possibility to jerk a suicidal loved-one back from the precipice, by the hair.

What do the parents say about this? Have you ever witnessed the writhing of a drug-addicted child? If not, please remain silent. The parents beg you to spank their beloved, drug-addicted son; *break his arms*—do whatever is necessary to rid him of that drug-death that is looming in the child's future.

Will you have complete community support for advocating this serious action?

In answer, is our society responsible?

One of the most difficult students we ever forced into the school, at the request of his mother, had turned from a Little League baseball pitcher at thirteen, gradually into a drug-user and gutter-bum at fifteen. He seemed to respond favorably to our Life Values School. But he would revert to drugs and the gutter, each time, just when we thought we had him saved.

One Friday, while retaining the boy for a weekend at school, at his mother's request, due to continued theft from the home, a heated argument ensued and the boy became physical. He attempted to push by Brad to leave. Brad stopped him, **spanked him**, and sat him in a chair. At that point the boy blurted out:

"I am not a homosexual!"

It was a surprise lead.

This was one of the few cases that we experimented with corporal punishment. Though it was effective with this boy, we don't use it now. In general, it tends to be ineffective and destructive.

Brad and Galen started following the boy at night. Days of extra work expanded into months. Finally Brad unlocked the secret. The boy was, and had been, all those years, the victim of a child-abusing homosexual teacher from a prior grammar school. It took Brad another six months night-after-night with cameras, tape recorders, the works, to finally put the child-abuser in prison.

What was Brad's reward?

Satisfaction, only, at two things: First that he was finally able to save the boy. But second, mental relief from the probability that he would get arrested and put in jail, himself, during his efforts. It seemed certain that he would. Outside of his brother's help, he had no help or encouragement, just threats—including serious death threats—and strong opposition. The attitude of one policeman, alone, scared me off. But I could not persuade Brad and Galen to give up the boy for their own safety and reputations. You can imagine the accusations made by the boy toward the school and his mother (for making him attend).

So the point is, no, you cannot expect community support unless you organize it first. That is the first job before using loving physical force with confidence.

Before we took the Canadian Indian experiment, I conducted extensive research; visited all of the seven bands that the school serviced. They were scattered in a circle over an almost 200 mile-square area. We were accepting the twenty-five to thirty *hardest cases* whom the band (tribal) chiefs selected. I soon ascertained that these teenagers would be mainly the sons and daughters of prominent tribal members and that they were totally *out of control*. With a couple of exceptions, the malady was irresponsible *love abuse.* The children had never been contradicted, never mind chastised physically.

In my research and informal negotiations, I established mainly the following point: We could obtain the indispensable community support we needed from the Native elders—who have a powerful voice. They had advised me that in the old days when the Native culture was healthy, strict discipline had been enforced, physically, not only on the youth, but on all tribal members. It was enforced not so much by parents, but by uncles and trusted tribal members. This was all we needed.

The spoiled, young Indians, of course, were unmanageable in the classroom. Brad and Galen, the teachers, did not even try to control them at first. Rather, as a part of the minimum necessary community organization, they taught the children some of the magic-like imagery-learning immediately. The young persons, of course, showed-off these unbelievable skills in their homes. Parents were understandably pleased.

But because of the chaos in the classroom, my sons, the new American teachers, were still being mocked. As one prominent Native leader mused at a school board meeting in an expression of futility:

"I knew those Yankee boys could never handle our rampaging young volcanoes."

After two weeks Brad decided he had to introduce class-discipline or see all the children drop out and drift back into heavy drinking, drugs, and crime. One morning, he announced to his half of the students (fifteen): "Henceforth, we shall abide by the type discipline used when the Indians were strong; the type that must be followed again if the Native culture is to be saved."

"Big," the informal student leader, soon, threw the gauntlet back at Brad. A few minutes after Brad announced the new regime of proper discipline, Brad left the schoolroom Quonset and walked the hundred yards through the mud over to the main school building that housed the "respectable" students. He found he had been followed by a girl student who told him that Big was tearing-up the classroom because of what Brad had said about starting the discipline. Brad got Galen from the gym along with the other half of the students and returned to the Quonset which, along with the furniture and books, was being destroyed by Big.

Galen had his students be seated and himself took a seat as if the youthful tornado was not in progress. Brad moseyed over in front of the large seventeen-year-old youth who was now completely berserk. Brad calmly warned him to stop. Despite it being a felony to hit a school teacher, the boy struck at Brad. Brad grabbed the boy by the shirt-front with both hands and slammed him against a row of metal lockers. Those lockers, when hit, you may recall, make a racket like the end of the world. Galen, by this time had walked to the front of the class with his roster book nonchalantly taking the roll to keep the other students uninvolved other than as spectators.

Brad continued to slam Big against the noisy lockers time and again. Big's conscious states changed from his initial, futile effort to fight back through wild-eyed panic—at having been crossed for the first time in his life—into puppy-dog submission.

The problem was resolved and not mentioned again. Eight cases of spontaneous violence during the rest of the year had to be managed with counter force. But there were no more cases of sober, planned acting out or direct challenges to the teachers' authority.

The results of that first year: Big was the first in the class to land a job in the white society. *Every* student in the class admitted at the end of the year that they would have dropped out if not forced, physically, to stay. All expressed gratitude for having been forced to learn. The event with Big was in a category by itself. But several of the Native children told me later that it not only saved Big; it saved the entire class.

Overcoming Love Abuse

Physical force is useful in retraining children who have been totally spoiled by permissive love. Children can be forced to learn. Of course the force must be accompanied by the type love that proves that you, as a teacher, are willing to make time- and work-sacrifices for the children. Counseling alone, we found, just makes the child worse—more deceitful. The children almost always insist that they can "chump" their counselors.

When another chief's son tried to drop out after the first month of school (he did not return to school after a weekend), the rest of the class bundled up for a walk in the Canadian October cold, to go get him, just as they had been warned would happen if anyone did not come to school without an excuse. This, Brad announced, was in conformity with *the old Indian motto,* taught to us by the elders: *The hurt of one is the hurt of all.* The problem was that the tribe of the truant lived one-hundred and forty miles north. It was to be a long walk. The chief was notified by phone that the class had started on its frosty way. On the second day, after sleeping out, twenty miles from the school, the class was met by the chief, embarrassed but pleased. He showed up in his car, bringing the son.

Once a community's responsible parents see the real menace of the combined failed-education/burgeoning-drug scene, and secondly, see that there are educators who know how and are willing to solve the problems, the parents will cooperate and support any necessarily drastic solutions. They must, or we are out of luck because the soft forces in society will force and perpetuate their socially destructive softness on us.

Without some toughening-up in our schools, our society will sink further into trouble. The drugs are everywhere, seen and unseen, and they are devastating. The best way to fight them successfully is not with drug education, but rather with real, constructive, total education for each child, which we do not now have in America. It requires a positive approach. All of the negative law-and-order ways, alone, will not work.

When we first implemented this program, Brad sought hard-core educational misfits for his classes in order to prove the effectiveness of the curriculum. He did not want to try it out on an average public school: too easy, educationally speaking. He wanted to prove that children whom educators had rated as uneducable could be educated. He proved it.

Ironically, the fact that we have been so successful with *uneducable* children has placed our curriculum into a category of last resort. *If all else fails, call the Life Values School.* That is regrettable.

There is no question that our curriculum is effective and adaptable to any school environment, but it cannot be watered down without losing some of its effectiveness. When any part of any interdependent component is dropped or modified, as has happened a couple of times with the Marines, the total program is weakened.

We have already disproved the myth of the uneducable child. This sets the challenge for the next decade: rejuvenate our nation by giving *all* the heirs to our society a complete or balanced values-based education.

THE TEACHER'S RESPONSIBILITY FOR THE USE OF FORCE

In the first week in the southern California school, Brad found himself facing a knife attack. It was not the last attack with a deadly weapon. Within a month, Brad and Galen walked out of the storefront classroom to face four young thugs from a neighboring gang armed with baseball bats. The two teachers immediately attacked the two gang leaders, aggressively, with football tackles, without a word, and then, while they grappled for the bats, called out for their own wide-eyed students to call the police. (The teachers made that attack defensively; otherwise they judged they were going to be attacked and beaten with those bats. Surprise was their only defense. It worked.)

Brad, Galen, and Jess continued, personally, to deal with these attacks—meeting force with force—during the eight years of experimentation just to determine if it could be done and would be successful if employed. It can be, and it is. But that burden should not be placed on teachers. All schools with violence problems should have good, handpicked, popular police on campus with the duty to control the students *but also keep them in school,* forcefully if necessary.

In closing these thoughts on the importance of using loving, corrective, physical force, it can sometimes be employed to teach valuable lessons with the teachers taking the pain. Galen used it that way early-on with our young Mexican-American dropouts to teach them tenacity. Lack of that quality seems to be the biggest *success-defeating syndrome* suffered by most dropouts. These troubled youth seem to give up on anything difficult; they simply can not *hang in there.* So, once, with our first class, in desperation to try to teach them this quality (and respond to a student's challenge). Galen (a lightweight novice fighter, 135 pounds) boxed with everyone in the class, all in succession, without rest in between thirty rounds; this, to show them what a person *can take and still hang in there,* if challenged.

The class applauded and began to try to learn the lesson. Jess accomplished the same feat four years later when he had the school, alone, and feared he was *losing one "quitter" back to crime.* It was again highly effective. Galen did it also with eight big Marine martial artists and so-called athletic studs to prove to them that good boxers can deal easily with trained martial artists. They all soon agreed.

CONCLUSION TO THE GENERAL SCHOOL REFORM LESSONS

Our Life Values Schools included eight-plus years of fascinating and heartrending case studies that illustrate the effectiveness of values-guided education. But Brad, Galen, and Jess must tell that full story. They spent those thousand-plus days in the classroom and those thousand nights doing proper truancy work because our communities are too irresponsible to take to those tasks.

During all those years, I only advised. So, I repeat, those three must tell that story. But don't wait. Build your own story of success in reforming the schools, your own story of success in restrengthening the nation, and your own story of personal involvement with your children. Use the educational revolt with the home school if necessary, especially if your young children are exposed to drugs in the local school. Currently, official America clearly does not seem to possess the understanding nor the resolve to stop that monster. Too many people are making too much money. It could be stopped if national leadership were responsible.

The reward for taking your children out of the failing school system or for building something better, will be a tremendous reduction of family tensions. If you serve your own children well, especially if you succeed in helping build a better world for them, you will be considerably more pleased with your own life than otherwise, no matter what else you do, or ever did. This too is the Law of Nature.

ATTACHMENT C

PART I

THE REASONS FOR UNDERDEVELOPMENT

Part I of this attachment is the copy of a lesson used all through my overseas military programs during the Cold War. Second only to the materials on human equality and STRIKE, this was the most important lesson in the entire program.

Lesson Purpose: To stimulate respect for the foreign peoples through a consideration of the geographic versus cultural reasons for poverty.

Instructions: Leaders should commit these facts, at least in general, to memory, and then present them at the relevant time. Don't turn off your personnel to these important materials by reading or presenting them as in a traditional school lesson. For most persons the memories of the school scene are too negative.

Earlier we discussed the tendency for a wealthy people to *look down* on a poor, uneducated, uncultured people. Let us return now to that topic. There is an idea in American popular philosophy that represents the problem. It is expressed by the needling comment that many of us have flung at friends: *If you're so smart, why ain't you rich?* It is only partially a joke.

There appears to be a tendency in the American culture to judge a man's intelligence by his wealth. it can contribute significantly to the unfair view that an entire nation is poor mainly because the people are stupid or lazy. Studies among overseas Americans indicate that we usually make the error of that destructive exaggeration. For example, ask several American associates outside of the these classes why the local people in any Third World country are poor compared to us Americans. Ask if it is because of the lack of intelligence and industriousness of the people or if it is because of limited natural resources and other geographic conditions.

Probably you will find that the majority of Americans believe that the local people themselves are to blame, and that we Americans, personally, can take the primary credit for our great wealth, completely aside from the benefit of superior natural resources.

Let us examine the validity of that position, first, by looking at a comparative situation here in the U.S.: Some of you may be from one of two adjoining areas, the Kentucky/Tennessee area, or the Illinois/Indiana region.

Now take a World Almanac and compare the two areas. Concentrate on the two adjoining states of Kentucky and Illinois. You will find that despite the fact that Illinois is only about one-fourth larger in land area than Kentucky, three times as many people live in Illinois and produce considerably more wealth per person than the people of Kentucky. From 1955 to 1960, the average income was about $2,500 in Illinois compared to only about $1,500 in Kentucky. This means the people of Illinois, with only three times the population of Kentucky, produce five times as much wealth as Kentucky.

How is it possible that the Illinois people can produce that *much more* than those of us from a little farther south? Is it because they are naturally smarter and more industrious than we are? They do spend more money per child on education. Is that the primary deciding factor? Or is the explanation more likely the superior abundance of natural resources enjoyed by Illinois? For example:

1. Illinois farmland compares favorably with the best in the world. Kentucky's is good, too, but on the average, it is not as valuable as Illinois land.

2. Next, more than two-thirds of the Illinois land can be used for farming, compared to substantially less than half of Kentucky's.

3. If that is not enough, a check through some atlases shows that Illinois also has an advantage in mineral deposits.

4. Also notice that Kentucky has good lakes and streams, but nothing compares with the Illinois position on the Great Lakes, and the Mississippi River which runs the entire length of the state's longest side.

Now, we'll consider whether there are any clear geographic reasons why some entire countries are rich while others are poor. Compare four general categories of resources that lead to wealth: good farm and fishing land, mineral wealth and healthy forests, geographic zones suitable for human habitation, and natural advantages for transportation and communication.

For an illustration, we will compare the United States and Bolivia. Bolivia is one of the poorest countries of the world. The question is: why? I have heard Americans stationed there denounce the Bolivians with this statement: *This country has great wealth if these people would only develop it.*

What are the facts? The following comparisons come from World Climate and Economic Tables in large library atlases such as Collier or Rand McNally, dated in the 1950s or '60s (during the time of our early programs).

1. What percent of each country's land is arable (*good for farming?*)

    The U.S.—24%

    Bolivia—1%

2. How much of the land is neither mountainous nor jungles?

    The U.S.—Around 65%

    Bolivia—Less than 25%

3. Estimate the percentage of the land that receives good rainfall, that is, 20 to 60 inches of well-spaced rainfall annually.

    The U.S.—At least 50%

    Bolivia—At best 25%

4. About how much of the land is in the temperate zone, rather than in the arctic or tropics?

The U.S.—At least 60%

Bolivia—0%

5. How many ice-free seaports and navigable waterways? (Rate many, several, few, or none.)

The U.S.—Many

Bolivia—None

6. How many major deposits of the chief minerals are shown on comparative charts?

Lead and Zinc

The U.S.—4   Bolivia—1

Oil and Natural Gas

The U.S.—9   Bolivia—0

Coal and Lignite

The U.S.—34   Bolivia—5

Iron

The U.S.—11   Bolivia—1

Ferroalloys

The U.S.—7   Bolivia—2

Copper and Tin

The U.S.—10   Bolivia—2

SUMMARY

When we Americans blame other peoples for their comparative poverty without knowing the comparative natural advantages that our well-blessed land gives us, it just makes us look foolish, as still uninformed.

ATTACHMENT C

PART II

LOOSE ENDS

The following questions and materials are taken from two sources: (a) the tapes and notes of final review and question sessions in many college courses, and (b) the questions and answers at the conclusion of several major educational conferences where a brief outline of the theory had been presented.

FOREIGNERS' INTERESTS IN U.S. RACE RELATIONS

The most frequent question I am asked by foreign nationals about implementation of the theory in America goes either to our U.S. black/white problems or to our white/Indian relations. To answer those two closely related areas of questioning adequately will require another book.

PROGRAM ORIGIN AND ITS NECESSARY LEADERSHIP

The next most frequent vein of questioning is personal, especially from foreign students. They ask, (1) how, I, as a big-business-oriented (Harvard-trained) legal student got into such a "financially unrewarding" (*"obscure," "impractical,"* or *"philosophical"*) offshoot of the law? And (2) (a variation of that) since this values-guided problem-solving method has been forthcoming from the law, why is it that our worst ethics problems seem so often to involve the questionable actions of lawyers: lawyers in business, lawyers in the

Congress, and even the entire legal system that appears to support criminals more than victims of crime? And (3), *if a study of the law includes values, why are so many lawyers getting rich through fees that often exploit persons already caught up in one of life's great tragedies?*

After I got over my defensiveness, and took the time to reveal pertinent, personal history and feelings, the following answer, in brief, has been well-received:

When I left home in Mud City, Missouri, as a teenager, it was not to become a lawyer. The departure and venture were mainly philosophically inspired. But it was also to seek survival without crime by joining the CCCs (for destitute, unemployable youths). Along with the excitement of the adventure, I held angry reservations about the unfathomable evil behind the Great Depression. It had stopped the joyous street music in my beloved hometown of Mud City and had traumatized too many happy families in that previously secure little town. It had stifled the roaring laughter of the 1920s all across America.

I was convinced that there had to be a better response to life's killing viciousness somewhere *out there in the bigger world.* All the responsible adults I knew said there was; they said it was available through *advanced education.*

So I started that long quest in and out of the CCCs, finished high school and Sidetown Junior College, and continued working, boxing, and seeking scholarships through twelve years of advanced academia, through eight universities, each a more renowned institution than the last, finally, into Harvard Law. Literally, I was *driven* by the thought that someplace up that academic ladder of superior knowledge, there had to be that superior answer, that greater wisdom. And where else than at Harvard Law?

I am sure you know what I found: that greater wisdom is not up there anywhere. I sat, finally, in head-reeling satisfaction along with the other students who had *made it* into the classroom of the greatest university. I sat there knowing that after all those years of struggle, now, finally, the answers would be forthcoming from the world's most-renowned teachers.

As one of those chosen few students in that illustrious classroom, at Harvard Law, I would be let in on the answers to peace and happiness that awaited only *the learning of those answers and then passing them along more effectively out to the masses in society.*

And what happened?

I was soon stunned with a sense of betrayal down into my unbelieving soul. The first words from the mouth of a distinguished professor, who walked out on that majestic stage, speciously defended the constitutionality of racist laws with all the vehemence of my red-necked friends back home. My roommate in the seat beside me was a black, and he had been blind from childhood. He had struggled harder, much harder than I, to get there. I felt and heard his whole body cringe in the creaking seat.

Since then, I have moved around a bit near the top of academia, big business, big philanthropy, and the military. Judging from those limited experiences, and allowing for the notable exceptions, do you know who is leading this *cat and dog society* at the top of most groups? I should have known: The fiercest cats and biggest dogs; and that puts it tactfully. I could have asked who is out front in the rat race.

THE UPSHOT—YOUR LEADERSHIP TOWARD WISDOM

The lesson from those experiences across the top of society is this: The open-minded leadership needed for us to escape the rat race, to find peace, and to stop violence, is not up there in general. There are only a very few original, objective thinkers. And they, similar to Socrates, (or Christ, for that matter) are not at all welcome in the ruling circles of the time.

The main problem is the closed mind; so above all else, try with bulldog tenacity to keep an open mind to new ideas including those that sound strange. Try to find better answers—a way out of this global violence.

If you endorse the Balanced Life Value, give your children its basic guidance to protect them from the philosophical foolishness generally taught in the schools. Those Dark Age philosophies still taught effectively are: selfishness, materialism, relativism, envy, and cynicism.

GOOD PHILOSOPHICAL GUIDELINES TO TEACH YOUR CHILDREN

Coach your children before they go to high school and again before they go to college with these three ideas. All else in the realm of values will take care of itself. But these three ideas are crucial:

One, warn your children that they will be taught one or more of these philosophies: that human nature is either (1) *all bad* (Freudian), or (2) *selfish* (mainly profit motivated), or (3) *all intellect, with no good or bad* (relativism).

Second, advise them that they will be presented with illustrious names or phrases ostensibly giving credibility to those descriptions of human nature: Locke, Skinner, Freud, Hegel, Nietzsche, Sartre, Adam Smith, the Invisible Hand.

Third, caution your loved ones to measure those views against the Balanced Life Value theory and decide for themselves which best describes their own feelings of self. The top measure of all things, earthly, is their own combined feelings and judgment.

The *life value* teaches that we humans have the three primary characteristics (which create our basic, equal-feeling Balanced Life Value):

1. The Individualistic Self-Preserving Drive,

2. The Social or Loving Species-Preserving Drive, and

3. The more-or-less Free-thinking Brain.

THE NATURE OF THE BRAIN

Recently, in my lectures and conferences, there have been many questions on the topic of the *more-or-less free-thinking* aspect of the brain is one of the more difficult concepts to consider with an open mind. Dwell on it a bit. Why do we all so often have to deal with persons with tightly closed-minds? We all see that troublesome phenomenon in others but not in ourselves. Here, apparently, is why human brains are so notoriously *closed*.

Our brains (our minds) apparently, cannot change easily. Putting the best light on it, human brains are not at all fickle or flighty. They are very conservative. Why? It is from a genetic, survival-serving cautiousness—a careful, life-protecting attitude *selected-in* during those years of early human development. Life was precarious then; all change was threatening. All carelessness was deadly.

Hence, when humans learn something and it works, that is, after we accept it, our brains seem to tend to set or *fix* on that knowledge. This fix is especially strong if we place a self-protective or possessive *value* on that knowledge, or if we perceive it as containing *morally right* content. The mere factual knowledge takes on some emotional importance. Consequently, something extra, something physical or chemical, probably, occurs in certain brain cells which, after that, does not allow the brain to respond to pure logic alone. Apparently that is why we learn values only from experiences that deliver emotional impact. Of course, sound logic is helpful in changing values (attitudes), but it is not absolutely necessary. Demagogues, rabble-rousers, and many average politicians exploit this fact. Some rely *exclusively* on appeals to the emotions.

THE NATURE OF RATIONALITY

In that same vein, understand that most people of the world do not view mere *thinking* (the ability to calculate and scheme) the same as they do *rationality or reasoning* (the ability to exercise *common sense or wisdom*). Thinking that is effective but exploits others is called by such terms as *clever, smart, or criminal genius;* it is also denounced as *irrational or unwise.* Thought (pure thought, including extremely clever criminal thinking) that is in any way threatening to life is denounced in negative terms connoting a lack of rationality. The negative evaluations range from *mildly foolish* through *irrational to maniacal.*

THE GREEN-EYED MONSTER: GREED

If fear is the most dangerous negative value, greed is a close second. Yet it seemed to me in all of my experience as a college and graduate student (twelve years) that the prevailing philosophy taught by American economists is that human nature is primarily profit-motivated (selfish). Small wonder our congressmen (and doctors, and lawyers, not to mention our Wall Street business leaders) are threatening the unity and strength of our nation by their insatiable chase for millionaire status rather than for national well-being and general happiness.

The profit-motivated or economic theory of human nature is absolutely unsound from the test of my worldwide experiences. As a description of universal human nature in the villages of the world it is simply wrong. Our greed is culture-*bound* to overly-specialized economic thinking.

Over forty years ago, our American economists took the *economic man theory* of human nature into all of the underdeveloped world. As a part of the U.S. AID development-plans for the *underdeveloped people,* our economists gave extra incomes to workers in many traditional societies, and then promised them even more income if they would work longer, harder hours. Representative economists of that profit-oriented philosophy told me smugly, *These natives are just like us, they will work harder now for the almighty dollar.*

The natives where I was at the time in the Middle East, and later in Latin America, did not do it!

After they got that extra money, up to the level of their life's needs, they baffled the American economists by taking more time off for non-economic values: to be with their families, to see more soccer games, to go fishing, or just to get the extra leisure.

Regarding Strength, Happiness, and Leadership

We do not need greater wealth in America. Rather, we need better values to guide us individually, privately in use of our wealth.

For Strength and Health. We might be better off with less wealth for greater strength and health. Too much wealth seems to lead to softness. If seems to result in too little exercise, which is destroying the health of our children currently on a national scale. That's a fact.

For Happiness. The happiest persons that I have encountered, by far, have been middle-income to lower-income families all over the world. These are the families that most often take the time to develop themselves and their small communities, wisely, into informal singing, dancing, and family groups for self-entertainment. There is much more of this, now, everywhere else, than in most parts of modern America (not counting our mountainous and a few other isolated areas). This is true in all parts of less-wealthy Europe, the British Isles, Latin America, Asia, and Africa. A much higher percentage of Americans, it appears, are much more tensed-up over the scramble for extra income—above necessities. And party-groups are not made up, primarily, of families. Rather, they are less socially healthy peer groups.

For Leadership Again. Let us all, at the grass-roots level, try to lead specifically toward more happiness through more human consideration with less time spent seeking money (within reason of course).

Let us back off reasonably and carefully from the wealth-chasing rat race. Strangely, we might even be better off financially, nationally, if we give more thought to human consideration. Germany and Japan are the two economic powers that concern the U.S. most as competitors. In trying to determine, through in-depth discussions in both countries, why they are so efficient and productive, I could find only two major, and to me surprising, differences from us. It seems to me, without adequate studies, that they do work harder, longer hours. But they do not *go so hard for the quick buck,* in the words of one Japanese businessman, but *take it a little easier, mentally, with longer-range views that protect their people.* And in the words of a German businessman, they *think first of the well-being of their workers somewhat as the Japanese do.*

What I am suggesting is that going too hard for the brass ring of wealth is like wishing on the monkey's paw. Do you know the story? Each wish made on the monkey's paw came true, but always at the cost of something terrible. For example, while the man of the house was away working, the mother and children of a young family wished for wealth on the monkey's paw. It came immediately as the payoff on a life insurance policy. The young man of the house—husband and father—had been killed in an accident.

A PEACEFUL POLITICAL REVOLUTION

To extricate ourselves from the rat race, perhaps we need another voters' revolt. In order to force our nation out of the *tension-filled scramble for vain wealth,* allowing for special exceptions, maybe we should decide against electing anyone to public office who is too wealthy—a millionaire, say, as many of our senators are. Maybe their leadership policies are too penurious, too selfish, too smugly indifferent to the cooperative needs of us average folk. Perhaps their attitudes are just too stingy for the welfare of the entire nation; perhaps their philosophies are just too close to the dangers posed by wishing on the monkey's paw.

It was not the departure of some mothers from the American home that undercut the family; it was the separation of working fathers from the home neighborhoods during the past fifty years. Let us do whatever is necessary to think a little less of appearances, fancy clothes, expensive cars, and zoning codes, in order to give more unhurried time and encouragement to the persons around us, especially the family unity and children. We definitely need to retain and protect our smaller farms and smaller communities versus the urban movement into overpopulated metropolitan areas; this, even though protecting those small social groups may be comparatively inefficient. But don't forget, the giant farms are often subsidized, too.

If the necessary enlightened changes in attitudes actually require a political revolt, then let us have it. That is the way democracy works.

Communism, Capitalism and the Life Value

In China, anti-capitalistic communism is still in control. Economically, communism is merely the fanatical, exaggerated dedication to the (social) species-preserving side of human nature. Rank capitalism is the similarly misguided devotion to the other side of human nature, or individualistic self-preserving side. For peace, the two exaggerated half-views of human nature can be reconciled. Since the fanatical *true believers* of both half-truths are sincere, rather than intentionally evil (as President Reagan, finally, happily admitted), their distorted views can be corrected. But it probably cannot be accomplished by words alone. On the American scene, it is probably going to require some rugged individualistic defiance of neighborhood pressures to keep up with the materialistic Joneses.

Some years ago, my wife and I were attending a fairly exclusive party at the home of a Pakistani diplomat in a Near Eastern capital. Among the dozen or so guests from five or six countries was a Russian couple from their embassy. We chatted, as my wife and I did with everyone at the small party. The events were limited, as most diplomatic parties are, to cocktails and talk. As the party ended and we were leaving, I used my one Russian phrase on the Russian couple: *Dosvidanya*, confident that it meant *goodbye*.

This Russian diplomat was a harmless-looking little fat man. But my brilliant little Russian *adios* started him absolutely sputtering. In anger and consternation, he objected to my leaving the scene. I was dumbfounded. Immediately I wondered, *What the hell does "dosvidanya" really mean?*

The guy actually called the Pakistani host over to us and blurted out his concern. "Your friend, Humphrey, here, speaks Russian and he did not tell us."

That was it; he was apparently afraid that I was a spy and had been eavesdropping on his conversation with his wife. (What could they have said that was so sensitive?)

The Pakistani officer was a subdued man but one full of quiet mischief. He knew me well for many years and knew that I did not speak Russian. He turned to me, pointed his finger at me as if it were a handgun, and said, *All right, Humphrey Bogart, up with your hands. I complied.* He pretended to frisk me quickly; then turned to the Russian and said very reassuringly. "He's clean; no wire and no weapon."

His obvious joking pulled me back from my embarrassment over possibly having embarrassed him. In that instant of relief, my Irish wife, with ever-ready wit but a tricky temper, flared. She said to the Pakistani, but loud for the Russian's ears: *Tell him that I found his Russian conversation with his wife very boring.* The Pakistani laughed but told me later that my wife's comment really blew everything, almost stimulated a full investigation (whatever that meant).

There were other similar incidents and the point is this: The Russian officials that I met seemed quite paranoid. I found the same thing inside Russia, only worse. This paranoia, if it still exists or returns makes them dangerous. Of course, as cultural detectives, we should not be surprised about their possible paranoia in their attitudes toward the West. Their nation has been invaded twice, lately in history, from the West. Do you recall how many persons in the USSR were killed by the last invasion from the Christian West? Over twenty million! So I don't blame them for some concern as a Slavic nation in relation to their Nordic neighbors. Still, that type paranoia down among their working-level officials is definitely dangerous. We have that fact to contend with. Possibly, as one Russian told me, it is an historic Russian thing, rather than the result of modern communism.

The Russian People. After brief but concentrated associations of the several members of my large family with common-folk Russians in Odessa and Moscow, one evening my wife teared up at dinner. "What is it, honey?" I asked." I don't know for sure," she answered, "but after this trip, I am so confused. I was always taught in my (Boston) Irish Catholic circles to distrust these people. But they are so nice; so now, I don't know what to think."

Collectivism versus Economic Individualism. What does the controlling Balanced Life Value promise for the new, possibly more democratic, former Soviet Union country?

As a cultural detective with some appreciation of geography, remember that some groups in Asia are compelled by a difficult environment to use considerable collectivism. That austere frozen land, just like Norway, Sweden, and Finland, forces cooperation among its peoples to avoid starvation. Until technology allows them to melt the winter ice and snow for longer growing seasons, that need for cooperative economics won't change drastically. Here is how it works off of the life value.

Human nature, as we have learned, consists of the two primary life drives: for species-preservation and self-preservation, plus the ability to reason. The need for the self-preserving drive is obvious. The cooperative inclination is hardly less indispensable.

Why?

It is because of our helplessness as babies and our historic semi-defenselessness, when alone, against our Stone Age enemies. However, our cooperative inclinations must be *especially* nurtured among those humans who have to live in the unfriendly icy lands of such places as Russia or northern Canada. (For Americans who do not already know, the Canadian people's socialistic lack of economic individualistic hustle is annoying to many other Westerners living up there. The latter do not understand.)

THE COOPERATIVE NATURE OF AMERICANS

For a closer-to-home clarification of humankind's cooperative nature, I'll return again for an example from my boyhood during the drought of the Great Depression. During those dust-bowl days of the 1930s, farmers, once fiercely individualistic, swallowed their pride enough to accept help for digging necessarily *deeper* wells than one man, alone, could dig.

Similarly, did you know that Japan's modern productive miracle in their factories rests on a strong tradition of communal-farms with collective governing needed for their labor-intensive rice growing?

Finally, despite our strong economic and political conditioning to individual freedom, even we Americans are always struck by the deeply satisfying stimulation of our cooperative nature while helping each other during and after life-threatening conflagrations such as floods, tornadoes, and earthquakes.

Our Individualistic Nature. Our collective tendencies in no way negate the facts that we also possess counterbalancing individualistic tendencies and the big, somewhat free-thinking brain. These militate in favor of individual flexibility for maximum survival chances and pleasant, easy, individual freedom. When changes are truly needed and the means are available for successful individual action, to have to wait on cooperation and collective decisions is foolish (life-destructive). It's the same as on any good, professional basketball team. Individualistic, every-man-for-himself play is the easiest, most enjoyable way to play. But to defeat another, better team of individuals, the men have to discipline themselves for the use of teamwork, but with the freedom for an individual "star" play when the opportunity arises. It is the balance, of course, that is best.

How Much Freedom in Life's Balance? The ideal amount of freedom and cooperation depends, at least in part, on the combination needed for the particular environment. Just as rigid communism (collectivism) has not been able to last without strong, dangerous challenges in China, it would have no chance at all in our resources-wealthy America. China's geography may fit a close balance between economic individualism and economic collectivism or cooperation. Eventually, the Chinese will find that ideal balance. *In the long run,* the land (natural resources) and human nature will be the determinants, not politics.

Raw, fanatical politics could try to put communism in America, rank capitalism in Russia, or a distorted combination in China. But the arbitrary political decrees would not last. There are laws of nature and of human nature that spell SURVIVAL. They eventually control economics/politics—through violence if necessary. As my Finnish friend once exclaimed: *If America, Russia, and China are ever stupid enough to go to war over the best economic system for the other guy, somebody should be shot.* (Regarding communism, we should not overestimate the extent of its demise in the world. Communism, recall, is an exaggerated belief in the species-preserving goodness of man. As such, it will remain an ideological force in many of the poverty-stricken areas of the world, including parts of China, until capitalistic leaders become kind, gentle, and protective forces in the world.)

Liberals versus Conservatives. The political struggle all over the world, I find, is all the same, because human nature is the same. It is the struggle of the persons who are strongly aware of the need to encourage the self-preserving, or the individual, side of human nature, versus those who lean more toward encouraging the species-preserving (cooperative) side. Respectively, these persons tend to be the champions of the *haves* of the world versus the champions of the *have-nots.*

Whether or not these intellectual adversaries understand that each is encouraging only half of the proper formula, the contest works effectively, gradually, despite tremendous backsliding at times and despite the stupid violence. Depending substantially on how much education there is in a society, and on how abundant the natural resources are in a particular land, the necessary balancing changes occur rapidly or slowly, peacefully or with violence.

Reconciliation between the two sides of the unnecessarily dangerous debate between Left and Right awaits recognition (and admission) by both the conservatives and the liberals that human nature has both sides: the individual and the collective. See Figure 3 in Chapter 21. The formula for a political-economy that recognizes properly balanced human nature calls simply for:

1) *All the economic collectivism necessary* (to protect the group—including the weak members), and

2) *All the economic freedom possible* in order to encourage individuals to produce as much as possible for both their

own gain and for the group. (I never had any problem convincing young Communist youths in Latin America that this interpretation of human nature is better—more complete—than communism's.)

Rational Control. How much economic freedom is possible and how much collectivism is necessary depends on the environment. More freedom is possible when there are good natural resources and well-developed human resources. In democracy, individual judgment, collectively expressed, must be relied on to establish and regulate the balance. See Figure 5 in Chapter 21.

The most important fact to remember is that the system is enforced by the Natural Law. Humankind feels a *Right of Revolution* (a right of life-defense for self and in-groups). That Natural Law is voiced in our Declaration of Independence. When respect for the Right to Life is withheld, it inevitably threatens *violence* because of the feared and likely injustices. Out of the human emotions, there will come rage; violence will tend to follow. Status quo forces are fond of saying, Violence *never solved anything.* What then of 1776, and 1914, and 1945 in American history?

Violence solves many problems; not always too well, but in the absence of justice, it will be called on, if possible, to try to solve major human problems. Consequently, now that one or two persons can assemble and carry an atomic bomb, self-serving injustice is foolish either for conservatives or liberals of any description.

FURTHER REMARKS ABOUT THE NATURAL LAW

Question from a Buddhist Student in an Asian Group: When I advise my American friends that there is something genetic in the individual human psyche that protects "other life," some argue back with pat-answer-rejections. They advise me, citing teachers, that such views are "religious superstition" and "super-sensory mythology." Some add that an individual's consideration for anything outside the "self" is merely social conditioning and not possibly genetic.

Is there anything of an accepted scientific nature that supports species-preservation, that cynical, factually oriented American students would be compelled to admit?

Answer: Yes, resort immediately to proof in the animal kingdom. Such reminders always establish conclusively that species-preservation drives are a fact of nature. You may recall that this was the same problem that weakened one of my own most important programs in Vietnam. Find the account of the leopard and baboons. It was a necessary inclusion to meet a similar problem of crisis importance.

For a vivid, recently observed example in my life, let me relate the following true story. You can use others from your own experiences.

There is a thrush-like bird that annually visits my former neighborhood in California. I think it is a mockingbird. Being a typical little bird, it is about the most skittish, apparently cowardly, thing on earth. For days and weeks, every time I saw it and eased my way carefully toward its tree, trying to get a photograph, it would, as if by some sixth sense, discover my silent approach and flit off.

Then one day, a baby chick fell into the grass. Suddenly, the little parent bird changed, like a timid person turned snarling aggressor behind the wheel of a car. Its entire constitution—every fiber in its previously nervous little body—completely reversed itself. It actually started dive-bombing our big family cat. It dove at old Sam time and time again with such fury that it brushed the hair on his back. Sam, king tomcat of our back-alley, wasn't unimpressed. He cowered down a bit under the repetitive dive-bombing attacks.

Species-preservation in most well-known species of animal life and, apparently, in all human in-groups, is the first law of nature. Self-preservation is only a strong second. We humans can control, distort, or even reverse these complementary halves of the fundamental life-drive with our big free-thinking brains; but that balanced, or dual, life-preserving inclination is nonetheless the instinct-like floor of our natures with the species-preserving side holding the edge over self-preservation in healthy human beings. (It simply fails in its natural functioning, to a degree, in selfish, or in other anti-socially sick—murderous or suicidal—persons. There are many misfires in the balanced life-preserving system; it is far from infallible, but it is basic.) See Figure 4 in Chapter 21.

Saying it another way, while properly emphasizing the prevailing species-preserving side of the life value: we humans, obviously in our natural, small-group habitats, as a life form, are not uniquely devoid of the species-preserving inclination (as has been too-frequently alleged). If we were, there would be *no way* to raise armies of honorable, altruistic, patriotic young men and women to protect the loved-ones against aggressive attack. And men would not behave the way I saw them behave, almost casually, self-sacrificially every day in the carnage called Iwo Jima. Under that ultimate, values-clarifying condition, combat, I saw some of our most previously chauvinistic Americans unconscionably denounce our most deeply conditioned patriotic values, yet matter-of-factly, risk their lives for their group-members.

In this vein, there is a popular myth among intellectuals who are inexperienced in the wild that we humans are the only animal that makes war. That is false. The other well-known groups, or related species, of animals that also make war are the communal insects such as the ants. They are not mainly self-preservers, but rather, species-preservers.

Planned warfare, for humans, involves a strong consciousness of deadly risk-taking. Consequently, the evil of warfare does not prove how bad we human beings are. Ironically, to the contrary: Aggressive warfare (if not by the leaders, at least by the masses) is a mistake caused by misguided species-preserving tendencies, not by selfishness gone astray. Unfortunately, that makes it more dangerous, not less, because species-preservation provides the stronger, more satisfying (patriotic) motivation.

THE BALANCED LIFE VALUE AND THE HUMAN BRAIN

Question: You mentioned in the seminar, yesterday, the interesting lateral division between the left and right sides of the brain – with the left side apparently managing the linear details of reading, writing, and arithmetic, and the right side, the more general concepts including total visual imagery. I read that the brain is divided-up vertically, top to bottom rather than horizontally with side by side parts. Which is it?

Answer: Both, as far as I know as a layman in the field. But the topic especially interests me ever since participating in a national/educational conference in Florida, last year.

I had completed my comments on the Balanced Life Value. The group of scholars, in addition to high school teachers, who were most interested and gathered around after the speech, advised me that they were students of the so-called *triune brain*—a fascinating and relatively new area of study.

Referring to our Life Values Schools, these scholars, besides corroborating the desirability of stimulating imagery for the right side of the brain, explained the vertical division of the brain in speculative relationship to the three key components in Life Value Theory. As I understood their explanations, the brain is divided into three parts, vertically:

1. The lower brainstem area is similar to the brain of the reptiles. This would be the locale of the strong self-preservation drive.

2. The middle brain is similar to the brain of the mammal and would accommodate the strong (stronger) species-preservation drive.

3. Finally, of course, is the upper brain, the human component that includes the cerebral cortex, the area, regarding our theory, that affords strictly human, free, rational controllability over instincts.

I am fascinated by the new evidence regarding these apparently somewhat independently developed parts of the brain because of the possible relationship to life-protecting rationality and wisdom versus mere thought and factual knowledge.

As it is with the right and left hemispheres of the brain, the three vertical parts also operate somewhat independently of one another, I was told. This may help explain why a person can possess a genius-like upper (cerebral cortex) part of the brain for mathematical calculations or fact-accumulation but still be inconsiderate and unkind to others and even self-destructive. Conversely, other persons who are not particularly adept in upper, left brain, linear academic matters, are often considered to be persons of *wisdom* and are consulted when there are values conflicts. This dichotomy is encountered almost routinely in the traditional villages of the world where everyone knows everyone else and knows their comparative strengths and weaknesses.

Follow-up Question: This is not a hostile question; I am asking it abruptly for clarity: Are you saying that the brain produces "thought" but the instinct-like drives produce "rationality"?

Answer: It is a good question for purposes of clarification. Different parts of the brain are apparently the loci of both thought (that is, so-called *cold calculation*) and also the instinct-like drives (the balanced human-life supporting inclinations). Both forces are seated in the brain.

However, *rational thought* or rational action must be not only free thought but also, on-balance, life-protecting. And the life-protecting aspect is the rationality part. That part, alone, is not necessarily calculated; usually, it is instinct-like. Life-protection comes out of the emotions—out of the life drives. All so-called dumb (unthinking) animals also possess it strongly, instinctively. So rational thought (the two things together) is the result of at least two functions of the brain working together. Without the harmony, a person might follow species-preserving inclinations (the life-drive) foolishly (irrationally) into certain death to try to save a loved-one where there is no chance; or another might figure out a brilliant but irrational (insane) plan to make a fortune for self by killing other people. Both have been done.

HUMANKIND'S PHILOSOPHICAL FREEDOM

Question: You said yesterday that you are not a trained philosopher; neither am I. Nonetheless, I want to ask you the question that two of our philosophy students discussed, emotionally, last night into the morning hours and seemed to be saying that it is one of philosophy's most important questions. If I understand, it asks whether or not we humans are truly free, or, conversely, are we merely the robot-like pawns of predetermining forces that are bigger than human beings and beyond human understanding?

Answer: I may not understand that *old* philosophical question either. (It is an old question.) Whether I do or don't, the new scientific philosophy revealed by the understanding of the Balanced Life Value raises the same issue. It is important; and, clearly, it has an answer, now:

Life—the Balanced Life Value—is not only humankind's most basic earthly value, it sets the measure of good and bad in human actions, and also, especially, of right and wrong—the key stuff of ethics and morality.

Good acts support the Balanced Life Value; bad acts harm it. *Right acts* or moral acts *intentionally* support the life value; wrong or immoral acts intentionally harm it.

Human nature's thought patterns adjudge degrees of moral (good and right) actions. The highest degree of goodness is that willing act in which the individual intentionally sacrifices his or her life for another. *No greater love hath any man...*

So here is the answer to that great philosophical question on meaningful choice in human life versus robot-like determinism. In the most important arena of life: the balance between the two sides of the life value, choice is not only possible, it is the daily essence of life. Life consists of daily giving-or-taking choices in all relationships ranging from little acts of giving or taking to the maximum choice expressed through selflessly dying for, or selfishly killing, another. Short of eternal life on Earth, how much more freedom of choice, versus robot-like determinism, could a mortal want?

INDEX

F

G

H

I

J

K

L

ORDER FORM

NAME_____

ADDRESS_____

CITY_____ STATE_____ ZIP _____

PHONE_____

E-MAIL_____

BOOK NAME	QUANTITY	PRICE EACH
VALUES FOR A NEW MILLENNIUM		$19.95
Shipping & Handling		$4.50
Total		

❏ Check   ❏ M.O.   Amount enclosed: $_____
❏ Credit Card

Name on Credit Card _____

Credit Card # _____

Exp. date ____ / ____

MAILING ADDRESS:

LIVING VALUES INSTITUTE
P.O. BOX 652
SPRING LAKE, NJ 07762

Order online at: *http://livingvalues.com*

A copy of *Values for a New Millennium* may also be obtained through

LIFE VALUES INSTITUTE
144 BOB WRIGHT ROAD
MAYNARDVILLE, TN 37807

Order online at: *http://mindbodyvalues.com*